COMMISSIONER

Commissioner

THE LEGACY OF PETE ROZELLE

John A. Fortunato

TAYLOR TRADE PUBLISHING

Lanham • New York • Boulder • Toronto • Oxford

Published by Taylor Trade Publishing
An imprint of The Rowman & Littlefield Publishing Group, Inc.
4501 Forbes Boulevard, Suite 200, Lanham, Maryland 20706

Distributed by NATIONAL BOOK NETWORK

Library of Congress Cataloging-in-Publication Data

Fortunato, John A.
  Commissioner : the legacy of Pete Rozelle / John A. Fortunato.— 1st ed.
    p. cm.
  Includes index.
  ISBN-13: 978-1-58979-291-3 (cloth : alk. paper)
  ISBN-10: 1-58979-291-2 (cloth : alk. paper)
  1. Rozelle, Pete.   2. Football commissioners—United States—Biography.   I. Title.
  GV939.R695F67 2006
  796.332092—dc22

                                                          2006006861

⊗™ The paper used in this publication meets the minimum requirements of American National Standard for Information Sciences—Permanence of Paper for Printed Library Materials, ANSI/NISO Z39.48-1992.

Manufactured in the United States of America.

CONTENTS

CONTENTS

FOREWORD

AS INCREDIBLE as Pete Rozelle was as commissioner of the National Football League, he was an even more amazing individual as a father. John Fortunato aptly portrays the life of my father as he nurtured and formed the NFL from its near-infancy to the full-grown, self-sustaining enterprise it is today. John relates the familiar details of how my father created and orchestrated his vision for a game he loved and for carrying it out in an organization that is unrivaled in its success. In mirroring that vision, he also applied the same principles of integrity and passion in the raising and nurturing of a daughter all on his own. Very few people could have had such success in all aspects of their life, but my father was no ordinary individual.

Dad always had a way of being successful and coming out on top, but it did not come without its share of battles. As a young girl, I envisioned him as James Bond, someone who was incredibly handsome, invincible, fearless, and always emerging from conflict calm, cool, and camera perfect. If Dad was my James Bond, Thelma Elkjer, his longtime secretary, was his Miss Money Penny. For Dad, she was everything—his right arm, his protector, his unfinished sentences. For me, a young girl in a single-parent family, she was a safe haven, and she was also a friend and confidant for me as a grown woman. Thelma was the special unsung hero who helped Dad weather many storms professionally and personally. Her devotion was consistent in victory and defeat.

Of all the battles my father won, the most important one to both of us was the long court battle in which he gained custody of me. While trying to endure the difficult times of my mother's mental illness, he made a decision that would change both of our lives forever. In a time that Pat Summerall would aptly refer to as the "dark days," my father fought and won in an unprecedented court decision, and this celebrity father with an unconventional lifestyle was awarded the custody of a daughter. This successful court victory set the stage for us to always be together and to finally bring some stability and calm to our lives.

Traveling with Dad was magical. Saturdays were spent in the NFL offices. Sundays found us at the stadiums. There were Thanksgivings celebrated during the halftime of a game, and other holidays shared at Ann and Herb Siegel's apartment or in a restaurant with them. Holidays with the Siegels and their sons, Billy and John, were special, and they were the closest surrogate family I could have had. Fishing with Ed Sabol, joking with Frank Gifford or Jack Landry, and later playing tennis with the Siegels, Tisches, and Mahoneys were Dad's greatest source of pleasure and true relaxation. Every Saturday night the Tisches, also owners of Loews Theaters, would host people for a first-run movie and many times with the stars of the film in attendance. There were also special League trips where we would spend time with the team owners, and most of the time the owners' wives babysat me while all the big deals were being worked out. Talk about your high-end babysitters! I will forever be grateful to all the owners, especially Norma and Lamar Hunt, Ann and Wellington Mara, Patty and Art Modell, and Patricia and Dan Rooney, who watched out for me and treated me as one of their own children.

On some of these trips together, we would finally end up in a hotel lounge at the end of a long evening listening to a piano player. It was at these times that he was no longer Mr. Commissioner but just Dad. I would beg him to dance with me, usually to something embarrassing like the *Hokey Pokey* or *Alley Cat*, and he would. Though I don't think he enjoyed being on the dance floor, he made it a point not to disappoint his daughter. Even with his schedule, there were many activities that he always seemed to find time to do with me. We spent countless hours sledding in the park and ice-skating at Rockefeller Center, and there was the occasional fishing and camping trip in Canada. When the World's Fair came to New York in 1964, Dad and I spent the day taking in the sights and sounds of that spectacular scene, and on a trip to Disneyland, he took me through "It's a Small World" eleven times in a row! I don't know how he did it all, but he always seemed to manage it. He raised a daughter completely on his own while doing one of the most visible and demanding jobs, and he did it well. He never missed a Christmas pageant, father–daughter dance, birthday, or graduation, and he always took my phone calls. Dad never broke a promise. As unconventional as our life was together, my dad's dedication to me never faltered.

As I grew up, I came to appreciate more and more the qualities Dad exhibited when dealing with people. It convinced me to want to work in an industry where people were the focus. By the time I became a young woman in my twenties, my father's contacts helped me to experience some tremendous job opportunities such as working for Roone Arledge at ABC News and Don Ohlmeyer at NBC Sports on the Moscow Olympic Unit, where I became acutely aware of the reasons conflicts arise between those who are the news and those who report it. Understanding that Dad approached each situation with complete honesty and giving each individual his full attention made me value the lessons I had unknowingly learned from him. This theory was put to the test again and again. In the political arena, I worked as an intern for Jack Kemp in Washington, D.C., and assisted Ethel Kennedy on the RFK memorial events. A memorable period of time was spent with Mary Jo Slater in casting for the soap opera, *One Life to Live*, and also in private business working for David Mahoney in public relations at Norton Simon Inc., culminating with eight years in public relations at Ralph Lauren. My father's principles helped me to weather all situations and all circumstances.

Life threw Dad a curve when he was diagnosed with a brain tumor. This thing neither played fair nor acknowledged the principles by which he conducted himself. When the tumor was first discovered, the doctors said he had a year and a half to live. Two weeks later we were informed it was worse than previously imagined; he only had three months. With tears in our eyes, we sat down at the breakfast table and discussed arrangements that needed to be made. We would sit and talk from then on about times past and good friends. He would continue to state that he was "very lucky for having such an incredible life and couldn't have asked for more." During the last few months, he would continue to go out to eat, even though it was difficult for him to walk and talk. Up until the last week of his life, Dad continued to go to the office. And every morning he would come to the breakfast room for coffee and to read the newspapers. Once, toward the end, when I was with him, I noticed that the paper he was reading was upside down. He couldn't see very well by this time. But he did not want me to know or worry, so he went through the motions.

Throughout his struggle with brain cancer, my father never lost his sense of humor. One day at the hospital, he got on the elevator and a stranger looked at him and recognized him, asking, "Aren't you Paul Tagliabue?" Dad responded by saying, "Fine, thank you. How are you?" Our friend Denise Harboush, who was with him, said, "You're both wrong. That's not Paul Tagliabue, and he didn't ask how are you." Dad laughed until he cried. Even at the very end he still had his mischievous twinkle and irreverent sense of humor. During the last few days, I would sleep on the floor next to his bed, and we would talk about everything. We reminisced about the wild summers spent with Pat Summerall, Bill MacPhail, and Bill Creasy at the beach house we all rented in the Hamptons. We thought back to my childhood and the trips to sea on his boat, the *Triple Eagle*, named after the *Double Eagle*, the ship Dad served on in the Navy. Dad would speak fondly of the crazy times at Super Bowls that he had shared with Joe Browne (NFL PR), Charlie Jackson (NFL Security), and with Wayne Rosen, his driver, who always added humor to any situation with his contagious and adventurous attitude. Finally, Dad would turn the conversation to his grandchildren, Miles and Alexandra, whom he so dearly wanted to see grow up. I pledged to him I would raise both of them with the same love he had given me and thanked him for the sacrifices, for the encouragement, for the kind words, for his love, and for the dances. In the end it was still about giving others your very best.

My father's great ability to live that ideal to its fullest continues to impact those that knew him best. Paul Tagliabue not only inherited the NFL from my father, but he also inherited my family and me. Today, the Super Bowl is my family reunion. We are fortunate to remain in the festivities surrounding the event and getting together with the owners, television people, and old friends who have filled the roles of my "aunts" and "uncles" all these years. It is no secret that my father did not like the spotlight, but his mission in life was to be the best commissioner for an organization and a sport he loved and to be the best father to a little girl who loved him dearly. Those who dealt with him professionally always knew they were getting an honest and fair shake in negotiations. The lucky ones, those who knew my father intimately, know that he also carried with him a passion and ability to make friendships work, acquaintances feel supported, and family know they are loved. Failure in any aspect of his life was unacceptable, but even though he lost this final battle, he still fought it with courage and integrity.

Integrity and humor were my father's greatest qualities. He was a kind, gentle man who always got teary-eyed at the first three notes of *Try to Remember*. He had a code of honor, and that code was his word. You were never to cancel a commitment for a better offer. He went to every wedding, birthday, graduation, funeral, or retirement party. He believed those were the most important days of his friends' lives, and he would be there for them. He always said, "If you are a true friend, you do what you have to do to be there." Only a few months before he died, he insisted on going to the Republican National Convention in 1996. Despite his failing health, he insisted on being there to support his dear friend, Jack Kemp.

After all these years, I still have many things my father gave to me: his letters, his desk, and the pearl necklace he gave me on my sixteenth birthday. These material things are very special because they remind me of him. But they are not the things I hold most dear. I am most grateful for the real inheritance my father left me: his sense of humor, his compassion for others, his integrity, and his belief that your word is your bond. To me, he was the best parent, adviser, and friend anyone could have dreamed of. I thank God for allowing him to be such a bright spot in what he used to call ... "life's ... rich ... pageantry."

—Anne Marie Rozelle Bratton

Special thanks to Michael Parker, teacher and friend, for helping me put the words in my heart onto paper.

Excerpts used from Pete Rozelle's Eulogy, 1996, by Don Philips.

PREFACE

WHEN I first began researching and writing about
Pete Rozelle, my intent was to document a Hall of
Fame career. It was surprising to me that a book
focusing exclusively on Rozelle had never been completed. I, like many other
sports fans, knew of Rozelle as a person who was instrumental in shaping not
only professional football but also the entire sports world, particularly the
way people experience these games and events on television. My thought was
that people might be generally familiar with many of his accomplishments but
not the particular details involving these situations and the difficult decisions
that Rozelle was forced to make. The details surrounding these events and
accomplishments illuminate Rozelle's many personal and professional skills
and lead many to conclude that he was the greatest commissioner of any sports
league, at any time.

As the project emerged, I quickly learned of the absolute reverence with
which so many spoke about Pete Rozelle the commissioner of the NFL and
Rozelle the man. To those whom I spoke with, Rozelle consistently proved to
be an inspiration and very much a hero, a man who in all instances acted with
integrity, humility, and loyalty. I am greatly appreciative to the people who
took the time to be interviewed and share their insights and experiences about
Pete Rozelle with me. They are: Peter Abitante, Ernie Accorsi, Bud Adams,
Dave Anderson, Chris Berman, Pat Bowlen, Gil Brandt, Anne Marie Bratton,
Joe Browne, Joel Bussert, Charley Casserly, Frank Deford, Steve Ehrhart, Frank
Gifford, Peter Hadhazy, Jack Kemp, Peter King, Red McCombs, Art Modell, Jay
Moyer, Gary Myers, Tommy Nobis, Carl Peterson, Neal Pilson, Gary Roberts,
Dan Rooney, Dick Rozelle, Ed Sabol, Steve Sabol, Duke Snider, Bob St. John,
Jim Steeg, David Stern, Pat Summerall, Paul Tagliabue, and Al Ward. Although

I did not get the opportunity to speak with him, I need to also recognize the late Wellington Mara, who, even after having surgery, sent me a letter explaining that due to his health his activities were limited, but writing, "I would like to cooperate in any effort to memorialize Pete Rozelle."

I would particularly like to make an extra special mention of Joe Browne for his help at so many instances in this project and for his demonstrating confidence in me to thoroughly and accurately represent his friend's career. Anne Marie Bratton, Pete Rozelle's daughter, was very generous with her time in sharing so many personal stories in addition to her library of materials documenting her father's career. I am also very appreciative of her writing the foreword for this book. To Dick Rozelle, this book would not have been as good without your valuable contributions. Jay Moyer provided me with careful and thoughtful responses regarding the particular legal situations that he was most involved with Rozelle. I am very appreciative of Paul Tagliabue for giving me some of his time and offering the perspective that only an NFL commissioner can provide. I want to thank Ernie Accorsi for the tremendous insight that stems from over thirty-five years of working in the NFL for men who were such an integral part of the NFL: Pete Rozelle, Wellington Mara, Art Modell, Robert Irsay, and Carroll Rosenbloom. I am grateful for his enthusiasm about this project from the very beginning and appreciative of his always responding to my inquiries. Finally, the people who contributed the comments that appear on the back of the book deserve an extra mention of thanks.

In addition to these direct sources, a good deal of research went into obtaining information from printed records and other media, particularly in trying to find quotes from Rozelle for his own perspective of events. Whenever possible I wanted the words of Rozelle to tell his own story. All of the work of the various newspaper and sports magazine writers provided valuable information about the stories and events involving Rozelle at the time they were occurring. The tremendous work of many extremely talented authors whose books were very helpful in assisting my research about Rozelle also needs to be recognized. I hope my work reflects and contributes to your extensive efforts. The authors and their books are: Jim Byrne, *The $1 League: The Rise and Fall of the USFL*; Bob Carroll, *When the Grass was Real*; Ed Gruver, *The American Football League: A Year-by-Year History, 1960–1969*; Mark Gunther and Bill Carter, *Monday Night Mayhem*; David Harris, *The League: The Rise and Decline of the NFL*; Jerry Izenberg, *New York Giants: 75 Years*; Mark Kriegal, *Namath: A Biography*; Michael MacCambridge, *America's Game*; David Maraniss, *When Pride Still Mattered: A Life of Vince Lombardi*; Jon Morgan, *Glory for Sale:*

Fans, Dollars, and the New NFL; NFL Properties, *The Super Bowl*; Phil Patton, *Razzle-Dazzle: The Curious Marriage of Television and Professional Football*; Harold Rosenthal, *Fifty Faces of Football*; Bob St. John, *Tex*; Shelby Strother, *The NFL Top 40: The Greatest Pro Football Games of All Time*; and Don Weiss with Chuck Day, *The Making of the Super Bowl*.

Several players and coaches also wrote their own books that helped provide some of their insights about Rozelle, some of their dealings with him, and some of the details of the situations that both they and Rozelle were involved in. These people include: Paul Brown (with Jack Clary), *PB: The Paul Brown Story*; Joe Foss (with Donna Wild Foss), *A Proud American: The Autobiography of Joe Foss*; Paul Hornung, *Golden Boy*; Alex Karras (with Herb Gluck), *Even Big Guys Cry*; Tom Landry, *Tom Landry: An Autobiography*; Joe Namath (with Dick Schaap), *I Can't Wait Until Tomorrow... 'Cause I Get Better-looking Every Day*; and Doug Williams, *Quarterblack: Shattering the NFL Myth*.

Finally, there are also the people who assisted me in gathering valuable information and coordinating interviews, and I am grateful. They are: Tina Bucciarelli, Paul Cammarata, Isabella Cunningham, Ed Farmer, Greg Frith, John Gault, Richard Irwin, Louis LaLuna, Michael Mastando, John Morsillo, Ryan Rebholz, Ronald Record, Lisa Searls, Jodi Lisa Smith, and Erich Zimny. The tremendous efforts of Rick Rinehart, Jenn Nemec, and the entire staff at Taylor Trade Publishing who assisted in this book and improving it at many steps along the way need to be recognized. Also, thank you for providing me the vehicle to write this book. I would also like to thank the faculty members of the University of Texas at Austin Department of Advertising for their tremendous support and encouragement of my working on this project.

In an interview in *Signature* magazine in 1979, Pete Rozelle asked, "Why would anyone want to read about me?" I hope the answer lies within these pages. In the end, the story of Pete Rozelle's career is one of how a man with a vision and the personal and professional skills to form the necessary relationships and persuade others to implement what at the time were revolutionary ideas transformed a league and created an enduring legacy. In researching and writing this book about Pete Rozelle, I constantly learned new things about his career, about his specific impact on the league and the entire sports world, and about NFL history in general. I hope that the readers of this book also have many moments where some information or detail illuminates recent sports history and the central role Pete Rozelle had in it.

INTRODUCTION

SOME CAREERS produce accomplishments that are of the moment. The greatness of the achievement is encapsulated at that time, at that place, and remembered as such. Others' careers produce accomplishments that transcend that one specific time and place. Their achievements are beyond memorable and have an impact that endures long after their careers have concluded. Such a career changes the landscape, how people within an industry think and behave, and how others outside of that industry perceive it. Things as they were before that person arrived on the scene are not the same when they leave. There are memorable careers and there are revolutionary careers. The career of Alvin Ray "Pete" Rozelle is one of revolutionary accomplishments that transcended his industry of professional football as well as the entire sports world.

He is probably not the first name that a person thinks of when one mentions the National Football League. Those recognitions are reserved for Tom Brady, Dick Butkus, Joe Montana, Jerry Rice, Emmitt Smith, Lawrence Taylor, or Johnny Unitas. He did not generate the vivid memories of Vince Lombardi stalking the sideline or Jim Brown running with an unmatched combination of power and speed. He never scored a touchdown, recorded a sack, kicked a game-winning field goal, or designed the game-winning play, but he helped design the stage for those who did those things. And, most important, he helped provide the vehicle for fans to witness and experience those skills and achievements. Pete Rozelle transcended sports off the field as much as those great players did on. He was Unitas in a navy blue blazer. He simply made the game of professional football a better industry for those involved and more enjoyable for the fans who watched. No, his name is not the first one mentioned by most fans when thinking about the NFL, but perhaps it should be.

Pete Rozelle was thirty-three years old when he was surprisingly named the commissioner of the NFL in January 1960. He had been the general manager of the Los Angeles Rams for only three years, and his total experience in the NFL was limited to another three years as the head of public relations for the Rams and working for the Rams while attending Compton Junior College. Rozelle came to the job of commissioner with one simple goal: make the NFL the premier professional sports league in the country, if not the world. He wanted to take a sport that at the time was not as popular as baseball, or many other sports, and by launching it into the consciousness of everyone, help it grow economically and in popularity. He approached that goal with an unflinching vision of what he and the league needed to do, the relationships that needed to be cultivated, and the personal and professional sacrifices that needed to be made.

The Rozelle vision began with a simple philosophy of putting the league first. Any and all decisions were to be made with the best interests of the entire league in mind. His vision was founded on a few uncompromising principles that he deemed absolutely necessary to grow the sport and have fans throughout the entire country maintain their interest in the league. The first principle of the Rozelle vision was that every NFL team must be equipped with the economic tools that would give the franchise the chance, if managed properly, to compete for a championship. To accomplish this, Rozelle needed to use all of his abilities of persuasion to convince the owners of the value of a league-first approach. He had to get all of the NFL's owners to agree to share the vast majority of their revenues equally. Large differences in revenues might allow only wealthier franchises to sign the better players, potentially creating a system where some teams could simply not compete. The fans in the cities of those teams not generating as much revenue might then easily lose interest in the games and the league if they believed their team did not have a chance to win. For Rozelle, not only was football an intrinsically entertaining game, but competition itself was entertaining. Revenue sharing was thus essential to create and maintain the necessary leaguewide competitive balance.

The second principle of the Rozelle vision, and a strategy closely aligned with the concepts of revenue sharing and competitive balance, was that the NFL had to have an impact and be entertaining on television. Because it was television that provided the league with its greatest source of revenue, it was the television money that would have to be shared equally among all franchises. To accomplish this economic strategy Rozelle had to convince the NFL's owners that they needed to change from a system where individual teams were making their own television deals with the networks to one where all of the teams would pool their rights and sell them to the highest-bidding network. Rozelle correctly predicted that a system of selling collective, pooled rights for all teams, with multiple networks competing for those broadcast rights, was the best way to increase the NFL's revenues.

After he convinced NFL owners to become partners with each other and share revenues for the betterment of the entire league, an economic system was in place to achieve substantial growth. In his three-decade career as commissioner of the NFL, from 1960 to 1989, Rozelle oversaw the NFL's growth from twelve to twenty-eight teams and the soaring of its popularity past all other sports. He negotiated television contracts worth billions for the NFL, consistently demonstrating an incredible understanding of the power of the television medium to help grow the sport. He was instrumental in developing the Super Bowl and transforming it into the premier television event. And with his belief that football would be a huge success in prime time, he cocreated the revolutionary idea of *Monday Night Football.*

Rozelle was as respected by his peers for his style in leading the NFL as he was applauded for his specific visionary ideas. He possessed a variety of personal skills necessary to implement his vision. Rozelle was very loyal to the game and league that he loved. He was also consistently loyal to the people involved with the NFL who shared his vision and passion for the league. The competence he demonstrated in performing his job and the integrity and humility with which he conducted himself would produce tremendous loyalty among those who knew him. Many would find his personal characteristics, particularly his devotion to his daughter Anne Marie, as valuable and endearing as his business abilities.

This combination of visionary ideas and personal leadership style also inspired confidence in his decisions. Always motivated by the league-first philosophy and what was best for the entire NFL, Rozelle's decisions were based on listening to others; carefully thinking things through; and once reaching a position, persuading others that it was the correct strategy in moving the league forward. For all of these reasons Art Rooney, Hall of Fame owner of the Pittsburgh Steelers, once said, "Pete Rozelle is a gift from the hand of the providence."

Rozelle fought hard to maintain his vision and the integrity of the game whenever necessary. He was challenged in many instances, and his vision at various times confronted by owners and players, rival football leagues, and the United States government, and he defended himself on several occasions in court and before the United States Congress. In addition to all of the other day-to-day operations of running a premier professional sports league and fostering relationships with all of the people a commissioner must, Rozelle would have to deal repeatedly with three major issues: expansion and franchise relocation, rival football leagues, and the complex interactions with the Players Association. Rozelle consistently had to monitor the growth of the league and the placement of new expansion teams. On the issue of franchise relocation, his vision for the league would never be as severely challenged as it would be by Al Davis and his moving of the Raiders from Oakland to Los Angeles. He helped withstand the challenge and was instrumental in facilitating the complex merger with the then rival American Football League. Later he withstood the challenge from two other rival leagues—the World Football League and the United States Football League. He would also see two players' strikes occur in the 1980s, marking the first time that regular-season games were cancelled because of a work stoppage. Rozelle was never afraid of a challenge, often vigorously and courageously confronting it if he thought it threatened his vision and the integrity of the game. In all of these situations Rozelle would prove to be as competitive as the players and owners whom he served. In the end, his vision would often prevail, and his accomplishments would become legendary.

Rozelle's accomplishments have been recognized by many media outlets. Rozelle was voted number one on the *Sporting News's* list of the most powerful people in sports for the twentieth century. In the *Sporting News* article recognizing his achievements, Paul Attner wrote, "with a vision that visits only a blessed few, he recognized the future of television, understood the need for competitive balance, realized the necessity of revenue-sharing among teams and grasped the power of having friends in high political places, all to turn a semi-major sports organization into the colossus we now recognize as the National Football League." *Time* magazine recognized Rozelle as one of the "builders and titans of the 20th century." *Sport* magazine, in a special collector's edition focusing on the forty people who changed sports, ranked Rozelle at number three, trailing only Jackie Robinson and Muhammad Ali. Rozelle appeared on the cover of *Sports Illustrated* in the January 6, 1964, issue for being selected as the sportsman of the year for 1963, the first and only time that a commissioner of a professional sports league was recognized with this honor. Finally, in 1994, he was picked by *Sports Illustrated* as one of the forty individuals who have most dramatically elevated and altered the games we play and watch and recognized as one of the most influential people in the then forty-year history of the magazine.

Introduction

The story of Pete Rozelle as the commissioner of the NFL is the story of a man with a vision, the dogged determination to pursue that vision, and an unparalleled personal skill set to implement that vision. It is a story of challenges and tribulations, and ultimately, many triumphs. There are seminal moments on the field and off the field that have shaped today's NFL. This book is a story of one of the chief architects of some of the major off-the-field events. It is ultimately a story of how a man came to the job of NFL commissioner as an unknown, "the compromise candidate," but left a legend.

CHAPTER 1

The Compromise Candidate

O CTOBER 11, 1959, was expected to be a normal NFL Sunday. Six games were going to be played in the third week of the twelve-team NFL season. The 1959 season was one in which the NFL was trying to capitalize on its significant landmark moment, the 1958 NFL Championship Game when the Baltimore Colts defeated the New York Giants in sudden-death overtime before a crowd of 64,185 at Yankee Stadium, but more important, before a national audience (except in New York) estimated at over fifty million people watching on television. The evidence for the growth of professional football was considerable. The 1958 season produced game attendance that reached the highest ever for the NFL up until that point, becoming the first year the league topped three million fans in attendance. The seventy-two-game schedule in the 1958 season also provided the NFL with its first season of having an average attendance of over 40,000, at 41,752. The NFL would never again have an average attendance of less than 40,000 for a season.

The NFL was also becoming a more stable league, as 1959 would be the seventh consecutive season in which no team had relocated to another city or folded. The Baltimore Colts, coming from the All-American Football Conference (AAFC), had folded after 1950, dropping the league total from thirteen to twelve teams. In January 1952 the New York Yankees football franchise was sold back to the NFL and a new group in Dallas would purchase the team and form the Dallas Texans. The Texans would begin playing in the autumn of 1952, but the season in Dallas was a miserable failure on and off the field. The Texans posted a 1-11 record, and the owners of the Dallas team turned their back on the franchise midway through the season. The commissioner's office operated the team until the end of the season, when the franchise was officially cancelled, marking the last time an NFL team failed. In January 1953, the holdings of the defunct Dallas franchise were awarded to a Baltimore ownership group headed by Carroll Rosenbloom, and the Colts would reenter the NFL for the 1953 season to complete the twelve-team league.

The person at the center of trying to capitalize on this emerging popularity of the league and the potential economic opportunities to grow the professional football business was the NFL commissioner, De Benneville "Bert" Bell. Bell had been the commissioner of the NFL since January 11, 1946, when he succeeded Elmer Layden, a man most recognized for being one of Notre Dame's famed Four Horseman. Bell had spent his lifetime in and around football. He had been the starting quarterback at the University of Pennsylvania in 1917, leading the team to the Rose Bowl, where his team lost to an undefeated University of Oregon squad. Bell would not play professional football but rather return to the University of Pennsylvania and serve as an assistant coach for the team throughout most of the decade of the 1920s.

Bell eventually entered into professional football when he and his former Pennsylvania teammate, Lud Wray, would lead a group in buying the NFL's bankrupt Frankford Yellow Jackets franchise. The Yellow Jackets had begun in an eighteen-team league in 1924 and finished their eight-year tenure in the NFL by playing only eight games of the 1931 season. Bell and his partners restarted the team in 1933 in Philadelphia. In that same year, with the country recovering from the Great Depression, President Franklin Delano Roosevelt introduced the "New Deal" policy through the National Recovery Administration, which had the eagle as its symbol. Bell would name his new Philadelphia football team the Eagles after the "New Deal" emblem.

With the Eagles struggling in their first two seasons, posting records of 3-5-1 in 1933 and 4-7 in 1934, Bell proposed in May 1935 what would become an essential component of the NFL's system of player allocation. Bell convinced the other owners of the league to approve a system where they would conduct an annual draft of college players, starting in 1936, where teams selected players in an inverse order of finish.

After a 2-9 record in 1935, for the 1936 season Bell would begin his tenure as head coach of the Eagles. Although winning the first game he coached in 1936, a 10-7 victory over the Giants, the Eagles would not win another game the rest of the season, being shutout on six different occasions to finish with a 1-11 record. Bell would be resoundingly unsuccessful in his five seasons at the helm of the Eagles, finishing in last place every year except one, a fourth-place finish in 1938. Bell ended his career as the Eagles' head coach with a record of 10-44-2.

Bell's involvement in the NFL took on a strange twist in 1940. Art Rooney, founder of the Pittsburgh Pirates NFL franchise in 1933, would sell his team to Alexis Thompson and become partners with Bell in Philadelphia in December 1940. Prior to the beginning of the 1941 season, however, Bell and Rooney traded the Eagles franchise to Thompson, and they would then become the co-owners of the Pittsburgh franchise and rename the team the Steelers. Bell would become the Steelers' head coach for the 1941 season, but only remained in that post for the team's first two games, both losses. The Pittsburgh Steelers would win only one game in 1941, but in 1942 the team finished second in the standings with a 7-4 record.

The connection of Bell to Philadelphia would come into play again in 1943, when at the height of World War II, with NFL players enlisting in the war effort, Pittsburgh and Philadelphia merged for one season. The team was called the Steagles by fans, and it divided its home games between the two cities, playing to a third-place finish and a record of 5-4-1. The merger was automatically dissolved at the end of the season. Pittsburgh would make a similar merger agreement with the Chicago Cardinals for the 1944 season, a winless campaign.

Although his teams struggled, Bell was well respected and well liked throughout the league. With the contract of Layden not being renewed, it would be Bell who was drafted to the commissioner position. Bell moved the league offices from Chicago to Bala-Cynwyd, Pennsylvania, a suburb outside of Philadelphia, and began presiding over what would be one of the more tumultuous periods for the NFL.

In January 1946, Bell inherited a ten-team league, with its championship team about to relocate to another city. Although the Rams won the 1945 NFL championship, a 15-14 victory over the Washington Redskins in Cleveland in a game played in below-zero temperatures at kickoff and before a crowd of only 32,178 fans, it would be their final game in the city of Cleveland. Rams owner Dan Reeves had failed in an initial vote to get approval to move the Rams to Los Angeles because other owners were concerned about travel costs to the West Coast. Reeves also mentioned Dallas as a possible new location for the team and even threatened to end the Cleveland Rams franchise altogether if he could not move the team. On the same day he took office, Bell approved the Rams' move to Los Angeles with an agreement that the team visiting Los

Angeles would receive $15,000 rather than the customary $10,000 road-team guarantee to help cover travel expenses. The move brought the NFL to the west. Previously Chicago had been its most western city.

Bell had to also immediately deal with the formation of a rival professional football league. The All-American Football Conference was created in 1944 and would begin play in 1946 with eight teams. One of the locations the AAFC was placing a team was Cleveland. The AAFC also had plans for teams in Los Angeles and San Francisco. These developments helped prompt Reeves to move the Rams out of Cleveland to Los Angeles, thus not allowing the upstart league to be the only professional football league playing on the West Coast. The AAFC created direct competition for the NFL in New York, Los Angeles, and Chicago and did produce some quality football teams, particularly the Cleveland Browns. Led by legendary Hall of Fame head coach Paul Brown, the Cleveland Browns would win all four of the AAFC championships, including an undefeated season in 1948. The AAFC would only survive four years, however, and although its teams were in financial difficulty, the NFL reached a merger agreement on December 9, 1949, allowing three teams to join the NFL for the start of the 1950 season—the Baltimore Colts, Cleveland Browns, and San Francisco 49ers. The Baltimore franchise had to pay the Washington Redskins $50,000 for imposing on their territory.

All three AAFC teams that merged into the NFL would make substantial contributions to the league in the decade of the 1950s. The Browns would quickly demonstrate their ability to compete on the NFL level by defeating the Philadelphia Eagles, the NFL's defending champion from 1949, 35-10, in their inaugural NFL game in Philadelphia. The Browns would go on to win the 1950 NFL championship in their first year in the league, defeating the team that formerly called Cleveland its home. With the game being played in Cleveland, the Browns beat the Rams 30-28 on a late two-minute drive by Otto Graham and a Lou Groza field goal before 29,751 fans in subfreezing weather on Christmas Eve. The Browns would be the NFL's most dominant team of the 1950s, appearing in seven championship games, winning three.

In addition to bringing another NFL team to the West Coast, the San Francisco 49ers would post winning records for four consecutive seasons from 1951 to 1954 and qualify for the playoffs in 1957, losing a divisional tie-breaking playoff game to the eventual champion, the Detroit Lions. The Baltimore Colts would struggle, playing only the 1950 season to a 1-11 record before returning as an expansion franchise for the 1953 season. Thanks largely to an eighty-cent telephone call in 1955 to sign then free-agent quarterback Johnny Unitas, in the

1957 season the Colts finally posted a winning record, 7-5. The Colts further improved to become the 1958 and 1959 NFL champions. Overall, during Bell's tenure as commissioner the NFL would fluctuate between ten and thirteen teams before becoming a twelve-team league in 1951 and remaining at that number through the 1959 season.

In the 1950s, the medium of television was continuing to emerge as a cultural phenomenon, and the networks were looking to all sports, including professional football, as a viable programming option, particularly for weekends. Bell and the NFL were continuously planning how to better incorporate the television medium into their business strategy. The broadcast rights to NFL games were controlled by each individual team in the 1950s. In 1950, the Rams became the first team to have all of their games televised, including their home games broadcast into the Los Angeles market. The Washington Redskins would quickly follow, with other NFL teams also making deals to get select games on the air. When the Rams saw a decline in attendance by televising their home games in 1950, however, they reversed their television policy and only broadcast their road games to the Los Angeles market in 1951. Bell declared in 1951 that teams could not sell the broadcast rights to their home games and must instead black them out on local television to protect ticket sales.

Bell was also concerned with other games being televised into a city when that team was playing a game at home. While Bell acknowledged that television would be a great tool for exposure and building interest in the NFL, he still believed the live gate always had to be protected. Therefore, Bell's plan was to continue to show only teams' road games in their home cities, ensuring that games that were otherwise unavailable would be accessible to fans.

This television-blackout policy would be challenged by the Justice Department as a restrictive restraint of trade and a violation of the Sherman Antitrust Act. On November 12, 1953, in a federal district court in Philadelphia, Judge Allan K. Grim upheld the legality of the NFL rule and preserved the right of the league to black out telecasts of home games and all other games in that city when the team was playing a game at home. Grim contended that the restriction of games into the territory of a team playing a home game was necessary for the league's existence and therefore was not ruled an unreasonable restraint of trade. The judge claimed that a decrease in ticket sales could be a financial disaster for the teams. Grim did, however, rule that the broadcasting of outside games when home teams were playing away was to be allowed because those games did not impact ticket sales. Bert Bell would comment about the verdict, telling the *New York Times* that professional football "won the most important part of the case because the league's most vital need is the protection of our home gate if we are to continue our existence." Although there was judicial approval to at least protect the home team's ticket sales, Bell would unsuccessfully push for a more permanent antitrust exemption from Congress.

The emergence of the NFL on television was clear. In 1951, the NFL broadcast its championship game between Los Angeles and Cleveland coast to coast for the first time, with the Dumont television network paying $75,000 for the rights. That same year, Dumont also televised five regular-season games, a number that would grow to twelve by 1954. NBC would assume the television rights to the title game in 1955, paying the league $100,000 to broadcast the game. In 1956, CBS would begin broadcasting some regular-season games to selected television markets across the nation at a fee of $1.8 million per year, demonstrating that all networks had now developed an interest in televising professional football. The growing success of the NFL on television in the 1950s culminated with the 1958 championship game.

On October 11, 1959, in the third week of the NFL season, the 1-1 Philadelphia Eagles were hosting the 1-1 Pittsburgh Steelers. Among the 27,343 people in attendance at Franklin Field in Philadelphia was NFL commissioner Bert Bell, watching the two teams he had once owned and coached. As the Eagles were wrapping up a 28-24 victory in the last two minutes of the game, Bell suffered a heart attack. He died just shortly after being admitted to University Hospital in Philadelphia. He was sixty-four years old. An article appeared the next day in the *New York Times*.

The National Football League at one time was regarded as a poor relation in the family of spectator sports until Bert Bell assumed command. Under his guidance the professional game rose to new heights of popularity and financial stability. . . . Mr. Bell's experiences in football were unlimited. Few men could match his background in the sport in which he served as a player, coach, and owner. At one time or another he performed just about every function in the sport, including the selling of tickets and advertising space.

A *Sports Illustrated* article also spoke of Bell.

He was, as much as any one man could be, responsible for the burgeoning of professional football, and he was the best commissioner any professional sport has had since the death of Kenesaw Mountain Landis.... [Bell] was responsible for the eminently sane policies of the league on television and procurement of personnel, the two factors which made pro football the success it is today.... He left a vacancy no one else can fill.

As the Eagles were defeating the Steelers on October 11, 1959, the Los Angeles Rams, under the leadership of their thirty-three-year-old general manager, Pete Rozelle, were defeating the Bears 28-21 in Chicago. In many ways, the Rams had been a revolutionary franchise. After moving from Cleveland to Los Angeles, the Rams signed the first African American players in the modern NFL in March 1946—halfback Kenny Washington and end Woody Strode— one year before Jackie Robinson would sign to play major league baseball for the Brooklyn Dodgers. In addition to their innovations in television, the Rams had also been the first team to put logos on their helmets, the horns being placed on in 1948. In 1957, the Rams would draw a record crowd of 102,368 at the Los Angeles Memorial Coliseum for a November 10 game against the San Francisco 49ers. The Rams would draw more than 100,000 for two more games in the 1958 season.

On the field, the Rams in the early 1950s were very successful. They won the NFL championship in 1951, played on the losing end of the championship games in 1950 and 1955, and qualified for the playoffs in 1952. In 1956, the Rams suffered their first losing season since moving to Los Angeles, ending the year with a 4-8 record. The team was also in the midst of a tumultuous ownership struggle. Rozelle would be named general manager for the start of the 1957 season and would prove to be a risk taker.

In the 1957 season the Rams improved to 6-6. Shortly after the season ended in January, Rozelle would be forced to deal with the unexpected announcement of the retirement of his quarterback, Norm Van Brocklin. Nicknamed "the Dutchman," Van Brocklin had been to the pro bowl six times as the quarterback of the Rams, winning the NFL passing title in 1950, 1952, and 1954. He was also instrumental in the Rams' winning the 1951 championship when he completed a crucial seventy-three-yard touchdown pass to Tom Fears. At only thirty-one years old, Van Brocklin would explain in the *Los Angeles Times*, "Nine years is a long time. I have a lot to be grateful for. It's tough to leave the game, but I've made up my mind and that's about it. I'm going to retire." Van Brocklin would claim his retirement was not due to an alleged rift with Rams head coach Sid Gillman and that he had no desire to play for another team. Instead, Van Brocklin was returning to Portland, Oregon, to work at his off-season job on a full-time basis, the northwest representative for the Philcoflex Corporation, which specialized in pipeline coating.

By the spring, however, Van Brocklin was beginning to have second thoughts about retirement, and the Rams were receiving numerous calls about acquiring the Dutchman. Rozelle would admit in the May 3, 1958, edition of the *Los Angeles Times* that he had discussions with many teams and on several occasions talks with the Eagles. By the end of May, Rozelle traded Van Brocklin to the Philadelphia Eagles for two players and a first-round draft choice. Van Brocklin would go on to lead the Eagles to the NFL championship in 1960, becoming the first quarterback to win an NFL championship for two different teams.

The trading of Van Brocklin would be minor compared to the deal that Rozelle pulled off the following season. Rozelle and the Rams traded eight players and a high draft pick to the Chicago Cardinals for Ollie Matson, a running back who had been selected for the pro bowl on five occasions. Rozelle told the *Los Angeles Times*, "It is axiomatic in trading that it is necessary to give talent to gain talent and on paper this appears to be a trade that will materially help both teams." The trade for Matson was praised by the *Los Angeles Times*, as an article by Cal Whorton on May 24, 1959, pointed out, "A lot of armchair experts already have declared that the Los Angeles pros have assiduously swapped their way into the Western Conference title."

The 1959 season for the Rams would, however, be their worst since 1937. Even though he was in the first year of a new contract, pressure would quickly build on Sid Gillman. Gillman had been the head coach of the Rams since the 1956 season, when he signed a four-year contract. He would agree to a contract extension in October 1958 that was scheduled to cover the 1959 and 1960 seasons. After defeating the Bears in week three, the Rams would be victorious the following week in Green Bay to even their record at 2-2. After two more losses dropped their record to 2-4, the *Los Angeles Times* headline on November 3 read "Gillman on Spot in 49er Battle." Ed Pauley, one of the team's owners, would clearly express his disappointment over the Rams' 1959 performance, being quoted in the *Los Angeles Times* saying, "I thought at the outset of the season we would win the championship. We spend more money to win titles than any other in the league." Rozelle would also claim he thought the team had one of the best offenses that the Rams had ever had and he thought the team would have contended for a championship in 1959. Even with a record of 2-4, he remained optimistic, stating in the November 3, *Los Angeles Times* article, "I still feel though, that we have the team to pull us out." He added, "We have six games to go. We could win those and still be a contender." The Rams would lose the game at home to the 49ers 24-16 to drop their record to 2-5.

While the criticism of Gillman continued, much of the blame for the team's disappointing performance was not being directed at Rozelle. In fact, a column by Jeanne Hoffman in the *Los Angeles Times* on November 23, 1959, began, "If the Los Angeles Rams could get things done with half the precision of their general manager, Pete Rozelle, they might not be hovering around the National Football League cellar these days."

The win against the Packers in week four would turn out to be their last of the 1959 season, as the Rams lost their final eight games to finish with a 2-10 record. Sid Gillman would finally be relieved of his duties at the season's end. His dismissal was described by Frank Finch in the *Los Angeles Times*, who wrote, "He didn't resign, but consented to surrender his job after the club's owners agreed that a change had to be made." Prior to the last game against the Colts, Gillman informed the Rams players that he was not returning to coach the team. Upon leaving the team, Gillman, who later went on to become a Hall of Fame head coach, recognized as revolutionary for his passing offense, described Rozelle and team owner Dan Reeves as capable people and wished them and the Rams the best. So the 1959 NFL season ended with Pete Rozelle as the leader of a last-place team, one that had compiled a 16-20 record during his three-year tenure as general manager and was now without a head coach.

As the Rams struggled, the NFL was still without a permanent commissioner when the 1959 season ended. A league that had been constantly striving for stability was now left without a leader at the crossroads of opportunity and the new challenge of another rival football league that was beginning to form—the American Football League. On October 14, 1959, Austin Gunsel, NFL treasurer, was selected to serve as interim commissioner, but when the NFL owners convened at the Kenilworth Hotel in Miami for their annual league meetings in January 1960, one of the principal concerns was to select the permanent successor to Bert Bell.

Initially the two leading contenders were Gunsel and Marshall Leahy, a San Francisco lawyer and the NFL's legal counsel. The candidates had sharply divided loyalties, with Leahy receiving the bulk of ownership support. The support for Gunsel was led by George Preston Marshall from Washington who wanted the league office to remain in Philadelphia and thought Gunsel was, according to *Sports Illustrated*, "amenable to suggestion." In addition to Marshall, Gunsel was staunchly supported by Frank McNamee, from Philadelphia,

Carroll Rosenbloom, from Baltimore, and Art Rooney, from Pittsburgh. With a three-quarter majority needed to elect a new commissioner, the first ballot had seven votes cast for Leahy, four for Gunsel, and George Halas from the Chicago Bears passing. Leahy would reach as many as eight votes on the second through fifth ballots, with Rooney switching from Gunsel to Leahy. The Leahy supporters thought that if Leahy had reached eight votes, Halas would break the logjam and cast the needed ninth vote. Halas, however, was at the time far more concerned with the issue of expansion for the league and how the owners might vote on that issue. Halas did not want to vote for a particular candidate and possibly alienate any of the owners whose vote he would later need on the expansion issue. Halas continued to pass and would, in fact, never vote for any individual for commissioner.

On the sixth ballot, Don Kellett, the very well thought-of and successful Baltimore Colts general manager was nominated. Kellett would receive the same four votes that Gunsel had received on the first ballot from the same four East Coast owners representing Baltimore, Philadelphia, Pittsburgh, and Washington. A fear to some owners with Kellett's nomination was that with him as commissioner, and coming from Baltimore, Rosenbloom might exert too much power over the league. Kellett would never receive more than four votes on the sixth through twentieth ballot. Upon Kellett's rejection, it would be reported in *Sports Illustrated* that Rosenbloom stated in the meeting to the Leahy supporters, "You don't want to compromise. If God Almighty came down from heaven and agreed to serve as commissioner, you'd vote for Leahy." Leahy, with a desire to move the league headquarters to San Francisco, where he had five daughters in school, would never receive the ninth vote he needed. On the sixth ballot Rooney had switched his support from Leahy to Kellett, pushing Leahy back to only seven votes.

On the tenth ballot Edwin Anderson, president of the Detroit Lions, would have his name placed in nomination. Anderson received five votes on the tenth ballot with Detroit joining the four eastern cities. Anderson's candidacy was short lived. On the eleventh ballot he received only three, with Rooney and Rosenbloom switching their support back to Kellett. The fourteenth ballot was the last that saw a vote for Anderson, one singular vote from his boss in Detroit.

As the struggle to find a suitable commissioner continued, names such as Paul Brown and Vince Lombardi were even mentioned as commissioner. Brown was more interested in coaching, and Lombardi, who had only been a head coach for one season with the Packers, had his name blocked from any vote by Packers president Dominic Olejniczak. On the twenty-first ballot Gunsel's name was brought back up for nomination. He would once again only receive four votes. In fact, the voting on the twenty-first ballot would be exactly the same as it was on the first ballot.

Having already hired Bob Waterfield to be the new head coach of the Rams, Pete Rozelle was present at the league meetings at the request of Rams owner Dan Reeves. With his experience in the NFL being limited in comparison to other candidates, the thought of his being named commissioner was not on the top of Rozelle's or anyone else's mind when the league meetings began. But with no agreement on a new commissioner being reached by the owners, a compromise choice was needed. On the tenth day of the league meetings, with the stalemate not being solved, Reeves would mention Rozelle as a compromise candidate in an afternoon session. Rozelle would be approached by Wellington Mara, the owner of the New York Giants, and Paul Brown, from Cleveland, but Rozelle would express his reservations about taking on the job to the two men. He would tell Paul Brown that he thought his being named commissioner "is the most ludicrous thing I've ever heard." Mara and Brown would explain to Rozelle that they thought he was capable and his candidacy would continue to be discussed. On the evening of January 26, 1960, Rozelle was asked to leave the room where the owners had convened while his candidacy for commissioner was considered. To avoid a lobby filled with reporters, Rozelle waited in the men's room, smoking and disguising his presence there by washing his hands every time a reporter entered.

Ironically, the advantage that Rozelle had was that his lack of experience and his youth had not given him time to make any enemies or develop adversarial relationships with any of the other owners. Whereas other candidates represented the fear of a power shift within the league, Rozelle was not perceived as a threat to most of the owners. Paul Brown would write in his autobiography that he told Rozelle, "You are the one person who has never indicated any interest in the job, so there are no active groups against you, and if you are elected you can come into the job as your own man." Tex Maule would describe Rozelle in *Sports Illustrated* as "an ideal compromise, acceptable to the Leahy bloc because he is from the west and acceptable to the anti-Leahy faction because he was a favorite of Bell."

When mentioned to some of the other owners Rozelle's candidacy would seem puzzling. Frank McNamee, the Eagles' owner, would confess he did not even know who Rozelle was. Mara and Brown continued to express their approval of Rozelle. While the owners still debated, it was Art Rooney who finally declared that if Rozelle was suitable for Reeves and Mara that he too would support Rozelle. Dan Rooney, who had developed a personal relationship with Rozelle, recalls his father asking him if Rozelle was someone that he could support with Dan responding "definitely." On a motion by Carroll Rosenbloom and seconded by Paul Brown from Cleveland, on the twenty-third ballot, the first ballot on which his name had appeared, Pete Rozelle was selected as the sixth full-time commissioner of the NFL. He passed with a vote of eight for; three abstentions from the Detroit Lions, Chicago Bears, and Los Angeles Rams; and one vote against from San Francisco, who remained loyal to Leahy. When Rozelle was summoned in the restroom, the newly elected commissioner was once again washing his hands. Upon rejoining the meeting Rozelle would joke to the owners, "I can honestly say I come to you with clean hands." It would be written in one of his hometown newspapers, the *Los Angeles Herald*, that "the enlisting of Pete Rozelle as czar of the National Football League has to be the zaniest act of the century." Ed Pauley, one of the Rams' owners would, however, tell the *Los Angeles Times* "The Rams have lost a most valuable man, but the league has gained the greatest asset it's ever had."

Upon his being named commissioner, Rozelle was quoted in the *Los Angeles Times* stating, "To say that filling the shoes of the late Bert Bell as commissioner is a challenge would be a gross understatement." He continued, "No one will ever fill his shoes. I never was so surprised in my life when I learned I was being considered. Up to now the steps followed in my career have followed each other in orderly fashion. This is beyond my comprehension." Rozelle also stated, "When I first heard my name being mentioned I could only think that it was a great honor to be considered, but I never dared believe I would be elected." Rozelle would tell the *New York Times*, "I would be silly to consider myself anything but a compromise commissioner. I only hope that I will be able to live up to the confidence that has been shown in me."

CHAPTER 2

The Fortuitous Journey

ALVIN RAY ROZELLE was born on March 1, 1926, in South Gate, California, a suburb of Los Angeles, but most of his childhood would be spent in the adjacent community of Lynwood. The Rozelle family, Pete's grandparents, moved from Indiana to Los Angeles in 1894, buying land on the Los Angeles River that they would farm. Pete's father, Raymond Rozelle, one of seven children, six boys and one girl, grew up working on the farm. After marrying Hazel Healey, Raymond Rozelle opened a grocery store in Lynwood that failed during the depression because he continued to generously extend credit to his customers before eventually going out of business. He later worked in an Alcoa aluminum plant as a packing clerk for eighty-five cents an hour. It would be from his father that Pete Rozelle acquired what he would later describe as one of his best attributes, his patience. Rozelle described his father as "a uniquely tranquil person." It was Pete's mother, Hazel, who had a more outgoing personality with many friends.

At a very young age Alvin Ray was given the name "Pete." His younger brother, Dick, says that there are two stories as to how the name change came to be, but even he is not completely certain which is correct. Dick Rozelle explains the one story he heard is that the name Pete originated from Raymond Rozelle's brother Glenn, an outstanding athlete who attended Occidental College on an athletic scholarship and who didn't like the name Alvin because he didn't think it was manly enough. The other story, which Dick thinks is more accurate, is that the name Pete came from Hazel's brother, Harold Healey, who was known as "Uncle Fritz." Dick, three and a half years younger than Pete, would not know his brother by any other name. Regarding the name change, Pete Rozelle would later state, "Considering my real name, I am forever grateful."

Much of growing up for Rozelle was spent with Dick and other family who lived nearby. Growing up during the depression Pete and Dick Rozelle mowed lawns during the summer to earn spending money. Pete would go out and line up the jobs, pushing the lawnmower all over the neighborhood. He and his brother earned seventy-five cents for cutting and edging the front lawn and fifty cents for the back. Pete would do the mowing and Dick the weeding and edging. The day often ended with what became a tradition for the two of them, stopping for milkshakes at the local malt shop. Although it was during the depression, Dick Rozelle describes Lynwood as "a stable area" and "a great environment to grow up in."

Rozelle excelled in school. Dick describes his brother as "innately bright" who would "get straight A's without ever cracking a book." Because he was so far ahead of the other students academically Pete was moved ahead an entire grade in elementary school. He was now, however, much smaller than the other kids in his class when he reached the junior high school. The school's principal, William W. Jones, suggested to Rozelle's parents that Pete be taken out of school for a year to allow him to grow physically. Although a very difficult decision, the Rozelle's agreed and Pete spent a year working in the vineyard on the ranch of a family friend, located two hundred miles north in Central California. The Rozelle's would only be able to visit Pete a couple of times during the year that he was at the ranch. At the ranch a basketball hoop with no net was mounted on the garage, and Pete would practice every day until dark developing the shooting accuracy for which he was known throughout his high school career.

Early on, Rozelle expressed a deep interest in sports. He would often play tennis with his father. Pete would also be heavily influenced by his junior high school coach, Bill Schleibaum. The area of California in which the Rozelle's grew up produced many Hall of Fame athletes, such as Joe Perry, a running back who was the first to rush for 1,000 yards in consecutive seasons in the NFL in 1953 and 1954 and Hugh McIlhenny, the first-round draft pick of the 49ers in 1952. Both played football, although at different times, at Compton Junior College and later played together in the San Francisco 49ers backfield. Growing up, Rozelle became friends with another person who would go on to sports prominence. Pete's Uncle Joe would tell him about an eighth grade student that he was coaching in football with a tremendous arm by the name Edwin Snider. After going to different junior high schools, Rozelle and the man who would be known to everyone as "Duke" both attended Compton High School and played together on the basketball team. The future baseball Hall of Famer describes Rozelle who played forward as "a good shooter." Rozelle characterized his contributions to the basketball team as getting the ball and passing it to Duke. Rozelle, who played first-singles and first-doubles on the tennis team with one of his cousins in high school, Lee Rozelle, described himself as "a frustrated athlete."

By the time he went to high school, Rozelle had developed another interest, that of writing, specifically with an eye toward the newspaper business. Growing up, Rozelle would say his goal was to become the sports editor of the *Los Angeles Times*. He had demonstrated some communication skills by winning an extemporaneous speaking competition in junior high school where he was elected student body president. In high school Rozelle became the sports editor of the newspaper and yearbook. Often later chided that his initials, P. R., were equally appropriate to mean public relations, Rozelle did in fact begin his career by promoting the exploits of Snider. Snider recollects that it was like he had his very own press agent, and when he would do something well in a game, it would appear in the newspapers. Rozelle explained in a 1959 *Los Angeles Times* feature on himself and Snider that "one day I watched him pitch a 6-0 no-hitter against Beverly High in his very first high school game and I thought 'something's got to be done about this.' Too often star athletes from outlying schools were overlooked." Rozelle would often call the newspapers about Snider's performances and write some press clippings himself. These efforts led to Rozelle getting a job as a high school correspondent for the *Los Angeles Times* and an early career in the newspaper business.

Duke Snider states that even at a young age Rozelle had "a special sense for sizing up a situation." The two remained close friends, and Rozelle attended Snider's Baseball Hall of Fame induction ceremony, paying for his Uncle Joe, and Bill Schleibaum to also be there. Sitting with Rozelle was another former classmate and longtime friend, Snider's wife, Beverly. Rozelle and Beverly were Lynwood Junior High School classmates where they would watch Snider's junior high team often defeat their school's sports teams. Rozelle would comment, "She thought this Snider kid was awful because he always whipped us. She changed her mind, she married him." Duke Snider would tell *Sport* magazine, "You knew he [Rozelle] was going to be successful. He had the savvy and the smarts. He had to have a lot of smarts because he dated my wife before I knew her."

Upon graduating from high school with high honors in 1944, Rozelle enlisted in the United States Navy and reported for duty on July 29, 1944. Rozelle served on an oil tanker for eighteen months; On the tanker he handled clerical duties, climbing to yeoman second class before his honorable discharge in 1946. While the tanker did enter dangerous regions in the Far East, Rozelle saw no combat in World War II.

When returning from the Navy, Rozelle enrolled at Compton Junior College. It was there he officially began his career in the sports communication business by working as the college's athletic news director. Rozelle was also working as a stringer for Long Beach and Los Angeles newspapers, including the *Los Angeles Times*, where he would be paid fifty cents per game to call in scores.

It was at Compton Junior College where good fortune and timing would meet up with Rozelle. For the 1946 season, the NFL's Rams left Cleveland for Los Angeles and chose Compton Junior College as the location for the team's training camp. Sensing an opportunity, Rozelle stopped at the Rams' offices and introduced himself to Bill John, the Rams' business manager. Rozelle was hired, and Maxwell Stiles, Rams public relations director, assigned him to duties that included delivering coffee, making sure press releases were free from typographical errors, and editing the Rams' home-game program, for which he received fifty dollars.

Upon graduation, Rozelle left Compton Junior College for the University of San Francisco, where he received a scholarship to finish his degree by being the student sports information director. At the University of San Francisco, with the help of the university's legendary basketball coach Pete Newell, whom Rozelle had met at a basketball tournament hosted at Compton, Rozelle took a part-time job as the athletic news director. Newell would comment about Rozelle, "He ran a first-rate tournament down there and made a good impression on all the coaches involved. A short time later we had an opening for a publicist at USF and I recommended Rozelle. He was only twenty years old, but he was so mature you never would have known it." Newell added that Rozelle "had an ability to relate to people and when there was a problem or crisis, he was able to take a step back and sleep on it before acting."

Rozelle's job would eventually become full-time when, in 1950, he graduated from San Francisco. His time as the athletic news director at the university coincided with a period when San Francisco was very good in sports. In 1951, Rozelle had the responsibility of publicizing the San Francisco football team. The 1951 team would have nine people who later went on to play in the NFL, a significant accomplishment for any school at the time, considering there were only twelve NFL teams and rosters were much smaller. The 1951 University of San Francisco team also included three players who were later inducted into the Pro Football Hall of Fame: Gino Marchetti, Ollie Matson, and Bob St. Clair. It remains the only university to ever place three players in the Hall from one college team. Another member of that team, Burl Toler, would be named by Rozelle as the first African American official in the NFL in 1965. The team also featured Joe Kuharich as its head coach. Kuharich would go on to be the head coach for the University of Notre Dame and in the NFL for the Cardinals, Eagles, and Redskins although unsuccessful with each of those teams.

Rozelle particularly tried to get the achievements of Ollie Matson, the team's fleet-footed running back, noticed by the national press. When the San Francisco team traveled to New York to play Fordham University at Yankee Stadium, Rozelle would get the opportunity to meet many press people of national prominence. Rozelle boasted of the talent of the San Francisco team in the week leading up to the game to the New York sportswriters. Rozelle even drove legendary writer Grantland Rice to the game. Rozelle's praise of his team would be prophetic, as San Francisco defeated Fordham, 32-26 behind Matson's three touchdowns and 302 total yards. The San Francisco team finished its season undefeated at 9-0, beating opponents by an average score of 33-8.

One of the people that Rozelle would become better acquainted with while at San Francisco was Tex Schramm, the general manager of the Rams. Schramm was hired in 1947 by Dan Reeves, the Rams' owner, who was looking for a publicity director to get the Rams more newspaper coverage. In 1949, Schramm would be promoted to be an assistant to Reeves. Schramm and Rozelle would often talk about some of San Francisco's talented football players whom Schramm might be interested in for the Rams. Schramm was quoted in Bob St. John's book, *Tex*, stating, "I was greatly impressed with his hustle, his thoroughness. Certain people just make a good impression on you, and Pete was one of those."

In 1952, the University of San Francisco decided to drop its football program, even after having its undefeated season. Rozelle became the assistant athletic director to Kuharich. Coincidentally, the Rams' public relations director job became vacant. Tex Maule had been the publicity director for the Rams, but left the team to go to work for the Dallas Texans in 1952. Maule would later go on to have a notable career as the NFL writer for *Sports Illustrated*. Schramm reached out to Rozelle and offered him the job. The negotiation for the job was described by Rozelle when introducing Schramm for his induction into the Hall of Fame in 1991. Rozelle explained, "We had a good discussion. Finally we got to salary. He said that the salary would be $5500 a year. I said well, perhaps $6000 would be more appropriate, so we compromised at $5500." On March 1, 1952, at twenty-six years of age, Rozelle left the University of San Francisco athletic department to join the Rams.

Rozelle worked for the Rams' public relations office until 1955, when he returned to San Francisco to join an international public relations firm headed by Ken Macker, a close personal friend. One of Macker's big clients was the country of Australia and its preparation for the 1956 Summer Olympics in Melbourne. Rozelle would focus much of his attention on this project, thus keeping him very much in touch with the sports industry. Macker, however, had the feeling that Rozelle missed football and always thought that he would return to football if the right offer came along.

In the years he worked for Macker the fortunes of the Rams had turned worse. Ownership of the Rams was embroiled in a power struggle among their five partners, who were no longer speaking to one another. The tension reached the point where disagreements by the Rams' ownership would result in Commissioner Bert Bell making the final decision. The turmoil even caused Tex Schramm to resign and accept a position at CBS Sports. Bell, also a close friend of Macker, actively recruited Rozelle to replace Schramm and run the Rams, sensing that he could help calm the tension in the Rams' ownership situation. Dan Reeves, who had a high regard for Rozelle from his days when he was the publicity director, called Rozelle virtually every night trying to convince him to take the Rams' general manager job. Rozelle, who felt he had made a commitment to Macker, was finding it difficult to leave, but Reeves would increase the salary of his offer with each call. The offer finally reached a point where Rozelle could no longer refuse and Reeves and Bert Bell would get their wish.

On April 8, 1957, Rozelle returned to the Rams, signing a contract to become the team's general manager. Rozelle would be quoted in the *Los Angeles Times* stating, "I'm extremely happy to be back. I have been with them [the Rams] since 1946 when they first came here [to Los Angeles]. I used to put out their programs. And even when I was in the north, I continued my association with the organization."

With his career successfully moving forward, on the personal side of his life, upon his leaving the Navy in 1946 a friend in the military convinced

Rozelle to visit Chicago before going back to California. The friend would set Rozelle up on a blind date with Jane Coupe. The two were immediately attracted to each other. Rozelle would make trips to Chicago to visit Jane and he would eventually convince her to come to California. Not an overly religious person, Rozelle converted to Catholicism to marry Jane. The two would have a daughter, Anne Marie, in 1958. The connection between football and his family life would be endless. Ironically, it was during the season opener on September 28, 1958, that Rozelle's daughter was born. Rozelle went to the hospital at halftime, but had time to get back to the Coliseum for the second half to see the Browns rally from a 27-14 deficit and defeat the Rams 30-27 on a field goal by Lou Groza with twenty-three seconds remaining. He would state, "We were ahead when she was born, but I wasn't able to pass out cigars for a double victory." He added, "We lost a football game, but I gained a daughter."

Jane Rozelle explained that "it's hard to get Pete's mind off football." In a profile of her and her husband she would tell the *Los Angeles Times* about one day when she had convinced Pete to go to a Van Gogh art exhibit at the Los Angeles County Museum. She said, "I made two mistakes. I forgot the Museum is next door to the Coliseum, and I bought a modernistic print of a shoe. Pete took one look at the print then at the Coliseum, and observed sourly, 'Now why did you buy that? It'll make me think of Lou Groza!'" In the same feature article Pete Rozelle would refer to football as "the most fascinating thing in the world" and remark that "there are few greater satisfactions than a winning team and performance before a capacity crowd: few more acute senses of obligation than to reward the loyalty of an entire city."

CHAPTER 3

The Rozelle Vision

P EOPLE WHO are visionaries have a clear idea of the direction to take an organization. Their decision making is guided by trying to implement and achieve that vision. Visionaries think big and are never satisfied with what they have already accomplished. They are always looking to the future and to the next opportunity, the next frontier. Perhaps when the NFL owners tapped the young Rozelle to be commissioner some of them might have thought they had selected a person whom they could mold and influence. It would be Rozelle, however, who would mold and influence them. Although not as experienced in the NFL as the owners who had elected him, Rozelle was not intimidated by the owners and would quickly win many of them over with his clear, visionary ideas about what the league could become.

When Rozelle was elected commissioner of the NFL he found himself as the thirty-three-year-old leader of a twelve-team league with combined revenues for the league and its franchises totaling less than $20 million. Attendance in 1959 was 3,140,000 for the seventy-two regular-season games (an average of 43,617). The 1959 championship game between the host Baltimore Colts and the New York Giants drew a crowd of 57,545 to witness the Colts victory and second consecutive NFL title. The attendance in 1959 continued to represent a dramatic increase, as the league attracted over one million more fans in 1959 than it had in 1952, with the average game attendance growing by more than 15,000 during that same time period. The challenge for Rozelle and the NFL was to continue this growth and continue increasing public awareness about the league. At the time, the NFL trailed baseball, college football, boxing, and horse racing in popularity. To amplify that point, in 1959, the subject of the NFL appeared on the cover of *Sports Illustrated* only once, the issue of October 5, 1959, featuring Johnny Unitas on the cover. The subject of horse racing would appear on the cover of *Sports Illustrated* on four occasions in 1959.

As for its position on television, the league as a single, collective entity was only selling the broadcast rights to its championship game, which in 1959 had earned $200,000 from NBC. Teams were individually selling their own television rights for regular-season games, creating wide-ranging disparities of revenue among all franchises, especially between those from larger markets and smaller markets. That approach to television was emblematic of a larger problem with the NFL's business model as Rozelle would see it, where franchises were being run more as individual team businesses rather than through any collective leaguewide economic system.

Rozelle immediately understood and demonstrated that the industry he was taking over was, and certainly still remains today, as he described it, "a sport slash business." Rozelle's clear vision for the NFL would be based on a simple overall philosophy: the league comes first. All decision making would emanate from having the best interests of the entire league in mind. His initial meeting the morning after his election as commissioner largely dealt with how a league-first approach would benefit all involved in the NFL. Rozelle believed that revenues would grow faster and be more substantial if the entire league was presented as a single entity rather than each team its own individual business.

It was at this initial meeting that he would provide an explanation of his ideas concerning the use of television. For any league-first vision to truly be fulfilled a dramatic shift in the NFL's television policy would be needed. Rozelle correctly saw that television money would become the NFL's greatest revenue source and quickly worked to formulate a comprehensive policy for the league regarding the medium. He knew, however, that to attain the largest revenue source for the league it would be necessary to sell the rights to all of the NFL's games collectively to a single television network, with networks bidding against each other for those rights. Less than one year into office, Rozelle convinced the owners to sell its collective television rights as a single package to the television network offering the most money.

The second part of Rozelle's vision was that the league would then share these television revenues equally among all franchises. His philosophical vision encompassed a simple indispensable economic principle that revenue sharing, especially the equal sharing of television money, is necessary to create and ensure competitive balance. In many ways he viewed his mission as commissioner as one to help attain league profitability and growth, but he knew for that to be accomplished there had to be competitive balance. Because television would become the league's largest revenue source, Rozelle understood that competitive balance was always strongly related to the concept of revenue sharing and the league's television policy.

A collective strategy would eliminate the potential advantage that franchises in larger cities might have, Teams in smaller markets, such as Green Bay, would now receive the same amount of television money as larger-market teams from New York or Los Angeles. In 1960, with each team still making its own individual television deals, there were incredible revenue discrepancies. Smaller-market teams earned approximately $150,000 each from television, while larger-market teams could earn approximately $500,000. Rozelle feared that without competitive balance, fans in many cities would become disinterested and weaker franchises would go out of business, creating a very unstable league. Rozelle believed that for fans to maintain an interest in the sport they needed to have a sense that the team in their city, if managed properly, could compete for a championship. According to Rozelle's thinking, it was not only great athletes playing a great game that people found entertaining, but also the competition itself. The phrase "on any given Sunday," so prevalent in the vernacular of professional football, would certainly coincide with Rozelle's vision.

Rozelle, himself, would explain the rationale for his vision for the NFL when testifying before a United States House of Representatives Select Committee on Professional Sports in 1976. He stated, "The NFL operates with the highest degree of internal profit-sharing of any professional sport. Partly this is the result of proven need, based on past experience, and partly it is a recognition that teams within a professional football league must sink or swim together." He continued to articulate the necessity for an economic system that called for revenue sharing of television income, explaining that "without such a policy, teams in major television markets would have an economic advantage over other teams—a decided one when you consider that broadcasting income represents approximately one-third of the clubs' total gross income. That economic edge would quickly be translated into a competitive edge built on a higher capability to spend, and the direct result would be the economic and competitive decline of many weaker franchises."

Rozelle, never wavering on these core visionary principles, offered similar testimony defending and explaining the league's economic system before Congress on many occasions. Speaking before the Senate in 1985, he argued,

> The shared revenues are jointly produced by all league members in co-producing their "league" product through the joint league enterprise. For the NFL, revenue sharing is essential, among other resources, to maintain the high quality of the league's product through league balance and to maintain league teams in relatively small markets—avoiding the emergence of "have" and "have not" clubs. Further, the immediate effect of revenue sharing would appear to be to make the member clubs and the league itself more competitive with other sports and entertainment. The league balance resulting from revenue sharing tends to make all clubs more viable, and the league as a whole more viable.

There were two extremely powerful groups that Rozelle would have to convince and get approval from to execute this economic vision of collectively selling television rights and then equally sharing the revenues: the owners of the NFL and the United States Congress. Convincing owners, some of whom benefited greatly from the individualized nature of the television business, would be difficult. Once owners approved, he would then have to secure an antitrust exemption and protection for the legality of this practice from Congress. The owners who benefited from the individualized system were obviously from the larger cities. For example, George Preston Marshall, owner of the Washington Redskins, was against any plan calling for pooling television rights, as the Redskins had their own individual network and their games were broadcast around the country, especially in the South.

In the fall of 1960 the individual team contracts with various broadcast networks created a completely cluttered television marketplace on a Sunday afternoon. NBC had contracts to broadcast the Pittsburgh Steelers and the popular Baltimore Colts, with their star quarterback Johnny Unitas. NBC would televise one national game per week. CBS had contracts with nine teams and was threatening to stop televising some of the smaller-market teams altogether. The Cleveland Browns had their own independent network. There was also the American Football League (AFL) game of the week beginning in the fall of 1960 being broadcast on ABC. With many games being played at the same time, CBS was concerned about the audience being dispersed on many channels and wanted to gain exclusive television rights to the NFL.

After much deliberation among the owners, in late January 1961 a motion was passed that allowed the commissioner to negotiate the television deals collectively for all of the NFL teams. The NFL would quickly enter into a pooled-rights agreement with CBS. The league would maintain its blackout policy, in that every road game would be broadcast back to its home market but home games would not be televised in the local area. Rozelle credited George Halas, from Chicago; Wellington Mara, from New York; and Dan Reeves, from Los Angeles for their willingness to adopt this strategy. David Harris quoted Rozelle in his book *The League: The Rise and Decline of the NFL*, stating, "They were wise enough to see the long term and they've been rewarded. All the franchises have seen their money increase from television as a consequence and the league as a whole has remained strong. All of the franchises have remained viable and have the means to compete with the rest of the league. That's what I think sports should be."

Once owners were convinced of the collective strategy, the next step was to ensure the legality of the practice and get a special antitrust exemption from Congress. The Sherman Antitrust Act protects the economic competitiveness of a marketplace. The Act is ambiguous, however, and is often realized in the interpretation of the courts. The language of the Sherman Act is broad where it can be interpreted that almost every type of agreement between businesses can be deemed illegal. The Supreme Court has held that only those agreements that are an "unreasonable" restraint of trade are in violation of the law. Major league baseball, already in possession of an antitrust exemption, would come under scrutiny from the Justice Department when it adopted a rule prohibiting one team from broadcasting a game into another team's home territory without the home team's consent in order to protect the local team's ticket sales. Bert Bell had implemented a similar television blackout policy in the NFL.

The NFL's television policy had come under direct scrutiny back in 1951, when the Justice Department filed suit against the NFL. The concern of the Justice Department at that time was that the creation of a system that did not permit open competition violated the Sherman Antitrust Act. In 1953, in the ruling of *United States v. National Football League*, Judge Allan K. Grim upheld the legality of the NFL blackout policy that prevented the telecasting of an outside game in a team's home territory when that team was playing a home game. Fearful that a collective television arrangement, with teams pooling their rights, might violate the 1953 ruling and would be considered an unreasonable restraint of trade under the Sherman Act, the NFL tried to secure a favorable ruling for its new policy through the courts.

On April 24, 1961, the NFL brought a petition seeking more government protection and a further interpretation of the 1953 ruling. The NFL would not be successful with the judicial branch. In the NFL's newly signed television agreement with CBS, CBS would have the right to determine entirely within its own discretion which games would be televised and where the games would be televised. Judge Grim felt that this clause in particular, giving CBS the right to determine which games were to be televised, violated the 1953 ruling, and thus he voided the NFL's two-year contract with CBS. In addition to ending the contract between the NFL and CBS, Judge Grim also prevented the NFL from entering into any other pooled-rights contract. In his judgment against the NFL Grim concluded that by pooling television rights the franchises eliminated competition among themselves in the sale of these rights. In ruling that the broadcast contract with CBS was an antitrust violation, Judge Grim declared, "Clearly, this restricts the individual clubs from determining from which areas the telecasts of their games may be made."

Having failed in the judicial branch of the government to get the antitrust protection desired, the NFL, as well as the other sports leagues and the networks, petitioned Congress for permission to pool and sell their broadcast rights to television networks. Rozelle spent the summer of 1961 actively lobbying Congress. His efforts would be successful, and the result was the Sports Broadcasting Act being approved by Congress and signed into law by President John F. Kennedy on September 30, 1961. The Sports Broadcasting Act altered Judge Grim's ruling and provided the legal protection that allows the practice of leagues collectively selling their television rights to the highest-bidding network. The Sports Broadcasting Act amended antitrust laws and provided sports leagues with what Congress termed "special interest legislation." Years later Rozelle would explain in an editorial he wrote in the *Washington Post*, that "in 1961, Congress was persuaded that it was in the public interest to permit the league to negotiate in a manner which would provide equal access to television facilities for each member club of the league. If the league's interests have been served by this statute, so also has the public interest."

The league-first philosophy and collectively selling the television rights to the entire league paid immediate dividends for the NFL. On January 10, 1962, CBS, already holding broadcast-rights contracts with several individual teams, paid $4.65 million per year, approximately $330,000 per franchise, for the broadcast rights to the 1962 and 1963 regular seasons.

Upon being named commissioner, Rozelle was given a three-year contract with a condition to keep the league headquarters east of the Mississippi

River. To more effectively execute the television strategy Rozelle immediately moved the league offices from Bala-Cynwyd, Pennsylvania, to the General Dynamics Building in New York City's Rockefeller Center. This move allowed Rozelle to have better contact and form personal relationships with pivotal television and corporate-sponsor executives. Rozelle worked extensively to cultivate and maintain these relationships, quickly establishing relationships with Bill MacPhail, the president of CBS Sports, and Jack Landry, an executive with Philip Morris, one of the NFL's main advertisers. Rozelle and MacPhail would negotiate several television contracts. Rozelle's relationship and friendship with Jack Landry would also pay dividends for the NFL. Landry was instrumental in including professional athletes in television commercials to promote Marlboro cigarettes. Although having a vast knowledge of the business and the game of football itself, Rozelle was always trying to learn more. In addition to the necessary business relationships for the league, Pat Summerall explains, Rozelle would often "cultivate friendships of players and ex-players so he'd have a finger on the pulse of those who were active in the game."

Rozelle's demonstration of his understanding of the television industry would be impressive to many. David Harris quoted Bill MacPhail, who said, "He and I went around the league together in 1960 and 1961. He became his own TV man so quickly. He understood the industry almost immediately. He would go to affiliate meetings and got to know the big stations. It was hard at first. Local stations made more money then by showing old movies than they did by showing professional football games. Pete got friendly with the affiliates and was willing to do things for CBS to help sell them on NFL broadcasts. It was a very smart attitude." Don Weiss, former NFL head of public relations, would write in his book (with Chuck Day), *The Making of the Super Bowl*, "Better than any other sports executive I have ever known or observed, Pete instantly recognized television's power and grasped how pro football could harness that power to drive its growth."

It would be Rozelle's visionary ideas that would inspire confidence from people around the league. For example, Tex Schramm agreed with many of Rozelle's policies, and the two were so close in their friendship and thinking that Schramm would often be referred to as the "assistant commissioner." Schramm is quoted in Bob St. John's book, *Tex*: "To be continually successful at the league level, we must pull together. Listen, when we play somebody on Sunday I hate the hell out of our opponent, but when the game is over, it's over, and we're all a part of the league again." Schramm would even take time in his Hall of Fame induction speech in 1991 to once again make this important argument. Schramm told the crowd gathered in Canton, Ohio, "I learned very, very quick that before any club can be successful or any individual can be successful, the league has to be successful. Because the teams and individuals get their recognition and their strength from the strength of the league so early on I made up my mind that I wanted to try to play a role in the development of our game, the development of our league. If necessary, a club has to sacrifice for the good of the league."

Jim Steeg, executive vice president and chief operating officer of the San Diego Chargers and former senior vice president of special events for the NFL, simply contends that "if the word visionary was ever designed for somebody it would be Rozelle." On many occasions, Rozelle would prove masterful at keeping the owners thinking that the interests of the league were in their individual interests as well, but never was it more important than on the issue of collectively selling television rights and sharing the revenue equally. Rozelle's political savvy in getting powerful owners to understand that they could each make more money through television collectively, by agreeing to pool the television rights for a "future" revenue stream—the money was predicted by Rozelle, but not yet in hand—would be an unparalleled accomplishment. Rozelle knew this "future" revenue stream would earn the owners exponentially more money than the individual network deals would earn. Don Weiss in *The Making of the Super Bowl* writes, "I don't think Pete has ever gotten the full credit he deserves for persuading pro football owners to pool their resources and interests." Bob Wussler, a CBS executive, was quoted in Phil Patton's book *Razzle-Dazzle* stating, "The owners ought to build a marble statue of Pete Rozelle at the Hall of Fame in Canton and bow down to it three times a day."

CHAPTER 4

The Rozelle Style

G REAT LEADERSHIP often entails more than great visionary ideas. It takes a style that inspires confidence and loyalty, where convictions about a strategy are the result of listening to others and the situation being carefully thought through. It is a style that gets others to respect your decision making and gets them to align with your thinking to implement that vision. It is an ability to persuade and build consensus to get everyone to move forward together. It is the combination of visionary ideas and leadership style that lends itself to tremendous accomplishment. Rozelle consistently demonstrated that combination and would be as respected by his peers for his style in leading the NFL as he was applauded for his specific visionary ideas. Rozelle demonstrated competence and comfort in many different settings, whether it was before the United States Congress or speaking with a group of players. Jack Kemp, former AFL quarterback, member of the House of Representatives, and vice presidential nominee, calls Rozelle "the ultimate diplomat" who he thought would have been "a great Senator." It would be Rozelle's style that permeated through the various activities in which the NFL became involved.

It would take a wide variety of professional and personal skills for Rozelle to execute his vision for the NFL. In presenting him for induction into the Pro Football Hall of Fame in 1985, Tex Schramm offered a litany of adjectives to describe Rozelle, stating that when the owners elected him commissioner, "they had obtained a man of tremendous intelligence, foresight, patience, preparation, tenacity, a will to win and a sense of class and he imparted that through the league." Rozelle would consistently prove to be adept at using certain personal characteristics at certain times depending on the situation. A few of those characteristics would never waver. Rozelle simply wanted everything involving the NFL to be conducted in a classy fashion and with an unshakable integrity. On the characteristic of integrity, Rozelle would lead by personal example, and the manner in which he conducted himself would be impressive to many who knew him. Dan Rooney says he "never heard Rozelle tell a lie." Art Modell describes Rozelle as a "very honest man who was committed to the NFL and his job." Ed Sabol, founder of NFL Films, points out that Rozelle would rarely, if ever, go out with any team owners because he did not want to appear partial to one particular owner. Ernie Accorsi, senior vice president and general manager of the New York Giants and former employee of Rozelle in the league office, comments that Rozelle had great courage and there was integrity in everything he did.

Maintaining the integrity of the game was at the core of everything Rozelle was trying to accomplish. He felt the public and the media must always have confidence in the integrity of the games. For example, he made sure that teams put out detailed and accurate injury reports about their players. He would also aggressively confront any players who he felt had behaved in a manner that threatened the integrity of the game. This would be most evident in his courageous stance on gambling situations involving NFL players.

The building and maintaining of personal relationships would be an important component of the Rozelle leadership style. For Rozelle, it was always leadership with a personal touch. Art Modell describes Rozelle as a "very gifted individual who was great at public relations and an extraordinary people person." There were two things about being commissioner that Rozelle really enjoyed: the challenge of building the NFL and the people with whom he got to embark on that challenge. Rozelle would surround himself with talented people who shared his vision for the league. Jay Moyer, former NFL counsel to the commissioner and executive vice president, explains that "those who worked for and with him were deeply devoted both to the man and the philosophy he embraced."

In the early days when the NFL office had moved to New York City, the small staff would often have lunch together to help create a strong bond. Rozelle was able to know all about the people in the NFL office. He consistently demonstrated concern for the people around him and took time to learn family names and perhaps what activities employees' kids were involved with. He always wanted to make sure his employees knew their efforts were greatly appreciated. For example, each year employees would receive a handwritten Christmas card from Rozelle.

One of those employees was Peter Hadhazy, who joined the NFL in a summer job following his sophomore year in high school. Even in the interview for this part-time job Rozelle sat in and asked a few questions. Hadhazy recalls that his first impression of the commissioner was that he was a bit shy, but he says that this aspect of innocence and appearing timid are part of Rozelle's charm. Hadhazy also recalls from the beginning of his working for the NFL that Rozelle always demonstrated a great concern and caring for him and was very much a father figure to him and the others in the NFL office. Rozelle gave Hadhazy a television upon graduation from high school in 1962, and when graduating from college he would advise Hadhazy, who desired to continue working for the NFL, to "talk to as many companies as you could, find out what they are willing to pay, and bring me the highest offer and I will give you $1,000 more."

Jim Steeg, executive vice president and chief operating officer of the San Diego Chargers, was twenty-nine years old when he joined the NFL with the responsibility of coordinating the events of the Super Bowl. He explains that Rozelle was a great mentor, teaching him the importance of the relationship aspect of business. He says that Rozelle always emphasized putting on events with style and class and that the relationships and money would develop from there. His idea was if you put together events in a first-class manner, sponsors would want to be a part of it. Tex Schramm explained at Rozelle's Hall of Fame induction in 1985 that Rozelle would often convey the idea to the people involved with the NFL, "I don't care what it is, what it takes, we are going to do it with class and with style, something we can be proud of."

Although in a position of immense power, Rozelle never wanted to give the appearance of being more important than those who were working hard for him. Ernie Accorsi points out that Rozelle had a natural humility that was disarming. When he was working for Rozelle at the league office, Accorsi explains, Rozelle wanted the NFL staff out at games with the simple directive and reminder that "you work for them, be humble and nobody acts arrogant." Rozelle stated in a 1975 interview in *Sport* magazine, "I don't like to be up front unless I have to. If you are up front all the time, you lose your effectiveness. In my job you can do a lot of things quietly." Always humble in trying to execute his vision, Rozelle would probably be the first to point out the many other talented, smart people responsible for the success of the NFL. For example, he spent the opening of his induction speech to the Hall of Fame detailing all of the accomplishments of Tex Schramm, the man who presented him for induction.

Rozelle had a knack for making people feel important. He would do that with everyone he met. He demonstrated class and confidence, yet in many respects he was also common and ordinary. Peter Abitante, an NFL executive, remarks, "You would be in an elevator with this iconic figure and he would make you feel comfortable by saying something simple like 'see that game last night.'" It was his unique leadership style that inspired others and made the NFL employees want to work hard for him. For these reasons, very few people would leave their job working for Rozelle in the NFL office. If at times someone did leave, it was often to take a job with one of the NFL's teams and often at the encouragement of Rozelle because he, too, thought it was an extraordinary opportunity for that person to further his or her career. When someone would ask advice of Rozelle about a promising job offer that he or she had received, it was common for Rozelle to say something such as, "If you were my child, I'd tell you to take the job."

Pat Summerall first met Rozelle when he began working for CBS after his career as the placekicker for the New York Giants. He describes Rozelle's style as courteous, polished, suave, and very confident, but it would be his loyalty that Summerall would value most about his friendship with Rozelle. Rozelle's loyalty toward friends and those who had assisted him was unquestionable. As an example, he contributed Super Bowl tickets to the University of San Francisco's Green and Gold Club fund-raising drawing every year. This type of loyalty to the game and to the people involved in it created a strong sense of loyalty toward Rozelle in return. Jay Moyer explains that Rozelle "prized loyalty. He didn't demand it, but commanded it by the strength of his personality and his track record and he reciprocated it. The league staff didn't just respect him—they liked him because they saw in him a kind and thoughtful and decent man. In that sense, at least, it's difficult to separate his leadership style from the kind of person he was." This respect and loyalty between Rozelle and his staff was especially evident in his relationship with his secretary, Thelma Elkjer. He had brought her from the Rams with him to be his executive secretary when he started serving as commissioner. She would remain Rozelle's secretary at the NFL until he retired and then move to California with him to continue being his assistant.

Rozelle had an inherent understanding of the complexity of being commissioner and all of the various people and constituency groups that someone in that position had to deal with. Jack Kemp explains that Rozelle "moved so easily through many different circles." He adds that even if the event was at the White House, with so much power in the room, Rozelle was "somebody the politicians wanted to talk to. They had so much confidence in his leadership."

Rozelle's appreciation and understanding for the responsibility that he believed a professional sports league had to other institutions was evident in his testimony at hearings before the House of Representatives in 1982:

> Leagues are expected to respect community commitments, fan loyalties, and public investments of funds. Leagues are expected to pursue sensible television policies in the public interest. Leagues are expected to assure competitive playing field balance so that communities throughout the nation may support teams with an equal chance at the championship. Leagues are expected to develop healthy relationships with college athletics and to avoid player eligibility policies that would destroy college athletic programs, and leagues are expected to assure the integrity of their contests.

All of these groups could clearly understand that Rozelle's objective was to grow the game so that all groups would prosper. Everyone sensed the respect Rozelle had for the NFL, its players, its owners, and the game of football in general. Rozelle's dedication to the league created a sentiment of trust among many, so that they never doubted his motivation for operating in the interests of the NFL. Gil Brandt points out that Rozelle was "ambitious with a great feel for the future and a love for the National Football League," and that "more than who wins, Rozelle was always more concerned with how are we going to get bigger and better." Rozelle would state in 1976 before the House of Representatives that "sports leagues are for the most part the product of trial and error based on experience. The NFL, for example, took 56 years to arrive at its present stage—with continual revisions of its policies and practices. Much of this experimentation was directed at achieving a workable balance among the multiple interests involved in professional sports—between stadium attendance and television viewing and among fan interests, player interests, and club interests."

As for his gathering information and his decision-making approach, Rozelle was not big on conducting formal staff meetings. Rozelle demonstrated a demeanor that some might even describe as shy in large groups, but Peter Hadhazy describes Rozelle as "the best one-on-one man that I ever met." Rozelle did keep in constant communication with his staff through letters typewritten by himself in all lowercase or often stopping by someone's office and casually talking about the day's events. Jim Steeg claims that Rozelle would always be aware of what people in the NFL offices were working on. He says that Rozelle "would stop in at the end of the day and go over events where you could not believe that he was aware of what was happening in that particular situation."

Rozelle would consistently demonstrate his intelligence and analytical ability in making decisions. His positions were not developed on a whim, but rather carefully thought out. He was quoted in the *Los Angeles Times* in 1970 about the most important lesson he had learned in his first ten years as commissioner, responding, "I think the basic thing is to take as much time as possible before acting. To talk to as many people as you can before you formulate a decision." Rozelle was a great listener and would ask for input on decisions from his staff, but often it would be to reaffirm his already established position. Paul Tagliabue, NFL commissioner, explains that Rozelle frequently said, "Don't make up your mind or at least don't express your opinion until you've listened to everybody." Rozelle's mantra, as he expressed in a 1979 interview in *Signature* magazine, was research gives you information, and patience ultimately gives you the solution.

Once establishing a position and becoming firm in the conviction of that strategy he would then work to convince others. Rozelle would not only get the decision he wanted, but would often be able to build consensus for that decision. Tagliabue adds, "He was able to build consensus because he knew what everyone thought." Peter Hadhazy explains that Rozelle had an incredible knack for convincing people to do what he wanted and being persuasive enough so that they felt that it was the right solution. Jay Moyer believes that Rozelle's greatest gift was his persuasiveness, saying, "His effectiveness in that regard was, I think, nearly always a product of thorough research and a well-thought-out position on the subject at hand, and the patience and persistence to see the discussion through." Ernie Accorsi claims that Rozelle would underreact to things and that he had a calm demeanor that always gave others the sense that he was in control. Accorsi states, "You always felt there was somebody in charge who knew what he was doing. I felt safe he was making the final decision."

Not afraid to defend his position, Rozelle would, in fact, prove to be as competitive as the players, coaches, and owners whom he served. Paul Tagliabue comments that Rozelle "knew that if you were going to be successful you had to have firm convictions, and part of being firm was defending what you thought was right." Will McDonough, former *Boston Globe* columnist and analyst for CBS Sports, once wrote, "The mistake people sometimes made about Rozelle was misjudging his toughness. Because he is such a nice guy, some people thought he was soft. He isn't. He made difficult decisions that affected football people he liked a great deal because he knew it was best for the league."

Rozelle proved early on in his tenure as commissioner his profoundly persuasive leadership skills by convincing all of the NFL's owners to collectively sell broadcasting rights and share the revenue. Once it was evident that his ideas would be successful, persuading owners on certain issues became easier. Gil Brandt explains that people came to trust Rozelle because his track record was very good and he possessed great communication skills. Rozelle demonstrated great respect for the owners and thought of the NFL as a league that was run by the owners, with the commissioner acting more as a steward for the entire game, representing all factions, including players and fans. Jay Moyer explains, "As commissioner, Pete had significant authority under the NFL's Constitution and Bylaws—he preferred to think of it as responsibility—but he couldn't govern consistently by fiat." Rozelle would have to consistently use his tremendous persuasive ability to bring the owners together and build consensus. Getting consensus from the owners would often be difficult, with many of them having their own agendas, normally what was best for their own team, and perhaps not always taking the league-first approach desired by Rozelle.

Bringing owners together would be attempted through many activities, including annual league meetings. Gil Brandt explains that league meetings would be well prepared and the charismatic Rozelle would get people to listen very intently to his messages. At the annual league meetings Rozelle would even try to foster some camaraderie and make the point that the league come together by organizing social events or golf or tennis tournaments.

To gather information and help build consensus Rozelle developed a system where owners would be put into committees to examine certain issues concerning the league and then report back to the entire ownership group. The committees would often know where Rozelle stood on a particular issue as they convened. Rozelle also knew when to insert himself into the deliberations of a meeting and use his political capital as a successfully performing commissioner. He was the master of the straw poll and being able to work the room, speaking individually with a critical swing vote whenever necessary. For example, when the league was debating its eventual move from a fourteen-game to a sixteen-game schedule for the beginning of the 1978 season, a disagreement would emerge between Rozelle and Tex Schramm who desired to keep the schedule at fourteen regular-season games and six preseason games. Rozelle would focus his strategy on speaking to the league's newest owner, Eddie Debartolo Jr. of the San Francisco 49ers. Rozelle is quoted by Bob St. John in *Tex*, explaining the tactic:

> Tex wanted to keep things as they were because the Cowboys were doing well with six preseason games. Their attendance was good and they were making money. Other teams were not. I needed one more vote for the change, so during a break in the meetings, I went to the newest owner, Edward Debartolo Jr. I told him that with sixteen games in the regular season we'd be negotiating a new television contract. I said there would be more meaningful games, more public interest and talked to him into coming over to our side of the voting.

When Rozelle convinced Debartolo of his position to adopt the sixteen-game schedule he had won the vote. Upon returning to the meeting, Schramm would stare at Rozelle and point out that he knew exactly what Rozelle was doing. Schramm commented, "I saw you corner him. Pick on the new guy who doesn't know any better, huh?"

Another example of Rozelle's understanding of timing and when to expend his political capital as commissioner was during the discussions regarding the continuation of instant replay. The owners had agreed to allow instant replay for the 1986 season, but the system was only for one season and had to again be approved by vote for its use to continue in the 1987 season. Rozelle had been in favor of instant replay, but some of the opponents were among the more powerful owners in the NFL, including Paul Brown, Wellington Mara, and Dan Rooney. The implementation of instant replay had passed by a 23-4-1 vote prior to the 1986 season, but with twenty-one votes needed, the measure was in danger of not being approved for the 1987 season. The recommendation of the competition committee was for a two-year renewal of instant replay. Straw polls conducted by Rozelle convinced him that the two-year renewal was a condition that appeared to have little chance of passing. Rozelle offered a compromise by making instant replay renewable for only one more season so that improvements could continue to be made. Instant replay would pass by a 21-7 vote. Jim Steeg says that when the issue was debated, Dan Rooney finally asked Rozelle his thoughts on the subject, and that got the measure quickly passed. Tex Schramm would comment in the *New York Times* on the instant replay measure passing, simply stating, "This wouldn't have happened were it not for the commissioner's role today."

Another prominent component of the Rozelle style was setting a standard for dealing with the media who cover the NFL. He would hire Jim Kensil, an Associated Press sports columnist, to become the NFL's public relations person and the Elias Sports Bureau to help maintain the league's statistics. Rozelle was adamant that the work coming out the NFL public relations office be accurate; to not be accurate was a sign of being unprofessional. Don Weiss explained the Rozelle philosophy toward the press in *The Making of the Super Bowl*, stating, "Pete Rozelle was unwavering in his insistence that the league level with the press and help them do their job. Moreover, by our providing them with information that helped them better perform their jobs, he reasoned, writers would follow pro football more intently and naturally tend to look with favor on the NFL—or at least be less inclined to go out of their way to criticize us."

Rozelle's personal, easygoing nature with his staff was also his approach with the media. Chris Berman, ESPN announcer, says that because Rozelle was such a football fan he simply loved talking about the game with people who shared his passion and enthusiasm for the sport. Berman calls his casual conversations about football with Rozelle some of his favorite moments in his career. Jim Steeg explains that before the press conferences were more formal, he would often just show up at the annual meeting with the media before the Super Bowl, turn the chair around backwards, sit down, and talk very casually with them. When the press conferences did become more formal, Rozelle would be sure to remain in control of the proceedings. Rozelle was always very prepared when having a press conference, knowing the strong points of the league he wanted emphasized and in some instances instructing people to ask certain questions if the topics he wanted covered were not yet addressed.

Tony Kornheiser, veteran sports columnist and commentator, actually offered a description of a Rozelle press conference. He wrote in the *Washington Post*, "He'd make a brief statement, and he'd take questions. After an hour or so, when his mastery was assured, people would turn to one another, marveling how all the media horses and all the media men never laid a glove on him. Then he'd gaze about at them all—surveying them with sharp eyes that would count every head in the house—and warmly thank them for coming." Kornheiser would also comment on Rozelle's physical appearance of being immaculately dressed, always having a nice tan, and flashing the smile of a winner, and how that contributed to his overall style and presentation. Kornheiser wrote, "His tan, which was always Pete Rozelle's best feature, was the copper color of a New Mexico sunset. Against it, his teeth were pearls. He wouldn't so much walk to the podium, as glide. And he wouldn't so much smile at the assembled multitude, as beam."

Rozelle was very accommodating and accessible to the media on an individual basis, an obvious extension from his work in public relations. Jim Murray would write in the *NFL GameDay Program* that was issued to commemorate Rozelle's career that "as a PR man, he's without equal. He could make Castro President of the U.S." Murray added, "Rozelle's great strength was in appearing to compromise without really doing so. He made everybody feel he was their best friend. He understood public relations as few people have in our generation."

Dave Anderson, a Pulitzer Prize–winning columnist for the *New York Times*, comments, "You could always get him to talk. He did not hide behind being the commissioner and he always had an answer." More than that, Anderson points out that Rozelle was simply "very nice, friendly, and an easy guy to be with." Peter King, senior writer for *Sports Illustrated*, says that Rozelle had a great respect for the power of the media and understood that it was "better to communicate with your public than try to shut them out." He claims if Rozelle thought the story you were doing was "serious and merited his time, he'd give you all of the time you needed." King describes Rozelle as very welcoming and when walking into his office he got the feeling from Rozelle of "come on into my living room and I'll tell you everything I could to help you do your story."

Gary Myers, an NFL writer who has covered the league for the *Dallas Morning News* and *New York Daily News*, says that he would even on occasion call Rozelle at home to get a comment on a major story. Myers recalls when Jerry Jones fired Tom Landry as the head coach of the Cowboys he was able to call Rozelle at his home on a Saturday night to get Rozelle's perspective on the situation. Myers also recalls when he was beginning a new job at the *New York Daily News* and wanting to do a profile on Rozelle that the commissioner made an extra effort to make himself available and help Myers out in the first assignment of his new job. Myers adds that even if you were critical of the NFL on a particular issue, Rozelle would always take your call.

How Rozelle treated the media was nothing more than an extension of how he treated people in general. He was generous with his knowledge and his kindness. Pat Bowlen recalls that when he bought the Denver Broncos in 1984, Rozelle gave him advice, saying, "If you really want to learn about how the NFL works, sit and listen a lot and you will be better off when you hear the twenty-eight different agendas and see where you fit in." When Carl Peterson left the NFL's Philadelphia Eagles to take a job as the general manager of the USFL's Philadelphia Stars he would receive a note from Rozelle wishing him well. Peterson says the note contained no animosity from Rozelle for Peterson going to the rival league and that "there was nothing negative about the decision and nothing negative about the USFL." Peterson also recalls that when the USFL folded Rozelle would speak to some of the NFL owners on his behalf. When Peterson did return to the NFL, taking a job as Lamar Hunt's general manger with the Chiefs, the first call he received was from Pete Rozelle welcoming him back to the NFL and wishing him luck. David Stern, commissioner of the National Basketball Association, comments that Rozelle was "very generous in sharing his expertise with commissioners of other sports." He recalls Rozelle telling him that you always have to do what's best for the league, even though not all teams will think the decision was the best for them.

Finally, Rozelle possessed an irreverent sense of humor, often poking fun at himself. His sense of humor could often defuse a tense situation. When forced into a disciplinary situation with Joe Namath, Rozelle received a letter that only contained the word "jerk." Rozelle would quickly quip about the letter, "Here's a guy who signed his name, but didn't write anything else." Pat Summerall recalls that when he was working on a morning radio station in New York, picking NFL games for that upcoming weekend, he often received a telephone call on Monday from a man disguising his voice chastising him for the wrong predictions. It would be some time before Summerall realized his friend Rozelle was the one joking with him.

Even Ed Garvey, the lead attorney of the NFL Players Association and a man who found himself opposing Rozelle on many labor issues, would tell a story to the *Washington Post* that depicted Rozelle's sense of humor. The story involved Rozelle serving as the arbiter in a dispute between Alan Page, Minnesota defensive end and later Minnesota State Supreme Court Justice, and the Vikings about the team not paying him a bonus. Garvey called Rozelle as a witness and asked him his salary. At that point, Garvey relates, "The management lawyer shouted, 'I object!' and I said, 'who's going to rule? We don't have an arbiter.' Rozelle asked if it was all right for him to go back to his arbiter chair. I said yes. He sat down and said, 'objection sustained,' and then calmly mosied back to the witness stand."

CHAPTER 5

Growing into the Job

UPON BEING mentioned as a possible candidate to be the commissioner of the NFL, Paul Brown suggested to Rozelle that he would "grow into the job." For Rozelle and the NFL, however, there would be no time for any growth to occur. The day that Rozelle was sworn in as commissioner also started one of the more tumultuous weeks in the history of professional football. Immediately claiming Rozelle's attention was the fact that the NFL was beginning to be challenged by a new league, as the soon-to-be-established American Football League was vigorously making plans for its inaugural season in 1960. Despite the positive trend in popularity for professional football, at the end of Bert Bell's tenure, expansion for the NFL was not a priority for the league's owners. That thinking was quickly beginning to change with the announcement on August 14, 1959, of the formation of the AFL. One person who wanted to become part of the burgeoning professional football industry was Lamar Hunt, son of Texas billionaire oilman Haroldson Lafayette Hunt. Despite the failure of the Texans franchise in 1952, Lamar Hunt believed that Dallas would support a professional football team. In 1958, he called Bert Bell with the idea of the NFL placing a team in Dallas, only to be told at that time that the NFL was not interested in expanding.

The other available option for Hunt to get into the NFL was to try to relocate one of its existing franchises. With there being two NFL teams in Chicago, and the Bears being much more popular than the Cardinals, in 1959 Hunt turned his attention to purchasing the Cardinals and moving them to Dallas. George Halas, owner of the Bears, had also offered $500,000 for the Cardinals to move elsewhere. The motivation for Halas was to increase the television exposure and revenue for his Bears. While all other teams could televise their road games back to their home cities, Halas often could not because when the Bears were playing away the Cardinals were often playing at home, and the NFL's blackout rules did not allow the televising of a game into a city where a home team was playing. The owners of the Cardinals, the Wolfson family, would not accept Halas's offer. The Wolfsons also only offered to sell Lamar Hunt 49 percent of the franchise, therefore not providing Hunt with the power to move the team. Similar failed negotiations with the Wolfson family were also attempted by Bud Adams from Houston, Bob Howsam from Denver, and Max Winter from Minneapolis.

When it became clear to Hunt that neither his desire of getting an expansion franchise nor of purchasing and moving the Cardinals would come to fruition, he thought of starting another professional league. He simply thought that professional football's growth was dramatic enough that the game could survive and prosper in several geographic regions that were not occupied by the NFL. Hunt began recruiting people and first called Bud Adams, whom Hunt knew had also unsuccessfully tried to buy the Cardinals. Adams recalls that when Hunt asked him if he was interested in forming a new professional football league, his response was "Hell yes!" Hunt also quickly secured Denver and Minneapolis, which made four cities. He then looked to New York and Los Angeles to obtain the two high-profile television markets to fulfill his original plan of a six-team league. Hunt convinced Barron Hilton, hotel heir, to own the Los Angeles franchise and Harry Wismer, a former sports broadcaster, to own the New York team.

Hunt then received a letter from Ralph Wilson, a millionaire who was in the trucking and insurance businesses and owner of a minority share of the Detroit Lions. Wilson had read about Hunt and the AFL in the *New York Times* and had become interested. Wilson asked Hunt about owning a team, with a particular desire to have one in Miami. In 1946 the AAFC did have a team in Miami, the Seahawks, and the team had a dismal season, winning only three of its fourteen games, with the largest game attendance being only 9,700 and the smallest a meager 2,250. The city still souring from that bad experience and refusing to let a new professional team use its Orange Bowl stadium, Wilson needed another location. Hunt, now believing that eight teams were needed to start the league, recommended several cities to Wilson that might be of interest, including Kansas City, Cincinnati, St. Louis, and Buffalo. Having never been to Buffalo, but aware of some of its success in the AAFC, including an attendance average of over 31,000 in 1947, Wilson selected Buffalo as the location for his team. The final team of the original eight AFL franchises would be given to Billy Sullivan in Boston. The AFL would thus bring professional football to six new cities: Boston, Buffalo, Dallas, Denver, Houston, and Minneapolis, and create direct competition with the NFL in New York and Los Angeles.

Initially Lamar Hunt did not see or desire for the AFL to be a threat to the NFL. He even invited Bert Bell to become commissioner of the AFL in addition to his remaining commissioner of the NFL. Another example of early harmony between the two leagues occurred in late July 1959, when Bell was going to speak before the Senate Judiciary Committee to try to secure an antitrust exemption for the NFL. To help his case that the NFL did not engage in business relationships that could be deemed an unreasonable restraint of trade, Bell had asked Hunt if he could mention the new league that was forming. It was in Bell's testimony before Congress, with Hunt sitting in the back of the room, that the public first heard of the AFL. In his testimony Bell would never mention Hunt's name, only identifying the founders of the league as "people from Texas." Bell would tell the Senate that the new league was not an "outlaw" to organized football and that no NFL owner "has an objection" to the new league. He would even quote George Preston Marshall, Washington Redskins owner, who had said, "If they're great, they'll help us. If they're not great, they won't hurt us." Bell also testified that teams in the new league would be allowed to compete for players against the NFL, that no agreement had been reached on player recruiting, and that none would be entered into by the two leagues, except that contracts with players in either league would be recognized by the other league. Although nobody had yet put up any money and there was no official announcement made to the public, the AFL appeared to be in business.

Bell's conciliatory testimony toward the AFL before the Senate would quickly be altered to a more aggressive, competitive position concerning the upstart league. Upon sensing some momentum from the AFL, and having been through the competition from the AAFC, the NFL would try to curtail the AFL's formation. In dramatically reversing the position that Bell had articulated before Congress months earlier, the NFL announced plans that it was now ready to expand with the newly named AFL cities as its primary targets. George Halas, the patriarchal figure in the NFL, having been in attendance at the league's organization back in 1920—was very focused on dealing with the AFL. Remembering the cost to the NFL of being in competition with the AAFC, Halas had even taken an informal poll of the other owners at Bert Bell's funeral about the possibility of expansion into Dallas and Minneapolis-St. Paul.

Rozelle now had to quickly learn to administer the league in the midst of a battle with the AFL over acquiring cities in which to have professional football teams. Upon being elected, Rozelle was aware of the importance of the expansion issue and the arising challenge of the AFL, stating, "The great growth of interest in professional football through the National League's promotion of the game has created a heavy demand for membership in several populated centers." Only one day into his being commissioner, the NFL owners voted to revise its expansion rule. Originally, Article 4, Section 1, of the NFL Constitution and Bylaws, stated, "The National Football League shall be limited to twelve teams unless enlarged or changed by the unanimous (twelve-twelfths) approval of the league." On January 27, by a 10-2 vote, the NFL announced a revised rule that now declared that expansion could be approved with only a ten-twelfths approval. Halas would get his wish for expansion by finally convincing Wellington Mara to become the tenth vote, and expansion would also pass by a 10-2 margin. Mara had wanted Baltimore to be shifted from the Western Conference, where it had been since it joined the NFL in 1953, but settled for having the owners of the Eastern Conference decide which of its proposed expansion franchises, Dallas or Minnesota, would join the East after the 1960 season.

One of the owners against expansion was George Preston Marshall, owner of the Washington Redskins, who particularly didn't want any expansion into Dallas. Playing in the 28,669-seat Griffith Stadium, Marshall's Redskins depended heavily on their television deals for revenue. Marshall, with holdings in several television stations, had made the Redskins the prominent NFL team in the South.

The Wolfson family was also against expansion, concerned that a Texas team would cut into the television exposure and the revenue generated by the Chicago Cardinals in the South. The Cardinals, although weak in attendance in Chicago, were still a coveted commodity—a franchise in professional football. When several people were trying to obtain the team and get into the professional football business, the value of their franchise increased. But, along with the AFL now starting up, expansion in the NFL would further decrease the value of the Cardinals because there would be fewer locations in which to move the franchise and fewer prospective owners available to buy the team.

On Saturday August 29, 1959, a mere fifteen days after Hunt had announced that the AFL was going to play football in 1960, Halas held a press conference to announce that Dallas, the city where Hunt was going to place his team, and Houston, the city where Adams was to put his, were being recommended for expansion into the NFL and would begin playing in 1961. Halas also announced that several other AFL cities were also being considered by the NFL for future expansion franchises. In addition to trying to acquire cities, the NFL would make overtures toward the people spearheading the AFL to try to prevent the new league from ever forming. The NFL plan was to grant NFL teams to the owners who were getting prepared to start the new league, notably Hunt and Adams.

Continuing to act as a point man for the NFL on expansion, Halas would have conversations with both Hunt and Adams about becoming owners of expansion NFL teams in Dallas and Houston respectively. Adams recalls that when he initially talked with Halas about an expansion team, prior to the official formation of the AFL, his getting an NFL franchise didn't look encouraging. Adams had even agreed to sponsor an exhibition game in September 1959 in Houston between Halas's Bears and Art Rooney's Steelers, paying each team a guarantee upward of $20,000 to play the game. Adams's idea was for two of the NFL's most influential owners to experience what Houston could bring to the league. But by the time the game was actually played, the AFL had already announced its plans, and Adams recalls that he did not even speak with Halas when he was in Houston for the exhibition game.

Had Halas and the NFL been successful in getting either Hunt or Adams to join the NFL, it would have almost certainly ended the AFL before a game was ever played. But both Hunt and Adams held steadfast in their commitment to the AFL and its other owners. Hunt refused the NFL offer to become the owner of the expansion Dallas franchise. Adams was quoted in Ed Gruver's book *The American Football League: A Year-by-Year History, 1960–1969*, stating, "When I met with Mr. Halas, he was ready to give Houston an NFL franchise in 1960 for $650,000. I said, 'I gave my word to Lamar, and I can't go back on it.'" One location where the NFL was successful in getting an AFL defection was in convincing Minnesota to join the NFL. Max Winter, Minnesota franchise owner, was entering the AFL's first-ever ownership meeting on November 22, 1959, when he mentioned to Ralph Wilson that he might withdraw from the AFL to join the NFL, claiming he couldn't pass up an NFL franchise for Minneapolis. Bud Adams recalls that Winter also told him that Halas was still willing to give Adams an NFL franchise, but once again Adams would remain loyal to Hunt and the AFL. One day after Pete Rozelle was selected as commissioner, on January 27, 1960, Minnesota did withdraw from the AFL, and one day later it was officially granted an NFL expansion franchise that would begin playing in 1961.

On January 30, 1960, with Minnesota pulling out, the AFL, at the urging of Los Angeles Chargers owner Barron Hilton (who wanted a West Coast rival for his team), would award Oakland the eighth and final original franchise. An AFL franchise in Oakland set up direct competition with the NFL in yet another geographical region, playing just across the bay from San Francisco. The NFL would also officially grant an expansion franchise to Dallas, with its owners Clint Murchison Jr. and Bedford Wynne, on January 28, 1960. Unlike Minnesota, however, the Dallas franchise would begin playing only nine months later in the 1960 season so that an NFL team would be in that city and could directly compete against Hunt's AFL franchise.

With the indications that Dallas was a prime target for NFL expansion, Joe Foss, the AFL commissioner, stated in the *New York Times*, "We would not consider it a kiss of love if the NFL expanded into Dallas." He continued, "It would be a clear sign they intended to continue their scorched-earth policy that caused us to surrender the Minneapolis-St. Paul territory." Foss, who was also a World War II Medal of Honor pilot and former governor of South Dakota, was also quoted in *Sports Illustrated*, stating, "This is an act of war. We will go to court or to Congress to prevent the NFL from putting the AFL franchise in Dallas out of business. You have antitrust laws to take care of such situations." Rozelle directly countered Foss's comment, questioning why the NFL should not be allowed to move into Dallas. He stated, "Should the NFL expand to Dallas it would hope to achieve the same harmony there with the AFL representative that it is seeking in Los Angeles, New York, and apparently San Francisco, where the AFL proposes to launch member clubs in NFL cities. We hope to get along in all four cities." George Halas would also comment in the *Los Angeles Times*, "The NFL has as much right to put a team in any city it wishes as the new league does."

Lamar Hunt would not see the NFL's expansion into Dallas in the analogous manner that Rozelle and others in the NFL had viewed the AFL's move into Los Angeles, New York, and the San Francisco area. Hunt stated, "It's not the same at all. In our case it's just like a little dog going into the big backyard of the big dog. But in their case it's the big dog going into the little backyard and asking the little bitty dog if there's not room for him. It's the size of the backyard that counts." When Dallas was officially announced by the NFL as an expansion city, Foss also commented, "They [the NFL] know this [Dallas] is a one-team city. They want to make Lamar drop out of this thing and make us all look bad. They want this league to fold. Well, Lamar won't quit and we're not going to fold. They made a big mistake. They promised to let us live." It was at that time that Clint Murchison would also convince Tex Schramm to leave CBS after three years to handle football operations for the Dallas Cowboys. Schramm commented, "In the final analysis it is going to be for the people of Dallas to decide which of the two teams they prefer to see." He added, "We don't feel that Dallas is either a one-team city or a minor-league city, Dallas has been an NFL member before and we are gratified that we are back."

Foss's comment about Dallas being a one-team city would turn out to be prophetic in that the Dallas Texans, despite having much better records than the NFL's Cowboys (in the three seasons in which both teams were in Dallas the Texans had a record of 25-17, and the Cowboys were 9-28-3, including a winless inaugural season in 1960), and despite winning the AFL championship in 1962, after the 1962 season the Dallas Texans were moved to Kansas City to become the Chiefs. Hunt, too, was correct that Dallas would support a professional football team, but supporting two teams in that size of a market was impractical. The NFL had even tried to get Hunt to agree to merge his Texans with the Cowboys and abandon the AFL after the first season. Once again, Hunt's resolve and commitment to the league he started did not waver. Los Angeles would also prove to be a one-team city, as after the inaugural 1960 season, the AFL's Chargers, with a better record than the NFL's Rams, would move from Los Angeles to San Diego.

To help establish its viability, the AFL actively pursued a television strategy. Sensing immediately the need for a collective approach, the AFL owners had decided to pool the broadcast rights to its games and share the revenue equally among all teams, rather than have individual, nonestablished teams try to negotiate their own individual television agreements. The idea, implemented by Hunt and the AFL, was due to Hunt being familiar with a revenue-sharing system that had been explained to him by Branch Rickey, an executive with major league baseball's Brooklyn Dodgers, when Rickey was trying to form the Continental Basketball League. On June 9, 1960, the AFL would obtain one of its early pivotal objectives toward survival when it signed a contract with ABC to pay the league a total of $8.5 million for the television rights for five years. This collective strategy, which packaged all games for sale to one network and then shared the revenue equally among all franchises, allowed each AFL team to earn more television money in its first season than the 1960 NFL champion Philadelphia Eagles. The success of the AFL's television system of pooling broadcast rights in providing substantial and equitable revenue was evidence that Rozelle had presented to the NFL owners to convince them to adopt a similar policy.

Despite an average attendance of only 16,538 for the fifty-six games of its inaugural year, totaling less than one million in paid attendance, with the television contract providing money and exposure, the AFL was in a position to survive and remain a threat to the NFL. For example, one small measure of success would come for the AFL in 1962 when the New York Titans and Dallas Texans were playing in a game televised on ABC. With the game running long, dominated mostly by incomplete passes, ABC cut away from the end of the game so as not to preempt *The Walt Disney Show*. The network was soon flooded with calls complaining about the game being taken off the air.

The year 1963 would bring two different situations that Rozelle would be forced to deal with: the issue of players betting on professional football games, and the assassination of President John F. Kennedy. Rozelle's handling of both of these situations would help define the early years of his tenure as commissioner. His handling of one situation would receive widespread accolades, while the other would be a point of contention.

When rumors of gambling by players had reached Rozelle's attention, in trying to uphold the integrity of the game that he felt was always of paramount importance, Rozelle calmly, patiently, but diligently conducted an investigation. Rozelle hired sixteen former FBI agents to investigate whether any players had bet on games. Two prominent players would come under the most scrutiny: Paul Hornung, Green Bay's all-pro running back and league MVP in 1961, and Alex Karras, a prominent defensive lineman for the Detroit Lions. During training camp before the 1962 season, Rozelle visited every team to remind the players that betting on games would not be tolerated and that there would be severe penalties for anyone caught gambling, including banishment from the game. There had been an NFL precedent for suspending players for gambling. In 1947, Bert Bell had suspended Frank Filchock, quarterback, and Merle Hapes, running back, of the New York Giants for their failure to report bribe offers.

The issue would begin to escalate when the Green Bay Packers defeated the New York Giants at Yankee Stadium to win the NFL title in 1962. On December 31, 1962, the day after the game, Rozelle called Karras to meet him. At this meeting Karras would admit to Rozelle that he had bet on professional football games, including the 1962 championship game. At Rozelle's request, Karras would agree to sign an affidavit that he had not thrown any games, nor ever bet against the Lions.

The situation for Karras would become worse when, appearing on NBC's *Huntley-Brinkley Report* on January 16, 1963, he would admit to betting on games that he was playing in. Karras was immediately summoned to New York by Rozelle. Rozelle requested that Karras take a lie-detector test. The main question Rozelle again asked of Karras was whether he had ever thrown any games. Karras would answer that he never placed a bet against the Lions, took money to throw a game, shaved points, or missed tackles. As Karras left the meeting, Rozelle would tell him not to mention the contents of their meeting or that they had even met at all.

On August 25, 1962, Rozelle visited the Green Bay Packers before an exhibition game to warn them about gambling. Rozelle would also meet with Paul Hornung individually after the meeting with the entire team. Hornung quoted Rozelle in his book *Golden Boy*, writing that Rozelle told him, "You're going to have to watch your associations. You have to be extra careful, Paul, because you're a bachelor and some people are always anxious to shoot down someone of prominence." On Tuesday January 8, 1963, while in Los Angeles for the Pro Bowl, Hornung would get a message to call Rozelle at his home. Hornung took the red-eye flight and was in New York the next morning.

At the meeting with Rozelle, Hornung initially denied gambling on any games. Rozelle told Hornung that he had been under investigation for ten months and that his telephone in Green Bay had been tapped. At this point Hornung did admit to betting on games, including Packer games. In *Golden Boy*, Hornung wrote, "I *always* [Hornung's emphasis] bet on us to win. But it was just for fun, more than anything. I don't think I ever won or lost more than $2,000 on a season." Once Hornung confessed, Rozelle asked him to take a lie detector test. Hornung refused and told Rozelle that he could continue to ask Hornung about his own gambling, but that he was not going to talk about anybody else.

Rozelle informed the owners of the investigation at a league meeting in January 1963. He would instruct that "No Gambling" signs be placed in team locker rooms before training camp. Later that year on April 6, Rozelle would meet with Vince Lombardi in his office, where Rozelle showed Lombardi the evidence that he had gathered against Hornung, including Hornung's signed admission. David Maraniss indicated in his book *When Pride Still Mattered: A Life of Vince Lombardi* that with the evidence overwhelming, Rozelle conveyed to Lombardi that his only choice was to suspend Hornung indefinitely. Lombardi would respond in agreement that the commissioner had no choice, according to Maraniss, saying to Rozelle, "You've got to do what you've got to do." Rozelle and Lombardi then spent the rest of the day together over a meal and drinks.

On April 17, 1963, Hornung and Karras would each receive a telephone call from Rozelle informing them that they were being suspended indefinitely for betting on professional football games, citing paragraph two of the NFL players' contract that empowers him to fine or suspend any player who accepts a bribe or bets on a game. The investigation would confirm that Hornung had placed bets of $100 to $500 on NFL games, including the Packers, and college games from 1958 to 1961, and that Karras had placed six bets of $50 to $100 on six NFL games since 1958. Five other Lions players would be fined $2,000 for betting on the 1962 championship game. The Lions would even be fined $4,000 because they ignored a police tip and because head coach George Wilson had minimized information that some players, including Karras, had been seen with people the league would deem undesirable, and that outsiders had been allowed to view games from the Lions' bench. On the fining of the Lions, Karras would write in his autobiography, *Even Big Guys Cry,* "The nerve of him [Rozelle] to say that some people had no right to sit on Lion benches. That sort of thing had been going on for years—all around the league. Comedians and actors, politicians and priests, cops and robbers—I've seen many of them sit on team benches. I've sat next to them. Some were friends of the owner, or the general manager, or Pete Rozelle himself."

In trying to sell the notion that the integrity of the game had not been harmed, upon announcing the suspensions Rozelle would state that there was "no evidence that any NFL player has given less than his best in playing in any game." He also added there was "no evidence that any player has ever bet against his own team" or "sold information to gamblers."

On March 16, 1964, Rozelle released a statement that both Hornung and Karras, having sat out one full season, would be reinstated. With the AFL mounting a serious challenge, Rozelle had demonstrated tremendous courage in suspending two all-pro players, especially the enormously popular Hornung. In analyzing his handling of the gambling scandal, Kenneth Rudeen would write in *Sports Illustrated,* "In that decision of wise severity Rozelle demonstrated strength, courage and his belief that the league's integrity was first among its possessions." Jim Murray wrote in the *Los Angeles Times,* "Rozelle had to protect the game rather than the players. He had to show the owners, the players—and the public—that pro football was a big boy now, a public trust that the public could trust." Tex Schramm called Rozelle's handling of the investigation, "the thing that made everybody accept him as commissioner and no longer a boy playing the part. He gained once and for all everybody's complete respect."

Friday, November 22, 1963, was a warm sunny day in Dallas, Texas. President John F. Kennedy was in Dallas on that day to give a speech to civic and business leaders. In the eleven-mile trip from Love Field Airport through downtown Dallas, the weather allowed for the plastic bubble top to be removed and the bullet-proof windows rolled down on the presidential limousine. As the motorcade entered into Dealey Plaza and turned from Houston Street onto Elm at 12:30 p.m., shots were fired from the gun of Lee Harvey Oswald who was on the sixth floor of the Texas School Book Depository Building, striking the president. President Kennedy was immediately rushed to Parkland Hospital, but shortly thereafter, assistant press secretary Malcolm Kilduff would announce to the press, "President John F. Kennedy died at approximately 1:00 p.m., Central Standard Time today here in Dallas. He died of a gunshot wound in the brain. I have no other details of the assassination."

With a nation demoralized, Rozelle would have to make a decision as to whether the NFL's scheduled games for that Sunday were to be played. Rozelle would receive telephone calls from both Art Modell and Dan Rooney urging him to cancel the games. He also consulted with Kennedy's press secretary, Pierre Salinger, a friend Rozelle had known from when they were classmates at the University of San Francisco. Salinger and Rozelle both agreed that President Kennedy would have wanted the games to be played. Both also factored into their decision that neither of the cities most impacted were hosting a game that weekend, with the Washington Redskins playing in Philadelphia and the Dallas Cowboys playing in Cleveland.

While many sporting events were cancelled on that weekend, including the AFL's games, Rozelle decided to proceed with the NFL playing. In a statement, Rozelle said, "It has been traditional in sports for athletes to perform in times of great personal tragedy." The statement added, "Football was Mr. Kennedy's game. He thrived on competition." Rozelle would provide more detail as to his decision-making process about playing on that Sunday in a *New York Times* interview with Samantha Stevenson in 1994.

> I was in my office the day Kennedy was shot. The first thing I did was try to reach Pierre. He was with some Cabinet members returning from Tokyo. The White House found him right away for me, and he returned my call right away. I said: "we've got planes with the players ready to get in the air and I don't know when the services will be. What can you tell me?" I was terribly upset. It

was difficult to talk to him about it. Pierre said: "I think you should go ahead and play the games." I hung up and thought about it some more. I discussed it with everyone in the office. Late that afternoon, I made the decision. I had to; our teams were calling, they wanted to know what to do.

Rozelle called just for football to be played on that Sunday, there would be no bands, half-time shows, pregame introductions of the starting lineups, or commercial announcements at the stadium, and the only music played at the stadium would be the national anthem. In fear of an angry reaction to anyone associated with Dallas, Browns owner Art Modell would tell his public address announcer to introduce the visiting team on that day only as the Cowboys.

The Cowboys, who had been practicing only three miles away from downtown Dallas, were informed of the assassination when one of their trainers came onto the field and told them the news. Tom Landry, Cowboys head coach, immediately dismissed practice. In his autobiography Landry described playing on the Sunday after the Kennedy assassination. He explained that after a moment of silence, "the Cowboys of Dallas were booed with a bitterness we had never encountered anywhere before. It was as if the events of that afternoon had suddenly tainted everything having to do with Dallas, Texas. We were booed lustily in every city we visited for the rest of the year and into the next."

The games that Sunday would not be televised, only broadcast on radio, and the NFL would return one-fourteenth of its broadcast money to CBS. In New York the Giants would offer any ticket holders a refund, but received no requests, and a capacity crowd 63,800 people filled Yankee Stadium. It was reported in the *New York Times* the next day that "the number of absentees was insignificant." To add to the confusion of the tragic weekend, on Sunday, November 24, 1963, Jack Ruby would shoot Lee Harvey Oswald on live national television in the basement of the Dallas Police Headquarters. On that Sunday, after going to church with his daughter, Anne Marie, Rozelle attended the game between the Giants and the Cardinals at Yankee Stadium. As reported by Harold Rosenthal in his book *Fifty Faces of Football*, Rozelle was confronted by Red Smith, columnist for the *New York Herald Tribune*, who told Rozelle, "I think you're doing the wrong thing playing today." When asked why by Rozelle, Smith argued, "because it shows disrespect for a dead president of the United States who isn't even buried yet." Rozelle replied, "There can be no disrespect where no disrespect was intended."

The next day in the *New York Times*, Arthur Daley described being at the stadium as similar to being at the Polo Grounds on December 7, 1941, the day of the Japanese attack on Pearl Harbor. Daley would contest, "Big men were playing a boy's sport at the wrong time." In the article he also described the moment when fans first actually responded like they were at a football game, when, by the sixth minute of the second quarter, Y. A. Tittle, the Giants' quarterback, asked the fans for quiet. Daley wrote, "They were caught up by the growing excitement and thoughts of their grief were swept aside. If that be an indictment, it would take a learned psychologist to offer interpretation."

Rozelle later described the Sunday being at the Giants/Cardinals game in the *New York Times*. "We had a moment of silence. I could not concentrate on the game. I brooded about my decision the entire game. You have to understand, I was more than depressed over the assassination. I had lost someone whom I'd respected as the leader of our country, but I was also a close friend of the Kennedy family." Rozelle did, however, lament on more than one occasion about the decision to play, stating "If I had a chance, I'd probably have done it differently." He would also state "One of the things that I regretted most was when we played games during the Kennedy assassination. The league took a lot of flak for that and it was a low period."

Years later after he announced his retirement, the Kennedy decision would often arise. "Reporters asked him often about his many successes," NFL executive Joe Browne says, "and eventually the conversation would turn to any decisions he regretted. Almost by default Pete would mention the Kennedy Sunday because he really had no major regrets. However, I don't really believe deep down he thought he made the wrong decision. Salinger said the Kennedy family wanted the games to be played in order to help get Americans out of their funk even if just for a few hours. The White House wanted to get things back to normal as quickly as possible."

Frank Gifford, who played for the Giants in the game at Yankee Stadium that weekend after the Kennedy assassination, also claims that he never heard Rozelle privately comment that he regretted the decision about playing games that weekend. Gifford points out, "The entire country was in such a malaise and football played a minor part, but it did help kick start the country." He also believes the Kennedy family wanted "America to get back to living."

Overall, in three challenging years, Rozelle had demonstrated an ability to achieve monumental things, deal with difficult situations, and make tough decisions. For his handling of these situations and the overall performance of his job Rozelle would be recognized in the January 6, 1964, issue as the 1963 *Sports Illustrated* Sportsman of the Year, the first and only time a commissioner of a professional sports league was recognized with this honor. Now having the trust and confidence in the league's owners, Rozelle could turn to dealing with the AFL and the eventual merger.

CHAPTER 6

Forming a New Frontier: The Merger with the AFL

I NITIALLY THE NFL had not been overly concerned with the AFL. The NFL had successfully withstood a challenge from the rival AAFC, and commissioner Bert Bell felt that the AFL helped relieve pressure that the NFL was receiving from the federal government. Whatever assistance the AFL might have initially provided to the NFL in its antitrust position, it would soon be the only positive characteristic of the AFL's existence in the thoughts of the NFL. The AFL even brought its own lawsuit against the NFL for alleged antitrust violations, charging that the NFL conspired against the AFL on the issues of securing a television contract, signing players, and placing expansion franchises, particularly when the NFL decided to expand into Dallas and compete directly against Lamar Hunt's Texans. The $10 million lawsuit brought by the AFL was seeking $1.5 million in reparation for the Texans. The suit initiated on June 17, 1960, was debated until May 21, 1962, when Judge Roszel Thompson of the federal district court in Baltimore finally ruled against the AFL. The ruling would be upheld on appeal in the U.S. Fourth Circuit Court of Appeals on November 21, 1963.

Early on, the AFL was able to gain some much needed exposure with the help of the NFL's blackout policy, which at the time prohibited NFL games from being televised in cities in which a team was playing a home game. Curt Gowdy, AFL broadcaster on ABC from 1962 to 1964 and on NBC from 1965 to 1969, explained in Ed Gruver's *The American Football League* that the NFL "opened the door for us. On Sundays, we were the only pro football game on TV in those areas where NFL teams were playing at home." Having fans not be able to see an NFL game, but still see an AFL game on television was "like opening the door to a vacuum cleaner salesman and letting him in. And that's what the NFL did." The NFL would revise its blackout policy for the next year so that if, for example, the Giants were playing at home, a different NFL game would be televised into the New York market, but according to Gowdy, "In that one year that the NFL had their blackout rule, the AFL was the only game on in some of those big cities. And that was a bad strategical error by the NFL."

The year 1964 would be crucial in the competition between the two leagues. In 1964, the NFL television contract for the first time was open for all networks to make a bid. Unlike the last television contract in 1962, when Rozelle had to legally negotiate with only CBS because of the network's ownership of several of the teams' broadcast rights, Rozelle could now have the networks compete against each other. His vision of a pooled system with multiple television networks bidding against themselves and the increased revenue that those negotiations could bring was finally coming to fruition. To finalize the negotiations, Rozelle utilized a purse-bid system, where each of the networks would submit their best bid in a sealed envelope. Rozelle would open the envelopes and the highest bidder would become the television network of the NFL. On January 24, 1964, at 11:00 a.m., with network executives present at the NFL office, the first envelope opened was that of NBC, who offered just over $21 million for the broadcast rights to the 1964 and 1965 regular seasons. As its television deal with the AFL was nearing its conclusion, ABC would also be involved in the negotiations for the broadcast rights to the NFL. ABC executives Ed Scherick and Tom Moore had discovered in the NFL's broadcast contract that it would be permissible for a network to broadcast NFL doubleheaders, putting a game on at 1:00 and a game on at 4:00. Moore explained in Phil Patton's book *Razzle Dazzle*, "I went to Pete Rozelle and said 'look, we're about to bid tomorrow and I don't want to lose my advantage to anybody else. If they don't know what I'm about to ask you, I don't want you to tell them.' He [Rozelle] said, 'anything you'll ask me is confidential.' 'As we've read this, we can do doubleheaders,' I said. He said, 'you're absolutely right.'" ABC feeling it could easily afford the cost with two games providing advertising income submitted a bid of $26 million to the NFL for the 1964 and 1965 regular seasons.

Finally the offer from CBS would be revealed. CBS, too, had realized the possibility of doubleheaders and offered the winning bid of $28.2 million for the two years. The bid by CBS more than tripled what the network had been paying for the rights to the previous two seasons. James Aubrey, president of CBS, explained the rationale for his network's historic bid in the *New York Times*, stating "We know how much these games mean to the viewing audience, our affiliated stations, and the nation's advertisers."

In fact, Aubrey had also called Rozelle and inquired about the possibility of doubleheaders. Tom Moore and ABC were surprised that CBS was also aware of the doubleheader possibility. Moore would ask Aubrey if anyone, implying Rozelle, had tipped him off about the doubleheader strategy. Again, as quoted by Phil Patton, Moore would state, "He [Aubrey] says no one told him and I believe him." Patton would also quote Rozelle, who claimed, "We didn't think it [doubleheader] was feasible yet. Eventually, though, we knew it would give us more national exposure, that there would be viewers who followed the league, not just individual teams." It would be the televised doubleheaders that would particularly help promote the national following of the NFL's Dallas Cowboys and Green Bay Packers (and eventually the AFL's Miami Dolphins, Oakland Raiders, and Pittsburgh Steelers after the merger). The doubleheaders would not be telecast in a city at the same time when the team was playing at home, keeping the league's consistent philosophy of protecting the team's home market and ticket sales.

Art Modell was in Florida waiting for the call from Rozelle about the outcome of the network bidding. Modell would then meet with the other owners to inform them of the news. When the NFL owners learned that they were getting $14 million dollars, their reaction was that the amount was not bad, thinking $7 million per year was still a good contract. But then they learned, to their amazement and delight, that the $14 million figure was for a single season. Modell says, "We were slapping hands with each other like we were kids." Each franchise would earn approximately $1 million per year, up from the $365,000 per year they had been earning, and more than ten times any team had earned in television revenue under Bert Bell. The new television contract would guarantee that no NFL team was going to lose money.

Not aware of the doubleheader possibility, NBC came in a distant third in the bidding for the NFL. When a frustrated Carl Lindemann, NBC's head of sports, returned to his office, he had a message from Joe Foss. Along with Sonny Werblin, owner of the Jets, who had relationships with many people at NBC, Foss would meet with Lindemann to discuss an AFL broadcast contract with NBC. The AFL and NBC would quickly come to terms, and on the same day that the NFL announced its television deal with CBS, the AFL agreed on a television deal that would pay the league $36 million over a five-year period, beginning with the 1965 season. The deal would be officially signed by the following Monday. NBC would also provide some up-front money totaling $1.25 million for the AFL to use to sign players.

Unlike the NFL's fourteen franchises, the AFL money was only divided by its eight teams, giving each team approximately $900,000 per year from NBC, a substantial increase from the $261,000 each team had been earning per year from ABC. In *The American Football League*, Ed Gruver quoted Billy Sullivan, Patriots owner, calling the day the AFL signed it television contract with NBC "the greatest day in our history." Lamar Hunt would state in an interview in the *Super Bowl XXV Game Program* that the television contract the AFL signed in 1964 with NBC "really insured that the AFL would stay in business. It was the most dramatic single development in regard to the competition of the two leagues. The first contract with ABC gave us some exposure, but the money was not large. The second one gave us the competitive ability to go and sign players, and it was much more stabilizing than the first one."

Three months after agreeing to new contracts for the regular season, on April 17, 1964, the broadcast rights to the 1964 and 1965 NFL championship games would be sold to CBS for $1.8 million per game, more than double what NBC had paid to broadcast the 1963 championship game. Unlike the regular-season bidding that was open to all three networks, the negotiations for the championship games was limited to CBS. Rozelle would explain in the *New York Times* that the loyalty to CBS was "because each of the other two networks have contracts with the American Football League to televise regular season games during the period of this contract, and one of these networks is committed to carry the AFL playoff game in 1964." He concluded, "It is considered the best interests of the National Football League to keep its championship game free of any possible conflict of interest, especially in the area of promotion."

The AFL had been disparagingly referred to by George Halas as that "damn Mickey Mouse league." Although the average attendance for the AFL had only grown from 16,538 in 1960 to 21,584 for the 1963 season, there was consistent growth in attendance. The economic fortunes of the league also dramatically changed in 1964 with its new television agreement. After both leagues signed lucrative television contracts in 1964, two things became abundantly evident, the AFL was now on the most solid financial footing of its existence and competition for players was about to escalate to unprecedented levels.

The NFL was decisively winning battles for attendance and popularity with its AFL counterparts in the various cities, but competition for players that had ensued was beginning to take its toll on both leagues and being noticed by all. Competition for college players between the NFL and the AFL was something that Pete Rozelle had intimate knowledge of. As general manager of the Rams, Rozelle had battled the AFL's Houston Oilers and owner Bud Adams for the services of 1959 Heisman Trophy winner, LSU's Billy Cannon. In November 1959, with its first territorial selection, Houston picked Cannon. To counter the AFL, the NFL would secretly hold its draft in November as well. The Rams also would select Cannon, whom Rozelle had described as "the finest football player in the draft," as their first-round pick. The challenge for Rozelle was now to sign Cannon before the Oilers did.

Initially, there seemed to be no concern as to whether the Rams would be the team that would sign Cannon. In the December 1, 1959, *Los Angeles Times*, a headline would read, "Cannon Had Rams Picked Out Long Ago." In this article Cannon would state, "As a youngster I used to watch the Rams on television. They were and still are my favorite team and I hoped to someday play for them." In claiming he had no interest in playing for the Oilers, Cannon explained, "Someone representing Houston called my home a few days ago and talked to my wife, but I never called the party back. I just wasn't interested in the new league." Cannon indicated he would officially sign with the Rams right after his LSU team played in the Sugar Bowl on New Year's Day.

In late November, Rozelle offered Cannon a financial package totaling $45,000 over three years, including a $10,000 signing bonus. Although Cannon would sign a contract with the Rams on November 30, the contract was not to be dated until after the Sugar Bowl so that Cannon would not be ruled ineligible for that game. Cannon would place the check in a bank in Baton Rouge, uncashed, until he played his final collegiate game.

In the interim, Bud Adams was still trying to negotiate with Cannon, but could not get him on the telephone. Finally, Adams was able to reach out to a mutual friend of his and Cannon's to get word to Cannon to give Adams a call— that he would double whatever the salary was that the Rams were going to pay him. Adams remembers that he told his wife, "I bet I get a call within an hour." He recalls that twenty-two minutes later he answered the telephone and the operator asked him if he would accept the charges on a collect call from Baton Rouge, Louisiana, from Billy Cannon. In this conversation Adams asked Cannon if he had signed with the Rams. Cannon admitting he had. Cannon asked Adams if he would in fact double his salary as indicated to him by their mutual friend. Adams would say that he did indeed offer to pay him that amount. Cannon's response was, according to Adams, "How do we do this?" Adams told Cannon that there would be a representative from the Oilers at the Sugar Bowl and he would sign on the field, under the goalpost, to the terms that he and Adams had already agreed to. The lucrative contract from the Oilers more than doubled the Rams' offer to a guaranteed $100,000 over three seasons, and as an added incentive, Adams also set up Cannon with ownership of several gas stations.

Perhaps because the contract with the Rams was not dated, Cannon felt the contract he signed was not valid and he was still free to negotiate with the Oilers as well. When Cannon returned to Los Angeles on a stopover from playing in the Hula Bowl All-Star game in Hawaii, he was served with court papers. The Rams filed an injunction in court to enforce the contract Cannon had signed with them. Rozelle would defiantly state, "If Billy Cannon plays pro football next season it will be for the Los Angeles Rams." He added, "We have his signed contract and we intend to force him to respect it." The court, however, ruled in favor of the Oilers, with Federal Judge William Lindberg declaring the Rams contracts invalid. The judge would also criticize Rozelle's handling of the negotiations, claiming that Rozelle rushed Cannon into signing the contract. Lindberg was critical of Cannon as well, calling him "exceptionally naïve" and "a provincial lad untutored and unwise in the ways of the business world." Bud Adams recalled in Ed Gruver's book, "We won the case, on the basis [that] the judge had said he thought Billy should have the maximum amount of money, and we had offered him the maximum amount, so he should play with the Oilers." Dan Reeves, Rams owner, defended Rozelle's handling of the Cannon negotiations in the *New York Times*, calling his general manager "the most honest man in the world."

In early February 1960, only a couple of weeks after being named commissioner, Rozelle would meet with Joe Foss and the two would reach a no-raiding pact on the other league's players. Rozelle was quoted in the *New York Times* about the meeting, saying, "Foss said his policy as commissioner would be to foster a policy in the AFL of no tampering with National League players—a policy I told him we would respect." Rozelle would also offer praise of Foss, commenting, "I was very impressed with Foss' sincerity and his whole outlook on how his new league should function." The sentiment of the winter meeting with Foss would not last that long. Rozelle soon became more aware of some of the difficulties involving player recruitment that would persist in his dealings with the AFL. After the 1960 season, Willard Dewveall, a tight end who had played out his contract-option year with the Chicago Bears, would become the first player to deliberately jump from the NFL to the AFL, joining the Houston Oilers. Fearing that the AFL might continue to tamper with some contract options, Rozelle would comment, "There is no war between the two leagues because it takes two rivals to make a war. There is a lack of harmony, since the basis for harmony is a mutual respect for contracts and options." Rozelle added, "We will continue to have our problems until both leagues respect each other's player contracts and options. We are concerned with protecting our rights. While the loss of an individual player might not mean too much, it is the precedent we are concerned with."

The nontampering pact would be honored by both leagues, and the AFL only bid with the NFL on players as they were coming out of college. The competition for signing players was so intense that players were often signed immediately after their college team's bowl game. On one occasion a fight would even occur between NFL and AFL representatives at the conclusion of the 1964 Orange Bowl game, when an NFL representative would see Nebraska lineman, John Kirby, speaking to a Chargers scout who was trying to sign him. To combat the competition from the AFL, the NFL instituted a system of recruitment of college players so that they would be more inclined to sign with the NFL. The strategy of "Operation Baby-Sit" was developed by Bert Rose, the first general manger of the Minnesota Vikings and later an executive in the league office. The idea of "Operation Baby-Sit" was for NFL representatives (people referred to in *Sports Illustrated* as "hand-holders") to simply contact and establish a strong relationship with the player prior to the draft, selling them on the advantages of playing in the NFL. The NFL representatives were to "baby-sit" and remain with the player until they were selected and signed to contracts. As Don Weiss explained in *The Making of the Super Bowl*, "Representatives weren't authorized to negotiate contracts per se but were expected to get a general idea of what players anticipated, what perks would interest them (cars, for example), and how much contact they had had with the AFL. At the moment a player was selected, a deal was to be struck over the phone and the player signed immediately." When learning that the Rams used the tactic for the 1964 draft and with the encouragement of his former boss from the Rams, Dan Reeves, Rozelle would endorse implementing the strategy for the entire NFL.

The intense competition for players would be highlighted by the recruitment and signing of Joe Namath. The battle for the rights to sign Namath in many ways symbolized the competition for many players. Having led

Alabama to a 27-3 record as a three-year starter, Namath was one of the most coveted players entering professional football in 1965. The New York Giants struggled in 1964 with a dismal record of 2-10-2, giving them the first pick in the draft. With their aging quarterback, Y. A. Tittle, set to retire at the end of the 1964 season, it seemed like Namath would be the prize of the NFL and play in New York. The Giants, however, didn't draft Namath and instead selected Tucker Frederickson, a running back from Auburn. Namath was not taken in the NFL draft until the twelfth pick by the St. Louis Cardinals.

Both the NFL and AFL conducted their player drafts on the same day. On the AFL side, it would have seemed that the Jets would not have had any interest in Joe Namath. The Jets still held the rights to quarterback Jerry Rhome, whom they had drafted the previous year. Not thrilled with Rhome, Sonny Werblin, Jets owner, traded him to the Houston Oilers for the second pick in the draft. Houston, also with the first pick, selected Lawrence Elkins, a wide receiver from Baylor. Although there was some debate as to whether the Jets should choose Namath or University of California quarterback Craig Morton, at the encouragement of Chuck Knox, then Jets assistant coach, and at the strong desire of Werblin, the Jets selected Namath. There was now an entire month before Namath would play his final college game in the Orange Bowl for the Cardinals and Jets to negotiate with Namath.

The Cardinals were first to speak with Namath. At the encouragement of Paul "Bear" Bryant, University of Alabama head coach, Namath would ask for $200,000 and a car. The Cardinals agreed to those terms but wanted Namath to immediately sign. Bryant would tell Namath that since the Cardinals agreed so quickly, he should also talk to the Jets. Namath would meet twice with Sonny Werblin, receiving an offer of $300,000 during the second meeting. The bidding between the two teams would go back and forth. Rumors were also circulating that the Cardinals were now negotiating on behalf of the New York Giants. The Giants had lost out to the Jets the previous year in a negotiating battle for the rights to running back Matt Snell and did not want to give an impression that they were openly bidding for Namath with the possibility of losing out again to the team from the rival league that they shared the city with. It was the thinking of some in the press that Namath was only interested in playing in New York. Namath would, however, refute those claims in his book written with Dick Schaap, *I Can't Wait Until Tomorrow . . . 'Cause I Get Better-Looking Every Day*, stating "Those stories were simply ridiculous. I didn't know enough about New York at the time to like it or dislike it, and I didn't know anything about St. Louis."

Eventually it was the Jets who would come up with the better offer and win the services of Namath. Namath would give Werblin his word that he would sign with the Jets, but could not do so until after the Orange Bowl so that he did not forfeit his eligibility for that game. On New Year's night in 1965 after leading a comeback that would fall one yard short, Alabama lost the national championship game to Texas, but Namath would be named the MVP of the Orange Bowl game. The day after playing on the field of Miami's Orange Bowl—a place where four years later he would cement his standing in professional football history and help attain national acceptance for the AFL in Super Bowl III, Namath would hold a press conference to officially announce he was signing with the Jets. In outbidding the Cardinals, the Jets agreed to pay Namath the most lucrative contract for a professional football player at the time, signing him to a three-year deal totaling $427,000. The New York contract included a signing bonus of $200,000 and a Jet green Lincoln Continental.

By that summer the Jets sold 35,000 seasons tickets, including 2,500 season tickets in the first week. With Namath, Shea Stadium attendance for Jets games would balloon to average approximately 60,000, more than many NFL teams. With results such as this, it would often be reported that Namath saved the AFL. While this may not be true—after all the league had signed its five-year, $36 million television contract with NBC in 1964—he would certainly help raise the profile of the AFL, not to mention help raise players' salaries in both leagues.

The NFL and AFL would together spend $7 million to sign their 1966 draft choices. For example, in 1966, both the NFL expansion Atlanta Falcons and the Houston Oilers drafted University of Texas all-American linebacker Tommy Nobis with their first draft choice. Nobis eventually signed with the Falcons for $600,000. Nobis comments that it was difficult playing for the University of Texas and being drafted by a team from that state but signing with Atlanta. For Nobis, one factor in his signing with the NFL was the history and tradition of the league. He explains that he was familiar with the NFL, watching the New York Giants and Lombardi's Packers on television with his father, and thought the opportunity to play in the NFL was special. If other players had a similar viewpoint, the money offered from the AFL teams would have to be much higher than their NFL counterparts to get them to sign. In 1966, the NFL would sign 75 percent of its 232 drafted players, with the AFL signing 46 percent of its 181 draftees. Of the 111 common draft choices, 79 signed with the NFL, 28 with the AFL, with four unsigned.

In addition to competition for players, competition was once again intensifying for expansion into new cities. Each league had two options: expand into a city in which the other league had already secured a team and directly compete with its rival league or find new cities that were anxious for professional football. In late June 1965, the NFL successfully recruited Atlanta by convincing owner Rankin Smith to join the league for the beginning of the 1966 season, becoming the fifteenth NFL team, at an expansion fee of $8.5 million. The AFL would respond by successfully securing Miami in August 1965 for an expansion fee of $7.5 million to begin play in 1966, making the Dolphins its first expansion team and bringing the league to a total of nine teams. The asking price for the expansion franchises in both leagues was increased largely because of the television contracts of 1964, with the Dolphins and Falcons now splitting those revenues equally with the other teams in their respective leagues. With competition for players and expansion into new cities intensifying, despite revenues rising through television, the cost of being in professional football was clearly starting to escalate.

With the exposure gained through the television contract of 1964 and the continued addition of popular players, the AFL was seeing its fan base grow. In 1965 the average game attendance of 31,828 for the AFL was an increase of more than 10,000 from only two seasons previous. The 1965 AFL average crowd was also larger than the attendance for any one game the league had played during its inaugural season. The NFL owners had to come to the realization that the viability of the AFL was long term. At this juncture, Rozelle and the NFL owners had two options: continue to escalate an ever-growing financial competition that was driving up the cost of being in the professional football business or devise a strategy for merging with the AFL.

Rozelle was not initially interested in a merger because he thought that eventually the NFL would win the conflict. Don Weiss in *The Making of the Super Bowl* points out, "Having endured more than six years of acrimony, nasty accusations, and legal challenges, Rozelle certainly was *reluctant* [Weiss's emphasis] to abandon this struggle." He would have to be convinced by the owners about the need to move forward with a merger. Rozelle did concede that the NFL could develop a plan for absorbing the AFL that the AFL's owners would find acceptable. He also thought the NFL had nothing to lose in offering merger proposals to the AFL. If any merger strategy failed, the strained relationship between the two leagues would simply remain. The only negative outcome of failed merger talks would be the competitive status quo that the league was currently in.

Talks of a merger had been occurring informally since the inception of the AFL in 1960. Any merger discussions would never substantially progress, however, if the NFL continued to suggest that only certain AFL teams join the senior league and weaker franchises, such as Denver, be forced to fold. Other early merger scenarios included the Jets and Raiders vacating the New York City and Bay Area markets, leaving the NFL franchises in those territories by themselves once again. The challenge of any scenario that involved teams moving was not only to get the AFL to agree, but also to get Congress's approval of the merger on antitrust grounds.

Tex Schramm would first call his former boss, Dan Reeves of the Rams, in late February 1966 with some ideas for a merger solution. Reeves would be encouraged by Schramm's ideas and tell him to consult Rozelle and explain the plan. At the encouragement of Rozelle, Schramm would continue to devise and present a plan to the AFL that would include all AFL teams becoming a part of the NFL. Schramm approached Lamar Hunt about the merger because even though Hunt was not the commissioner he was the founder of the league and Schramm thought he would be able to cordially negotiate with him.

Schramm called Hunt and the two initially met in complete secrecy on April 4, 1966, when Hunt, flying to Houston for an AFL meeting, stopped over in Dallas. The two sat in Schramm's Oldsmobile in the parking lot of Dallas's Love Field Airport, where Schramm explained his proposal. Schramm indicated to Hunt that Rozelle was aware that they were speaking. The major result of this initial meeting was an agreement to talk further about a merger.

Schramm would provide a detailed account of how the merger occurred in the June 20, 1966, issue of *Sports Illustrated*. In the article, he said of Hunt, "We wanted an owner who had the prestige, the desire for peace, time to work on the problem, no personal prejudices—and who could keep his mouth shut. Lamar filled the requirements perfectly." Hunt also possessed the critical characteristic of thinking league-first, similar to the philosophy of both Rozelle and Schramm. Billy Sullivan, owner of the Patriots, when presenting Hunt for induction into the Hall of Fame, described him saying, "We saw him at league meetings time after time after time when Plan A would help his team and Plan B would help professional football and as the night would follow the day you could always be sure that our honoree would vote for what was in the best interest of the game."

It appears that the choice between a merger and a continuing hostile and expensive economic environment was understood by both Hunt and Schramm. In a lengthy interview about the merger in the *Super Bowl XXV Game Program*,

Schramm commented, "It became clear to me that something had to be done because the whole framework of professional football was being destroyed. What was basically happening in their league, and eventually in our league, was that players were no longer being drafted on their ability and potential. Instead, they were being selected on whether or not they could be signed." The economic climate would prove to be the variable that had been missing in the other informal merger discussions, as Schramm felt that the competition would eventually kill the weaker franchises in both leagues. In the same interview, Hunt stated, "I believed a merger was desirable because the economics in pro football were not good for either side. I felt it would be a good thing if we could stabilize the sport." Hunt also contended that another strong reason for a merger from his perspective was that it would ensure that professional football would continue in all of the AFL cities.

Schramm and Hunt continued to meet in relative secrecy. Relations between the NFL and AFL owners were volatile, exacerbated by the continuous battles to sign players. And there was a profound lack of trust stemming from the formation of the AFL and the NFL's acquiring the Dallas and Minnesota territories for expansion franchises. With Hunt having a home in Dallas, not far from the Cowboys complex, meetings could easily occur without the knowledge of people from either league—or the press. The two would meet on May 3, and again on May 10. Schramm would detail the result of the meeting on May 10 in *Sports Illustrated*, saying "Until this meeting Lamar had been non-committal. Now he felt any problems could be solved, and for the first time I thought we had a good chance for success. I called Pete and told him of Lamar's reaction."

On the NFL side, Schramm's planning involved Rozelle as well as, at the request of the commissioner, Wellington Mara, New York Giants owner, and Lou Spadia, San Francisco 49ers executive, the two representing teams still in direct geographical competition with the AFL. Both Mara and Spadia were concerned about the Jets and Raiders joining the NFL in their respective markets. Schramm and Rozelle would meet with Mara and Spadia prior to a league meeting scheduled to begin on May 16. Mara and Spadia would waver at different moments throughout the merger discussions. Mara was skeptical at first but held that if a plan was strong enough for the other owners, he would not prevent a deal. With Mara and Spadia expressing some doubt, Rozelle and Schramm decided not to bring the topic of a merger up to the NFL's full ownership group, but instead to approach them on an individual basis to feel them out and gradually build consensus.

At the AFL league meeting that Hunt eventually attended after his initial meeting with Schramm at the airport in Dallas, Joe Foss would resign as commissioner. Upon his resignation Foss called for professional football to replicate major league baseball and have two leagues merged under one commissioner. Foss also thought the merged league should have an annual championship game like the World Series. Suggested by Wayne Valley, Raiders owner, and encouraged by Sid Gillman, Lamar Hunt, and Ralph Wilson, on Tuesday, April 8, Al Davis, the thirty-six-year-old head coach and general manager of the Raiders, was named commissioner of the AFL by one vote.

Al Davis, who thought of himself more as a football coach, represented a shift from the leadership philosophy of Joe Foss. Davis provided insight to his leadership style in his induction speech to the Pro Football Hall of Fame, stating, "I learned early on in life that if you are going to lead, if you are going to dominate, the golden rule do unto others as you would have them do unto you is not necessarily right. You must treat people in a paramilitary situation the way they want to be treated, not the way you want to be treated."

Davis was more willing to escalate the battle with the NFL rather than merge and claimed in the *New York Times* that as commissioner of the AFL he would have "dictatorial powers." Davis explicitly stated his opposition to the merger saying, "I've never been for it." Instead Davis was pushing for expansion of the AFL, favoring cities such as Chicago, Los Angeles, or Anaheim. Davis claimed that he had assurances from the AFL owners prior to accepting the job as commissioner that they would spend whatever money was necessary to acquire players. He declared, "We will fight for players. We'll do anything we think necessary."

Meanwhile, Hunt saw the merger talks as an opportunity for future stability. And while Davis saw himself as in charge, it was not until early May that Hunt even informed him and the other AFL owners of the talks. The merger received a mixed reaction by the AFL owners, with its newly elected commissioner adamantly opposed. After informing the other AFL owners, Ralph Wilson and Billy Sullivan were included on the AFL side in the merger negotiations.

On May 17, with some owners on both sides still skeptical of the idea of merging, an event occurred that threatened to scuttle any agreement. The NFL's New York Giants signed Pete Gogolak, placekicker for the AFL's Buffalo Bills, who had played out the option year of his contract. Gogolak was the first successful soccer-style kicker and the second leading scorer in the AFL in the 1964 and 1965 seasons. The Giants were in desperate need of a kicker, having converted on only four of their twenty-five field goal attempts in the

1965 season. Wellington Mara would defend the signing, stating, "We honor contracts of other organizations just like we honor the ones in our own league. We would not have talked to Gogolak, or any other player, prior to his becoming a free agent."

The signing of Gogolak did, however, break the verbal pact between the two leagues that neither would sign a player from the opposing league. Rozelle would still approve the transaction, creating friction between himself and the NFL owners. The signing of Gogolak was criticized by George Halas, and even Vince Lombardi criticized Wellington Mara, his former boss. Halas commented about the Gogolak signing in the *New York Times*, stating, "I think it was a mistake in judgment." Tex Schramm described the impact of the Gogolak signing in a June 20, 1966, *Sports Illustrated* article. He said the Giants signing of Gogolak was "perfectly legal and aboveboard, but it obviously came at a bad time for peace negotiations. Far from triggering an agreement between the leagues, it almost ended the possibility of peace. At a time when we wanted the owners in as harmonious a mood as possible, it created division and anger."

Gogolak's signing also highlighted the developing disagreement between Rozelle and the NFL's owners about a merger. Although he approved Schramm's continued efforts in negotiating with Hunt, Rozelle would continue to express lack of interest in a merger. Don Weiss explained, "Pete felt in his heart that the AFL's failure was inevitable. He had no reason to compromise, he insisted." The owners, however, still not wanting to continue the escalating economic war, continued to maintain their position in favor of a merger. George Puscas of the *Detroit Free Press* even quoted one unnamed NFL owner as saying, "Rozelle will get this settled properly, or we're all in trouble. He'll get it done or he's through." It would be Tex Schramm who would confront Rozelle, requesting that he lead the NFL owners in the merger but letting him know that the owners would continue to support the merger even without Rozelle's support. The talks between Rozelle and Schramm even got to the critical point where, according to Don Weiss, "if Pete Rozelle wanted to continue as NFL commissioner, he was going to have to stand front and center for something that he really didn't believe in." Schramm is quoted in Bob St. John's *Tex*, telling Rozelle, "It was decided that if you're not going to lead us in the merger, then we're going to go ahead without you." An emotional Rozelle would finally consent to the owners' wishes and support the merger. Once agreeing to work on the merger, Rozelle once again became a pivotal leader working hard to make sure the merger occurred and was successful.

Dan Rooney contends "the merger would have never happened without Rozelle. He was the person who ended up pulling all of the particulars together, convincing some owners that the merger was the right thing to do." Rooney adds, "if Rozelle really wanted to kill the merger, he could have easily gotten the votes to do so."

The signing of Gogolak also gave the antimerger voices of the AFL more ammunition—the NFL could not be trusted. Al Davis saw the Giants' signing of Gogolak as an invitation for the AFL to actively pursue NFL players, particularly the league's star quarterbacks. Lamar Hunt commented, "The signing set people in the AFL in motion, specifically Al Davis, and Al devised his own plan to sign NFL players and began to implement that plan without consulting with the AFL ownership as a group. He talked to individual AFL clubs and they began a recruiting campaign for NFL players." The Raiders in 1966 would sign Roman Gabriel, Rams quarterback, and the Oilers signed John Brodie, 49ers quarterback, and offered Mike Ditka, Bears tight end, a deal to join them after the 1967 season. To some, the reaction by Davis actually helped quicken negotiations to merge, providing more economic evidence to the other owners of both leagues who didn't want to further escalate the cost of player salaries.

While he accelerated discussions by recruiting NFL players, Davis was not part of the merger negotiations and would find out about the merger just the same as the AFL owners. Don Weiss claimed in his book that Davis didn't learn of the details of the merger until the night before its announcement. Tex Schramm also said the role of Davis in the merger was limited. Schramm is quoted by Bob St. John, stating, "Davis always has said that he was the man who forced the merger when he went after some established players, but that just wasn't true. The wheels were already turning before he came into the picture and, in fact, Lamar was smart enough not to tell him about our discussions, because he knew Al would try to stop the entire process."

Despite the tensions between the owners from both leagues, the relationship between Schramm and Hunt would remain amicable throughout the negotiations, perhaps each man understanding the situation that the other was dealing with. Schramm stated, "We both had the difficulty of trying to sell our leagues whatever we were going to be agreeing to. And he [Hunt] had the biggest problem because we were in essence dictating the terms."

In late May 1966, a series of meetings between Hunt, Schramm, and Rozelle occurred. After meeting with Lou Spadia to finally convince him of the merger, Rozelle flew to Dallas and stayed at Schramm's house for the weekend to finalize the general terms of the merger proposal. Schramm's daughter nicknamed

Rozelle "sneaky Pete" after being instructed by her father not to mention that Rozelle was there and what they were working on. The two made notes and called the NFL owners, when necessary, to develop a plan that all on the NFL side were in agreement with. On Sunday night, after their weekend of work, Schramm called Hunt to tell him of a proposal, with details he had not yet heard. This would be the first time that Rozelle talked directly to Hunt about the merger issue, assuring Hunt of the commitment and good intentions of the NFL.

Hunt and Schramm would meet on May 31, this time at Schramm's home, where the most detailed merger plan was presented. Schramm ended the meeting by telling Hunt, "If you accept, this deal has been approved by every NFL club. If you alter it too much, it will blow up." Hunt would take the proposal to Wilson and Sullivan for their input. On the AFL side, the details of an agreement would be worked out by Hunt, Wilson, and Sullivan operating on behalf of all of the league's owners. Hunt explained, "We were free to resolve issues at the end; we never had total formal agreement among the AFL on all of them. If it always took everybody's approval, you'd have an impasse." The AFL trio would provide a series of twenty-six changes and additions to the deal. Rozelle and Schramm would find one-third acceptable, one-third not acceptable, and the final third negotiable.

After a series of telephone calls between Schramm, Rozelle, and Hunt, Schramm and Hunt met a final time on June 5 at Schramm's house. The two would go over the plan point by point. The final point of contention would be on the issue of expansion. It would finally be agreed that the AFL teams would provide the players for an expansion AFL franchise, but the payments for the new franchise would go directly to the NFL.

The next day, the two would speak by telephone on several occasions to clarify any last points. At approximately 1:00 a.m., a tentative agreement was reached. Schramm called Rozelle, who then consulted one last time with the NFL owners, confirming their consent to the deal by late morning on June 7. Even as the last days of negotiations were occurring, Al Davis would continue to convey a sense of pessimism about the merger, stating in the June 7 *New York Times* that "this is still all speculation and conjecture. It is very doubtful anything will be done." Davis would be mistaken.

Schramm, Rozelle, and Hunt agreed to make an announcement to the press and met in Washington, D.C., to set up the arrangements. Not wanting to alert the media, Schramm arranged a suite at the Sheraton-Carlton under the fictitious name "Ralph Pittman" and told Hunt to go right to the room and not register at the hotel. He forgot to inform Hunt of the name, but it didn't matter; because of a delay in his flight, Hunt arrived in the lobby at the same time as Rozelle and Schramm. They went quickly to the "Ralph Pittman" suite and finished the wording on the press release announcing the historic merger.

On June 8, 1966, just after 6:00 p.m., the agreement for the merger between the NFL and the AFL was officially announced at a press conference at the Warwick Hotel in New York City. Among the provisions of the agreement were that there would be no relocation of existing franchises and the AFL would pay $18 million in indemnities to the NFL over a twenty-year period ($10 million to the Giants, and $8 million to the 49ers). Two expansion franchises would be added by 1968, one in each league, and a common player draft would be established after the 1966 season. Interleague preseason games would begin in 1967, but there would be a four-year period before becoming a single league with a common regular season beginning in 1970. Meanwhile, the two leagues would continue their current respective television contracts with CBS (NFL) and NBC (AFL) for the four years that they had left on them, with each league keeping its own income. A world championship game was to be played between the two leagues, with the inaugural game to be played following the 1966 season. Finally, Pete Rozelle would be retained as the commissioner of the newly expanded NFL.

The owners from both leagues were pleased with the outcome. From the NFL, Art Modell commented, "The merger will allow the league to expand scientifically giving it stability and insuring that no franchises will be moved." Art Rooney stated, "It was inevitable. We feel that for the good of the public this is the only way the game can be presented to the entire country." From the AFL, Bud Adams, added, "It will end the financial strain on pro teams." Even Wayne Valley, owner of the Oakland Raiders, concluded, "The merger was desirable and necessary."

With the leagues planning to merge, Davis would only serve three and a half months as commissioner, rejoining the Raiders on July 25, 1966, as their general manager and part owner. Milt Woodard would become the president of the AFL. Although he was not in favor of merging with the NFL, Al Davis would later acknowledge its success. He told the Senate in 1982, "I think that is the quickest expansion and the best expansion we have ever had in this country because the National Football League took nine of the American Football League teams into their league, and we all become one, and it was based on competition, and it was based on something that is inherent in the American way of life."

The next hurdle to completing the merger would be the approval of Congress. Immediately after the merger was announced, Philip Hart, senator from Michigan, chairman of the Senate Anti-monopoly Subcommittee, and former Detroit Lions minority owner, claimed that he felt the merger was in compliance with a sports bill previously passed in the Senate. Hart would even state, "As a fan I have been aching for a world's championship game for some time." However, getting the merger through the Congress would not be so simple. By the autumn of 1966 the Justice Department was threatening to bring an antitrust lawsuit against the NFL, and without Congressional approval the merger would be halted. Rozelle clearly knew what was at stake if a lawsuit was brought, telling the *New York Times*, "It is conceivable that the sum total of financial risks resulting from legal actions could easily be larger than the total value and net assets of all the existing franchises." Any lawsuit would also probably extend past January 1967, the time when the first championship game between the two leagues was now scheduled to be played.

The headline in the October 14, 1966, *New York Times* would describe an ominous environment in Congress, reading, "Dispute Over Language Dims Hopes for Pro Football Merger Exemption." The major obstacle was Emanuel Celler, chairman of the House Antitrust Subcommittee. The seventy-eight-year-old Democratic congressman wanted detailed hearings on the merger, and with the Congress set to adjourn the following week, it appeared a vote would not occur. The other members of the subcommittee were in favor of granting the NFL its antitrust exemption.

Rozelle would try several political maneuvers to achieve his desired outcome of an antitrust exemption and approval of the merger. Rozelle contacted David Dixon, a New Orleans businessman who was working on bringing professional football to that city. Dixon would reach out to House majority leader Hale Boggs, whom he knew while attending Tulane University. Russell Long, senator from Louisiana, would also be instrumental. Long would even be quoted in the *New York Times* stating his motivation to get involved, "Maybe we can get one of those teams for New Orleans." Rozelle would be able to convince the other NFL owners that New Orleans would be the next expansion city. With the Superdome plans already developed, it was not a difficult job. The NFL had to add another team per the merger agreement anyway, and there was already interest in New Orleans as the logical expansion location, so it seemed as though an agreement could be reached.

Rozelle and the Congress would also find a way to circumvent the powerful Chairman Celler. Senate Republican Everett Dirksen would attach the antitrust immunity to the Johnson Administration's anti-inflation tax bill that was sure to pass through the Congress. It would be Senator Long from Louisiana who accepted the Dirksen amendment. The House and Senate overwhelmingly passed the bill, with both Long and Boggs being part of the Senate-House conference committee that would settle any discrepancies between the two bills. Celler would admit defeat on the legislative end around, stating, "They caught me in bathing and sold my clothes."

On October 21, 1966, the NFL-AFL merger was approved by Congress in legislation that exempted the agreement from any antitrust liability. Less than two weeks later, on November 1, New Orleans was added as the sixteenth NFL team, joining the league in 1967. One unnamed NFL owner would tell the *New York Times*, "I didn't think we had a chance. But Pete found a way as usual." Cincinnati would be the final AFL expansion city, bringing the total number of AFL teams to ten for the 1968 season.

The first-ever common draft between the two leagues would feature yet one other condition of the merger agreement. To combat the popularity of Joe Namath with the Jets, the New York Giants would be given a once-in-a-lifetime privilege pick at the top of the draft that they had to use to select a quarterback coming out of college. The pick could also be traded for a quarterback on another team or postponed until the 1968 draft. After scouting Bob Griese, from Purdue University, and Steve Spurrier, the Heisman Trophy winner from the University of Florida, the Giants would instead trade three draft choices and a player to be named later to the Minnesota Vikings for Fran Tarkenton.

Although heading toward a merger, a rule was established that teams from the AFL could not trade with teams from the NFL until 1970. The order of the draft was determined by the inverse order of the combined final standings of both leagues, but the expansion New Orleans Saints were given the first pick in the draft. The Saints would deal the selection to the Baltimore Colts for quarterback Gary Cuozzo. The Colts then made Bubba Smith, Michigan State defensive lineman, the first choice of the combined draft on March 14, 1967.

Pete Rozelle attended his first AFL game in November 1966, fittingly in Kansas City as a tribute to Lamar Hunt, but there was still a final challenge to completing the merger, and it would not come until years later in 1969, when the new league would have to realign its conferences and divisions. An initial announcement by Rozelle to the media called for a sixteen-ten team conference arrangement, with no change as to how the NFL and AFL were presently constructed. With the NFL having more of the major television markets, CBS was very much in favor of this type of alignment. However, Paul

Brown, now the owner of the Cincinnati Bengals, was adamantly opposed to the alignment proposal. Brown would be quoted in Harold Rosenthal's *Fifty Faces of Football*, stating, "I paid my million dollars to come into the National Football League, and a sixteen-ten breakdown won't be any National Football League." Brown would be joined by Al Davis and Phil Iselin from the Jets to block the proposed conference alignment. NBC was also interested in adding some larger television markets to its lineup. Rozelle was forced to un-announce the sixteen-ten alignment, and a thirteen-thirteen split would then have to be negotiated—meaning three NFL franchises would have to join the newly established American Football Conference (AFC).

Finding the three teams to switch leagues would be difficult. As the owners continued to negotiate to a stalemate, Rozelle called for round-the-clock negotiations until a conference alignment agreement could be reached. All teams were mentioned in discussions to switch leagues except for the Rams—CBS not wanting to lose the large television market of Los Angeles—the Giants, and the 49ers, the AFC already having the Jets and Raiders in those markets. With debate intense, Rozelle would offer teams a one-time $3 million payment as an incentive to switch leagues. Carroll Rosenbloom would be the first to move, bringing his Baltimore Colts to the AFC with the appeal of creating a rivalry with Joe Namath and the Jets. With two teams still left to move, Art Modell would claim he had a "responsibility to serve," and to help the AFC achieve parity, at dinner with Rozelle, Rankin Smith, and Tex Schramm, Modell announced his willingness to move the Browns, so long as Art Rooney and the Steelers also joined him. Modell recalls that he did ask Wellington Mara if it would be acceptable to him if the Browns moved. Mara agreed, with the condition that the Browns and the Giants continue to play in the preseason.

Dan Rooney explains that he was initially against the idea of the Steelers moving to the AFC. Wellington Mara tried to convince him of the move. Finally, after meeting all day about the issue, Dan Rooney and his father went to dinner in New York. Upon returning from dinner to the NFL office, Rozelle handed Dan a piece of paper with the names Pittsburgh, Cleveland, Cincinnati, and Houston on it. Dan Rooney recalls handing the paper to his father, telling him "this is our new division." A three-day stalemate ended when the Rooneys saw the rivalry possibilities of Rozelle's newly created division, which matched Pittsburgh and Cleveland with Cincinnati, giving them both a natural geographic rival. Houston was also attractive, with the Oilers playing in the recently constructed Astrodome. Dan Rooney indicates that he had so much trust in Rozelle's judgment that it made the shift to the AFC an easier decision with his endorsement. The rest of the AFC was easily aligned geographically, based on the remaining AFL teams, with the Baltimore Colts simply joining the eastern division. Rozelle would speak about the thirty-six-hour nonstop negotiation session in the *New York Times*, describing the owners who finally switched conferences as "three of them who felt strongly about maintaining the identity built up between the AFL and NFL, and who have deep faith in the future of the American Conference."

Negotiating the National Football Conference (NFC) divisions would also be intense. The owners met on two separate occasions without any resolution on a new divisional alignment. Rozelle often joked about realignment meetings, saying, "Each owner wanted his team to be in a division with at least one warm-weather site or a domed stadium, with teams with large season-ticket sales and with teams that are pigeons." Finally, immediately after Super Bowl IV in 1970, with the merger taking effect the next autumn, the NFL ownership group met again. On this occasion, after three days of meetings, five proposals were still being debated. When no agreement could be reached Rozelle drafted the five potential divisional alignment scenarios on separate pieces of paper. Each of the five plans were individually put into envelopes and placed in a glass vase. Rozelle would then suggest getting his longtime secretary, Thelma Elkjer, to select the winner and end what had now been a total of over sixty-four hours of meetings over the eight-month period. Elkjer would select plan three, innocently changing the course of NFL history.

Plan three was the only one that placed the Cowboys in the eastern division (along with the Cardinals, Eagles, Giants, and Redskins) and the Vikings in the central (along with the Bears, Lions, and Packers). All of the other four plans had the Vikings in the eastern division and the Cowboys in either the central or west. Rozelle would explain in the *New York Times* that there was some objection to every plan. He said, "I told them we had to resolve this and since we couldn't get agreement any other way, we would do it my way. In effect, I did it without their consent. There was never any formal or informal concurrence." To complete the realignment system, each conference would send its three division winners and one "wild-card" team, the second place team with the best overall record, to the playoffs.

CHAPTER 7

Architect of a Television Image

O NE CONCLUSION that is difficult to dispute is that the AFL was instrumental in helping the sport of professional football grow, particularly in geographic regions that the NFL had not yet placed a team. In 1965, fans surveyed in the highly respected national Harris poll would for the first time choose professional football, and not baseball, as their favorite sport. With the merger now complete, Pete Rozelle was the leader of a combined, solidified league with what appeared to be an incredibly bright economic future. For example, television revenue would only increase, as networks were competing with each other now for the broadcast rights to a single professional football league.

Though he and the NFL often acted to protect ticket sales, Rozelle always understood that the television event of an NFL game was an even bigger part of the league's product than the in-stadium event. He knew that developing programming strategies that would increase the value of the television product, such as he had done with the implementation of doubleheaders, would lead to more revenue from the networks. The centerpiece of the merger, having a championship game between the NFL and AFL winners, provided the league with its premier television event. Joe Foss, the first AFL commissioner, had pushed for a championship game with the NFL from the early days of the AFL. In 1964, NBC and the AFL even tried to entice the NFL into playing a championship game by offering to donate $500,000 of NBC's money to the Kennedy Memorial Library Fund if a game was created. Rozelle would deny the request, pointing out that NFL had already donated to the fund.

There were two major reasons that Rozelle had consistently dismissed the possibility of a championship contest with the AFL. The first reason was that the AFL had brought an antitrust lawsuit against the NFL. Rozelle told the *Washington Post* in 1961, "It's an incongruous proposal. You don't consider playing games with people suing you for $10 million." The second reason was that a championship game early on would have given the AFL tremendous credibility, a signal of recognition that Rozelle and the NFL were not interested in providing at that time. William Wallace had written in the *New York Times*, "The NFL policy is to ignore the competitor when possible, and certainly never to agree to enhance its image by playing [a championship game]." Now, only months after the merger, with a championship game agreed to, the broadcast rights to that game would provide immediate financial rewards when they were sold for four years to CBS and NBC for $9.5 million on December 13, 1966.

Although exhibition games between the two leagues had been played, the first true on-the-field test of the NFL versus the AFL would come in what was then known as the AFL-NFL World Championship Game between the Green Bay Packers and the Kansas City Chiefs. The game would not officially be called the Super Bowl until Super Bowl III. Rozelle initially felt that calling the game the Super Bowl was undignified. He stated, "To me 'super' was a corny cliché word that we used during my school days at Compton High in California in the 1940s." The name of the Super Bowl would emerge from Lamar Hunt innocuously mentioning it at a meeting. His children had been playing with the toy balls named "super balls"—highly compressed rubber balls that kids would bounce high on concrete. When Hunt asked if there should be a week off before the championship game, someone questioned which game he was referring to, each league's championship game or the championship game between a team from the AFL and NFL. With the name "super ball" subconsciously on his mind, Hunt replied, as quoted in the *Super Bowl XXV Game Program*, "I mean the final game, the last game, the Super Bowl." He described the reaction, "Everybody looked at me kind of funny and smiled, and kiddingly thereafter we would refer to the game as the Super Bowl. It just caught on within this committee, and the media heard about it and kind of grabbed onto it." Rozelle would later acknowledge the name's importance to the overall event, stating, "I am the first to admit that I was mistaken about the name of the game. 'Super' takes on a different connotation when it is applied to this event. I think the name has played a big part of the game's success."

From the beginning Rozelle saw the potential for the event and envisioned the championship game to be something special. Rozelle had some immediate ideas about what the event of the final game should look like. It was his idea to select a neutral site. Previously the championship game had been at an NFL team's home stadium. He also wanted two weeks in between each league's championship game and the final game so coaches could better prepare and the league could have two weeks to build up the game in the media. Rozelle even convinced Packer head coach Vince Lombardi to travel to Los Angeles to prepare for Super Bowl I earlier than he had desired in order to help promote the game.

The first AFL-NFL championship game was played in the Los Angeles Coliseum. Rozelle had first thought of having the game at the Rose Bowl in Pasadena, but executives at the Rose Bowl did not want a professional game intruding on college football's preeminent location. The game began at 1:00 p.m. local time and the Coliseum was far from a sellout, attracting only 61,946 fans, an attendance figure that disappointed Rozelle. The game would, however, be the only Super Bowl that was not a sellout. It was later thought that the steep ticket prices of $12, $10, and $6 were partially to blame for the low attendance.

The inaugural championship game would not be shown on television in Los Angeles—one newspaper showed a diagram of how to attach a coat hanger to a television antenna to try to watch the game. Local NFL fans had refused to believe that the game would be blacked out in Los Angeles; however, Rozelle held to the league's television policy at the time. Some people drove to Santa Barbara or San Diego to watch the game. The game was televised by both CBS and NBC, with each network paying $1 million to share the broadcast rights. CBS charged $85,000 for a minute of commercials and NBC $75,000. CBS Sports president, Bill MacPhail, commented, "We wanted exclusivity of the Super Bowl. You always want things you can't get. This thing is extremely complicated. However, we wouldn't have agreed to this Super Bowl arrangement if we weren't satisfied." Having two networks broadcast the game did produce an awkward moment when NBC had not returned from its commercials as the second-half kickoff occurred. Officials stopped the play just as it had begun, making the Packers kick off twice to start the second half.

The game would be intense for players and coaches with the credibility of their respective leagues at stake. Shelby Strother's book, *The NFL Top 40: The Greatest Pro Football Games of All Time* describes Vince Lombardi, Packers head coach, telling reporters that he had never seen an AFL game either in person or on television. When one reporter commented, "Come on, Vince, even Pete Rozelle has seen at least one AFL game." Lombardi responded, "Maybe Pete has more time than I do." In the week leading up to the game Lombardi would receive messages of support and encouragement from many NFL owners. Wellington Mara, Lombardi's former boss from when he was an assistant coach with the Giants, wrote to Lombardi, "I could think of no other standard-bearer that I wanted to carry our banner into battle." Frank Gifford, who was broadcasting the game for CBS, would interview Vince Lombardi before the game, and described it in the *Super Bowl XXV Game Program*, "During the five minutes or so we talked, (Lombardi) held onto my arm and was shaking like a leaf. It was incredible."

With the score close at halftime, a 14-10 Packer lead, the AFL's Chiefs had made a strong showing of their abilities. The second half, however, would be controlled by the Packers, with Green Bay winning by a final score of 35-10. The next day, in an NFL league meeting, Lombardi would receive a standing ovation upon entering the room for leading his Packers and the NFL to victory. As for the result of the game, Rozelle commented years later, "I was pleased that it was a close game for more than a half. I think we all feared that it might be a one-sided blowout. I was very happy with the 35-10 result." The Packers would dominate the second AFL-NFL championship game too, defeating Al Davis's Raiders 33-14 and enforcing the notion that the NFL was clearly the more dominant league. That game played at the Orange Bowl in Miami would be a sellout, with the NFL increasing its efforts to sell tickets, including leaning on television networks and advertisers to purchase tickets.

Super Bowl III was supposed to be another NFL romp when the heavily favored Baltimore Colts lined up to play the AFL's New York Jets in Miami's Orange Bowl. The eighteen-point-favored Colts had lost only one game all season, but had avenged that loss with a complete domination of the Cleveland Browns in the NFL championship game, 34-0. Tex Maule would write of the Colts victory over the Browns in *Sports Illustrated*: "Seldom in the long history of NFL championship games has one team so thoroughly dominated the other as did Baltimore in shattering the Browns." In that article Lenny Lyles, Colts defensive back, who had covered future Hall of Fame wide receiver Paul Warfield in the championship game, was asked who he would be covering on the Jets. Lyles responded as quoted in *Sports Illustrated*, "The Jets? I haven't the vaguest. I haven't thought about the Jets. This was the game I thought about. This was the one that got rid of all the frustration. This was it."

Joe Namath was outspoken before the game, claiming that there were a number of quarterbacks in the AFL who were better than the Colts' starter Earl Morrall, including the Jets backup, Babe Parilli. Dave Anderson was a beat reporter covering the Jets and recalls that during the week leading up to the Super Bowl the entire Jets team was very upbeat and positive, thinking they could win largely because of Namath's attitude. Anderson, too, had confidence in the Jets, and picked them to win the game on Brent Musburger's radio show in Chicago. Anderson says his confidence in the Jets was largely a confidence in Namath. After Namath became the first quarterback to pass for 4,000 yards a season in 1967 Anderson had written a magazine article with the central question: Could Namath perform at that same high level if playing in the NFL? Anderson heard praise from Paul Brown and Vince Lombardi, who referred to Namath as an almost "perfect passer."

On the Thursday before the Super Bowl, Namath attended a banquet for the Miami Touchdown Club where he was recognized as professional football's player of the year, the first AFL player to win the award. While giving his acceptance speech a heckler yelled out to Namath telling him to sit down. Namath responded with the famous proclamation for which he would forever be identified, "We're going to win Sunday. *I guarantee it!*" Namath and the Jets would back up the guarantee and defeat the Colts, 16-7, before a crowd of 75,389. The win was more than a victory for the Jets; it was also a win for the AFL, demonstrating that the "Mickey Mouse" league could play with the NFL. For perspective on the importance of the Jets win on behalf of the entire AFL, when the Jets opened their next season in Buffalo to play the Bills, Buffalo would salute the Jets for their Super Bowl victory.

The result of Super Bowl III was a great surprise to all involved with the NFL. Pat Summerall, although an employee of CBS, was working on the game's broadcast as the sideline reporter for NBC, through an arrangement made between the two leagues and the networks. With the result of the game no longer in doubt, Rozelle would ask Summerall to tell him everything he knew about the Jets so he could have some information before going into the Jets locker room and presenting the championship trophy to them. As for Rozelle's own sentiments, years later in the *Super Bowl XXV Game Program*, he was quoted saying, "I really did not care who won the game, but I was hoping against hope that we could have a close game." He continued, "After Namath and the Jets prevailed 16-7, the NFL owners were upset, of course. It was crushing for the old-line people. But I was secretly pleased because I realized that this shocking turn of events was going to do nothing but help pro football."

If Rozelle was "secretly pleased" with the result of the Jets win, the victory by the Kansas City Chiefs the next year over the Minnesota Vikings in Super Bowl IV was equally pleasing, proving that the first AFL victory was not a fluke. The Vikings had been a twelve-point favorite to defeat the Chiefs, but were beaten convincingly, 23-7. In accepting the Super Bowl trophy, Lamar Hunt, Chiefs owner, would state, "It really is a satisfying conclusion to the ten years of the American Football League."

To Rozelle, the Chiefs' victory helped give him what he had always desired for the NFL, competitive balance. Steve Sabol, president of NFL Films, explains that Rozelle initially thought the Super Bowl was a novelty and was not sure it would be a major sporting event until the public accepted the competitiveness of the game. According to Sabol, Rozelle felt the game truly would be a "Super Bowl after the Chiefs dominated the Vikings because he knew it was a viable league that was merging with many competitive teams, not only from the old NFL." This sentiment was consistent with his philosophy that competitive balance helps grow the sport and that one of the primary reasons that fans watch the NFL is because of its intense competition. Rozelle didn't want fans in the AFL cities to think their teams would simply not be able to compete with their NFL counterparts. With the merger taking effect after Super Bowl IV, Rozelle was now taking over a more credible league in his estimation. He could also proudly tell the press the day after Super Bowl IV that more people had watched the game on television than had watched Neil Armstrong walk on the moon.

Rozelle stated in the introduction of the book *Super Bowl*, and reprinted in the *Super Bowl XXV Game Program*, "I can honestly say that there are only three Super Bowls in which I was rooting—silently of course—for a team. I wanted the Packers to win in both Super Bowls I and II because my NFL loyalties still were strong. And I wanted the Steelers to win in Super Bowl IX for the sake of the finest, most decent man I ever knew apart from my own father—Art Rooney." Rozelle would also state, "I am not ashamed to admit that I had tears of joy in my eyes when I presented the trophy to Art Rooney that January, 1975, day. No man ever deserved it more."

The Super Bowl is now more than the culmination of an NFL season and the crowning of a new champion. It is simply the greatest spectacle in sports, viewed by more people every year than any other television program. The game has also emerged as the best promotional communication of the image of the NFL as the premier sports league in the world. Don Weiss, longtime NFL executive, would write in *The Making of the Super Bowl*, "Saying the Super

Bowl got to be what it is by accident, luck, or happenstance fails to recognize the amount of planning, preparation, and pure sweat that has gone into it." Rozelle acknowledged the spectacle and the event of the Super Bowl, but still would often remind the NFL staff, "Don't forget about the game." Rozelle would tell the media at his press conference prior to Super Bowl XIII in Miami that the game still gave him a lump in his throat and that "it will be a real upper just to see that crowd."

Starting with the first game in Los Angeles, the Super Bowl was not televised in the city in which the game was being played. This was consistent with how the NFL had previously been broadcasting its championship game. No NFL, or for that matter AFL, championship game had ever been carried on television in the city where the game was being played. Rozelle was quoted in the *Los Angeles Times* prior to the inaugural championship game explaining, "We've got to have a consistent policy. If we televised here, people in other places would be demanding that other games be shown locally. They'd be saying, 'you did it in L.A. Why not here?'" In the same article Art Modell commented, "If Pete lifted the blackout here, I wouldn't sell 45,000 seats in Cleveland next year."

Rozelle and the NFL would even have to defend the NFL blackout policy in a Fort Lauderdale, Florida, courtroom the day before Super Bowl V. With the game to be played at the Orange Bowl in Miami, a Florida attorney named Ellis Rubin campaigned to have the NFL lift the blackout and allow Super Bowl V to be televised in the Miami area. Rubin believed that everyone had a "right" to see the game. The court ruled in favor of the NFL, claiming that it did not have the power to force the broadcasting of the game. The judge, Arthur Franza, would, however, take the opportunity to communicate his thoughts on the television rule to Rozelle. According to Don Weiss, Judge Franza called the blackout "a transgression and a usurpation of the airwaves" and said that he would "applaud a decision by Pete Rozelle" to remove it.

The league would eventually be forced to adopt a change in its television blackout policy against its wishes. The blackout rule would be challenged by the Nixon administration and Congress. Rozelle was firm in his convictions that the league felt that it owned the rights to the games and he and its representatives would decide when and where the games were televised. The NFL's blackout policy had been challenged by the Justice Department on several occasions, with the courts repeatedly siding with the NFL. The legality of the NFL's television blackout policy of games within a seventy-five-mile radius of the home team had been upheld by Judge Grim in 1953. The policy was once again upheld by Judge Edward Weinfeld in the federal district court in New York, denying an injunction that would have forced the 1962 championship game between the Giants and the Packers played in Yankee Stadium to be televised in the New York City area.

Rozelle's thinking on the blackout issue was consistent with that of Bert Bell and held that televising games to the home geographical region would damage the long-term finances of a team. After all, fans could buy a ticket to a home game. Both Bell and Rozelle could point to the Rams' failed experiment in 1950 when the televising of their home games in Los Angeles hurt the team's attendance. Fear of a sellout was also a great incentive for fans to buy season tickets, something all owners desired. If fans were not sure they could buy a ticket to a game anytime they desired, a sense of urgency was created, forcing them to buy the entire season up front. Also, if tickets are bought in advance, people are more apt to go to the games and teams can be more confident that attendance will be good than if they relied on game-day traffic. Finally, if fans really wanted to see the game on television they could also travel outside of the seventy-five-mile blackout radius to watch the game. The league did remain adamant in fulfilling what it thought was its responsibility in requiring the broadcasting of all of a team's road games back to its home market.

Rozelle would provide an explanation of what he thought might happen without the blackout policy in a *Los Angeles Times* article prior to Super Bowl I. He explained, "Suppose we sold all our tickets and announced, that because of the sellout, we were going to have the game on local TV. Now suppose you have already committed yourself to spend $30 on the game. You've bought two tickets and you'll have to pay for parking and the babysitter. Now I tell you I'm not going to buy a ticket. I'm going to stay home and watch the game for nothing. That's the last time anybody will sell you a ticket to that event. You can't just lift a blackout like that and keep faith with your public." Rozelle even wrote an editorial in the *Washington Post* on the subject in 1973, claiming, "If the public becomes accustomed to receiving without charge the same product which it is being asked to buy, there will inevitably be a steady erosion of ticket-buying interest. Ultimately, ticket-buying habits and actual game attendance will be significantly affected—to the benefit of no one."

Even with increased television exposure ticket sales were not suffering. In fact many teams were beginning to sell out all of their games, especially the Washington Redskins. After thirteen years without a winning record, the Redskins hired Vince Lombardi as their head coach in 1969, and the team posted a 7-5-2 record. Lombardi's tenure lasted only one season after he became gravely ill. In the early 1970s the Redskins hired George Allen as head coach, a man who had a successful record as head coach of the Rams. With Allen, the Redskins became consistent winners. With tickets difficult to get in the 55,677-seat RFK Stadium, and the games still blacked out in Washington, D.C., the politicians, including football fan President Nixon, were not pleased. Congress now wanted a rule that would allow them to see the Redskins when they were playing a home game, and the NFL knew it was up against an opponent that it could not defeat. When the bill passed through the Senate by an overwhelming vote of 76 to 6, Rozelle was not surprised. He said, "We weren't exactly even money going in, we are realistic enough to think that some action will be taken by Congress. But it is beyond question that the bills being considered will be damaging to professional football."

As the Senate was passing its bill, hearings were being held in the House of Representatives on the NFL's blackout policy. Torbert MacDonald, the Democratic chair of the House subcommittee, would chastise Rozelle, saying, "You're a monopoly. You are the only game in town. I never said this wouldn't hurt you financially. It will. But I believe you have enough fat so that some could be cut off and you'd still have the pot of gold." Art Modell testified at the hearings on behalf of the NFL and argued that the proposed law "would be disastrous to us." The House of Representatives passed its version of the bill 336-37. Jack Kemp, member of the House and former quarterback for the Buffalo Bills and San Diego Chargers, would comment, "In retrospect, I think the Gulf of Tonkin resolution was the last thing that passed the Congress this fast."

In 1973, Congress adopted legislation requiring any NFL game that had been declared a sellout seventy-two hours prior to kickoff to be made available on television in the local region of the game. Rozelle would not even wait for President Nixon to sign the legislation and announced that blackouts were immediately ended if the game attendance complied with the seventy-two-hour rule. After the first Sunday that the televising of home games was implemented, and when some stadiums were not filled to capacity, Rozelle would continue to argue against the lifting of the blackout policy. The first week after the local blackout was lifted, Rozelle attended the Steelers game against the Lions in Pittsburgh, where there would be over 1,400 no-shows. Rozelle was quoted after the game in the *Los Angeles Times*, saying, "Potentially this could be the biggest threat in the history of pro football." He added, "I am a fan myself. I would want to see the games on TV for nothing. I would like to get a hamburger for nothing. I would want to see the best Broadway show for nothing. But when you're in business you can't afford to give things away for nothing. Pro football is no different from other sports or businesses." Rozelle concluded, "It will hurt concessionaires, stadium, parking. In the long run, if lifting of the ban continues, everybody will be hurt." The policy was continued by the league even after the three-year law expired, out of fear that Congress might pass a permanent law giving the NFL even less control over the television exposure of its product.

Despite the change in its broadcast policy, the league was flourishing on television under Rozelle's leadership. At heart Rozelle was a public relations person, which gave him an acute awareness of the importance of the media and of knowing when and how the NFL should appear on television. In addition to the obvious spectacle of the Super Bowl, Rozelle would be the architect in creating many television initiatives designed to increase the revenue and exposure of the NFL.

Any time a sports league can get multiple networks competing against each other for its broadcast rights there will surely be an increase in the rights fees paid to the league. The other strategy that a sports league can adopt is to take a portion of its games and create another television package that they could sell to the networks. With the popularity of the game increasing, making more of the NFL product available for television was a pivotal strategy; however, Rozelle was also concerned with maintaining the value of the NFL television product and thought that overexposure could dilute the value of the product in the estimation of the television networks and advertisers. Although trying to create the right balance, Rozelle had already seen what the prospect of more games available for television could mean for NFL revenues with the 1964 broadcast contract increasing largely because of the network's ability to broadcast doubleheaders.

Greater exposure and more revenue for the league provided the rationale for the next television frontier. Always looking for ways to better promote the league, Rozelle would be instrumental in cocreating another American television institution—*Monday Night Football*. Rozelle had long thought that the NFL could be effective in prime time and greatly increase the visibility of the league to a much larger and more general audience than the traditional NFL fans who watched on Sunday afternoon. And a prime-time package of games would also be another product that the networks would bid for.

In 1964, the NFL had reached an agreement with ABC and the Ford Motor Company to televise and sponsor five prime-time, Friday-night games. The plan would be reacted to with much criticism from the NCAA and the National Federation of State High School Athletic Associations. Both groups would contact Congress to express their displeasure with the NFL. The fear from the NCAA was "creeping professionalism"; the high school athletic associations argued that a large percentage of their games were played on Friday night and they didn't want the NFL intruding on that schedule. The NFL would decide not to broadcast the games on a national basis, but only televise them in the city of the road team. Since then, the NFL has continued to respect the wishes of the NCAA and high school football by not scheduling any Friday or Saturday games when their seasons are being played. To further illustrate that point, when hurricanes forced the shifting of Dolphins' games in Miami— against the Tennessee Titans to a Saturday in September 2004 and against the Kansas City Chiefs to a Friday night in October 2005—the games were only televised into the geographic markets of the teams playing in the game. The games would not even be televised live on the NFL's satellite broadcast partner, Direct-TV.

Because of some stadium conflicts with baseball, there would still be some prime-time games played in 1964. The Giants played a home game on a Friday night against the Redskins, their first night game since 1938, but the game would only be televised in the Washington, D.C., area. Two other games were played on a Monday night. In September 1964 the Detroit Lions hosted the Green Bay Packers on a Monday night before a crowd of 59,203, then the largest crowd to see a football game in Detroit. On October 12, the Baltimore Colts would play a Monday-night game in St. Louis. Neither game would be televised nationally. Two years later Rozelle would persuade CBS to televise a Monday-night game between the Chicago Bears and St. Louis Cardinals. These games on Monday night in the 1960s received very good ratings.

Sensing the potential, Rozelle desperately wanted to make a weekly prime-time game a part of the NFL's regular schedule. Rozelle would have discussions with ABC Sports president, Roone Arledge. ABC had been out of the professional football business since losing the AFL contract to NBC. Arledge couldn't convince ABC executives, and the network was initially not interested in a weekly prime-time package. Rozelle would also shop the idea of a prime-time package of NFL games to CBS and NBC, but neither wanted to preempt their successful prime-time lineups, with CBS featuring *I Love Lucy* and NBC televising *Rowan & Martin's Laugh-In* and not wanting to delay the start of *The Tonight Show*. Rozelle would then get the Hughes Network involved in the negotiations. When Hughes put an offer on the table for a prime-time package of games, Arledge could now go back to the ABC executives with the threat of ABC losing many of its affiliates who might decide to buy the games from

Hughes and broadcast them instead of ABC's programming. ABC was more apt to take what at the time was considered a gamble by televising professional football in prime time on a regular weekly schedule. The network didn't want to risk losing those affiliate stations, and it was already trailing CBS and NBC in the Monday-evening time slot. ABC simply had everything to gain and little to lose. Finally, in 1969 ABC agreed to pay the NFL $8.5 million for the rights to *Monday Night Football*, beginning the following year. Joe Browne, NFL executive, comments, "One of the ways Pete made this package more attractive to advertisers and fans was that he got ABC to guarantee that all of the games would be televised in color." Browne adds, "That was a major selling point in those days."

On September 20, 1970, *Monday Night Football*, in full color, became a reality as the game between the New York Jets and Cleveland Browns from Municipal Stadium in Cleveland would begin a tradition that lasted on ABC until the end of the 2005 season. After attending the first game Rozelle was convinced that having a game on Monday night would be a huge success and have a positive impact on attendance when people witnessed how exciting it was to attend a prime-time game.

Arledge was the visionary that would lead the broadcast of *Monday Night Football*. He was an innovative producer, instrumental in pioneering the use of multiple cameras, including hand held cameras, isolation cameras, split screens, field microphones, graphics superimposed on the screen, making instant replay a more intricate part of the broadcast, and providing a more personal approach to covering athletes. His philosophy can be summed up in a memo he wrote to Ed Scherick, an ABC executive, upon his arrival at ABC. As quoted in Marc Gunther and Bill Carter's book, *Monday Night Mayhem*, the memo read, "Heretofore, television has done a remarkable job of bringing the game to the viewer—now we are going to take the viewer to the game!! We will utilize every production technique . . . to heighten the viewer's feeling of actually sitting in the stands and participating personally in the excitement and color. . . . We must gain and hold the interest of women and others who are not fanatic followers of the sport we happen to be televising." The memo also included strategic statements about the production of the games such as "we will have cameras mounted on jeeps, on mike booms, in risers or helicopters, or anything necessary to get the complete story of the game." The memo concluded, "In short, we are going to add show business to sports!"

Steve Rushin would write of Roone Arledge in *Sports Illustrated*, "Television is largely responsible for having made sports the global and moneyed enterprise that it is, and Roone Arledge is largely responsible for having made sports on television look and sound and succeed the way it does." Overall, Gunther and Carter provide a succinct summary in *Monday Night Mayhem* of the relationship between Rozelle and Arledge as one of the major reasons for the success of *Monday Night Football.* They wrote, "Arledge knew better than anybody what sports could do for television. Rozelle knew better than anybody what television could do for sports." Because of *Monday Night Football,* the sports television landscape would forever be changed in America, and it served as a precursor to many other sports moving into prime time.

Perhaps the biggest decision Arledge would make in terms of the broadcast of *Monday Night Football* was to hire Howard Cosell to be one of the announcers on the telecast. Cosell was joined by Keith Jackson and the popular and charismatic Don Meredith, the three-time all-pro quarterback of the Dallas Cowboys who had retired in 1968. Arledge had the final decision on all announcers, which was the first time Rozelle had given a network partner that authority; however, the hiring of Cosell was encouraged by Rozelle. Feeling that the prime-time audience would be different from Sunday afternoon, Rozelle mentioned to Cosell, after being interviewed by him for a local program in New York, that he thought he would be terrific on the Monday-night games.

After a few games Cosell was being routinely criticized by some in the press, by viewers, and even by advertising agencies whose clients sponsored the telecasts. Upon hearing that Cosell was upset by all of the criticism during the first season, Rozelle visited him at his apartment in Manhattan and encouraged Cosell to disregard all that was being said and simply have fun doing the broadcasts. It would eventually be Cosell who gave *Monday Night Football* its signature identity. Tony Kornheiser wrote in *Sport* magazine, "Cosell's presence turned a game into an event. People tuned in to see him. Conversation the next day wasn't about how they played, but about what he said." Kornheiser would add, "Cosell was something unique—a serious, intelligent man with moral principles, someone pledged to tell it like it is." Cosell, always the polarizing figure, would be voted in a *TV Guide* poll as both the most liked and disliked sportscaster.

Monday Night Football was not only a television success, but a cultural success as well. Because of *Monday Night Football,* bowling alleys, movie theaters, and some restaurants were closing early or not even opening at all on a Monday. Don Ohlmeyer, an associate producer when *Monday Night Football* began, identified ABC's approach as instrumental in the game's success. He stated, "I think the key thing in the beginning was that we treated this as a happening." Ohlmeyer added, "It was far more entertainment oriented. We tried to reach out for the non-football fan. We tried to create an excitement like the old *Tonight Show* where something outrageous would happen and you would be afraid to turn it off." Having games on a third network did create one dilemma for Rozelle. A game that would otherwise be slated for NBC or CBS based on its conference affiliations and the location of the game would now be provided to ABC. With the success of *Monday Night Football* Rozelle now had to deal with the complaints of NBC and CBS, who were claiming that ABC was getting all of the good matchups.

In 1973, all three networks were negotiating to renew their broadcast contracts with the NFL. CBS agreed to pay $88 million for four years, an increase of 20 percent. NBC would increase its contract by 6 percent to $74 million. At only $8.5 million per year in rights fees, the success of *Monday Night Football* was an economic bargain for ABC, who was earning over $20 million in advertising revenue. The NFL would finally get a chance for ABC to increase its payment, getting the network to agree to continue broadcasting *Monday Night Football* at a price of $72 million for four years, more than double what the network had been paying. Marc Gunther and Bill Carter explained the negotiating climate in *Monday Night Mayhem*: "None of the networks saw any reason not to give Rozelle what he wanted. They weren't going to pay the increases anyway; the advertisers were. And enough advertisers were lined up to get into the games so that if a few dropped out, selling their sports would be no problem." The league would also help the networks by expanding commercial time so that they could sell extra time to advertisers as a consolation for the higher rights fees that they were now paying. The league had previously instituted a two-minute warning, which provided a guaranteed time-out opportunity to sell commercials.

Rozelle had appointed Art Modell as the chairman of the broadcast committee to assist him in television negotiations. The two became friends and worked closely on the development of the NFL's television product. Modell describes Rozelle as "a very good working partner" and explains that together they would not make a deal with a television network where the network was not also almost guaranteed a profit. Modell describes the relationship between the NFL and the television networks as a "partnership that was not adversarial" and we always tried to "protect the network." Modell explains that the television negotiations for the next cycle would generally start with *Monday Night Football*. Once a benchmark price could be established with the prime-time package, guidelines were set for the Sunday-afternoon and eventual Sunday-night packages.

Neal Pilson, former president of CBS Sports, describes what it was like to negotiate a television deal with Rozelle. He explains that the initial negotiation session would begin by confirming that the network was still interested in broadcasting the NFL. Pilson confirms that none of the networks were seriously interested in intruding on another network's package, but Rozelle might on occasion hint that there was some other network interested to strengthen the NFL's bargaining position. In the negotiations Rozelle would have access to CBS's sales figures and information about the production costs and approximate revenue projections and profits for the network. Rozelle would also gather information independently of what the network allowed him to see. Pilson claims that he was "amazed at the intelligence Rozelle was able to secure."

Finally, Rozelle would provide the dollar amount that he was seeking for the NFL. Pilson reports, "We'd throw up our hands and come back with a lower number that Rozelle would respond to as not being interested." Always confident that the NFL had great value and the network would eventually ante up, Rozelle would wait for another offer from the network before revising his position. Pilson explains that after Rozelle's declining of the initial offer, CBS would submit another bid much closer to Rozelle's initial demand. Pilson recalls that Rozelle's reaction might be to tap his cigarette and indicate that they were "getting there." At this point Rozelle would drop his figure slightly and a deal was agreed to.

Roone Arledge had developed one other innovation in the *Monday Night Football* broadcast that became immensely popular, having Howard Cosell offer a narration of Sunday's games' highlights during halftime. With other networks not making widespread use of NFL highlights (and long before the days of HBO's *Inside the NFL* or ESPN), the *Monday Night Football* halftime highlights were often the only chance for fans to see video of other games. The halftime highlights became such a staple of the entire game broadcast that it was a matter of prestige for teams and players to appear during the segment. ABC would receive several letters from fans in various cities complaining that their team was not featured enough in the highlights. Fans in Pittsburgh would even threaten to take ABC to court because the network was not showing the Steelers enough in the highlights.

The halftime highlights featured the work of another visionary company that Rozelle was helpful in recruiting to promote the league—NFL Films. The film company, founded by Ed Sabol, would shoot the game highlights and provide them to ABC for its use at halftime on *Monday Night Football*. In addition to live television, Rozelle believed that football should be captured on film to demonstrate the talent, strategy, and emotion of an NFL game. Sabol had read about a film company named Telra that had paid $1,500 for the rights to film the 1961 NFL championship game and the fact that the rights to film the 1962 game were open for bidding. At the time Sabol was selling overcoats in Philadelphia for his father-in-law. Unhappy with that line of work, Sabol, who loved football, decided to bid for the rights to film the 1962 NFL championship game. Sabol and representatives from the other film companies would meet in Rozelle's office and deliver their bids in sealed envelopes. Sabol's bid was double that of the next highest.

Ed Sabol's credentials were essentially that he loved the game of football and that he had a hobby of taking motion pictures. His only experience up until then largely consisted of filming his son Steve play football, some local high school football games, and his company, Blair Motion Pictures, producing a few educational films. But Sabol was the consummate salesman and convinced Rozelle to award him the contract to film the 1962 game.

Rozelle was so impressed with his work he hired Sabol to film the 1963 and 1964 championship games as well. Sabol would then approach Rozelle about the NFL having its own film company, with the idea of shooting all of the league's games and producing a team highlight movie at the end of the year. Rozelle loved the idea and convinced the owners to make an investment in Sabol's company. Each owner contributed $12,000 and the NFL bought Sabol's Blair Motion Pictures and created NFL Films. Ed Sabol points out that Rozelle had "an unrivaled handle on public relations for a commissioner." He simply states that "there would be no NFL Films without Rozelle. He was visionary enough to see what it meant. All of the owners did not understand the importance of NFL Films."

Ed Sabol explains, "Football lends itself perfectly for film, the shape of the football field is the same as the shape of the camera." Sabol's films were an important component of the NFL's growth as fans experienced the game as they never had before through his innovative techniques. The use of slow motion was able to perfectly capture a pass spiraling in midair or the breath coming out of the mouths of the players on a frigid Green Bay or Minnesota day. The films conveyed an image of the NFL's players as not just athletes, but men engaged in a dramatic struggle. The music that would accompany the video and the narration of the legendary John Facenda added to the lure of NFL Films.

Sabol was also able to microphone players and coaches to produce memorable moments such as an angry Vince Lombardi screaming at his defense "everybody's grabbing out there, nobody tackling. Just grabbing, everybody—Grab, Grab, Grab, nobody's tackling." Or Hank Stram, coaching his way to victory in Super Bowl IV asking his offense to "just keep matriculating the ball down the field," or euphorically laughing after calling the "65-Toss Power Trap" for a touchdown.

Steve Sabol, Ed's son and president of NFL Films, comments that Rozelle's understanding of public relations and marketing developed his vision that for the NFL to grow it must prosper on television. Steve Sabol points out, "The closest thing to a mission statement for NFL Films was to create an image and mystique to help the league grow." The mission for NFL Films was also to preserve history. Steve Sabol says that Rozelle deserves credit for "what he did and what he didn't do." He describes Rozelle as hands off, and never giving instructions other than a general philosophical approach that "you are not making films for owners, players, or coaches, but for the fans." Sabol says Rozelle gave NFL Films autonomy to do their work and had confidence in their judgment and talent because they had the same creative vision as Rozelle. Rozelle could be confident that NFL Films would never produce something that would harm the NFL.

Neal Pilson, former president of CBS Sports, also recalls that Rozelle was not intrusive into how CBS broadcast the NFL's games. He comments that Rozelle had a philosophy of "we provide the football, you provide the coverage." Pilson adds that he felt that Rozelle was "confident we [CBS] knew what we were doing and confident we understood our business." Pilson does recall the one issue where Rozelle did mention something about the coverage, indicating that he didn't want the networks to promote gambling in any way. *The NFL Today*, CBS's pregame show that featured Jimmy "the Greek" Snyder, would try to not mention the actual point spread. Pilson describes this as the only real "interference," but says that it was more subtle guidance and that he doesn't recall Rozelle ordering a change in the broadcast. Rozelle would state in an interview in *Sport* magazine, "We have no control over how the networks choose to present our games. I like the way they do it, but I have not influenced it."

Jim Steeg comments, "Rozelle could see what was going to happen ten years down the road." This was especially true for the television medium. For example, when Rozelle approached Chet Simmons at ESPN about covering the NFL draft it would initially be voted down by the owners for fear of giving the players' agents a forum. Rozelle would then tell ESPN that the network could cover the draft without broadcast rights, simply as a news event. Rozelle understood the promotional value of the draft as introducing the players coming into the league and creating an excitement for fans that their team might be improving. The draft also provided an event that allowed for the NFL to be relevant in the spring. Chris Berman explains that ESPN wanted the draft because it gave the network an opportunity to associate itself with the NFL. For these reasons, Rozelle eventually moved the NFL draft from beginning on a Tuesday morning to the weekend to increase the event's exposure. Steeg explains about the television coverage of the NFL draft, "Rozelle took a non-event and made it into an event."

Even when the NFL might have some public-relations problems, such as a decline in television ratings in the mid-1980s or a 1984 *Sports Illustrated* cover that asked the question "What's Wrong with the NFL?" Rozelle would demonstrate an ability to look toward the future and to understand the television medium like few in the sports industry ever had. In 1987 the NFL's television contracts were up for renewal; however, this time Rozelle had to deal with a decline in television ratings for the NFL. For the first time he didn't have all of the leverage in negotiations with the networks. It was clear that the networks were not going to provide any massive increase in rights fees, if any increase at all. In the negotiations, Rozelle also had to deal with owners who were accustomed to the cash cow that was network television continuing to produce. ABC would agree to a slight increase for *Monday Night Football,* but the CBS and NBC contracts in 1987 would represent decreases from what the league was earning in 1986.

To make up the difference in television revenue in 1987, the NFL would sign its first cable-television contract, a three-year agreement with ESPN. Art Modell, chairman of the league's broadcasting committee, would state in the *New York Times,* "We are, by far, the last of the major sports to involve itself in cable." He added, "The reason we're in cable at all is that there was a shortfall in dealing with the networks. They are coming off a soft television market, with increasing costs. So we turned to cable to help fill that shortfall for our member clubs." The package with ESPN was for a total of thirteen games, eight games on consecutive Sunday nights covering the last eight weeks of the season and the five prime-time specials that had previously been on ABC. On November 8, 1987, the New York Giants and the New England Patriots played in the first regular-season NFL game broadcast on cable television. Chris Berman recalls that because of its limited household penetration at the time, the playing of games on cable was greeted with much skepticism, but not on the part of Rozelle. In fact, Rozelle would also encourage ESPN to develop the *Primetime* program that showed all of the day's highlights, the first NFL recap show on Sunday of its kind. Berman summarizes, "Next to coming on the air, getting the NFL is the biggest thing to happen to ESPN."

The move to cable had been hinted at by Rozelle in testimony before Congress in both 1982 and 1985. Just as he had done with the NFL and AFL merger and in other television matters, when the NFL signed its first cable-television rights contract with ESPN Rozelle had to defend the policy before Congress. In doing so, he pointed out that other professional sports and college sports had already been making extensive use of cable or pay television. Rozelle, conscious of everyone not having cable television and not wanting to make the NFL an exclusionary product, described ESPN's televising games as "entirely consistent with public and fan interests. It is also a decision reflecting the realities of the television marketplace." He explained that fans of the local team would not lose the opportunity to view them if they were the ESPN game but did not have cable, stating, "Under our ESPN contract, we have required that every game televised by ESPN on cable be simultaneously telecast on a broadcast station in the home city of the "visiting" team and, if the game is sold out in advance, in the city of the "home" team as well. Thus in the markets of the two participating teams there will be simultaneous coverage by both a broadcast television station and ESPN." The NFL was, and is, the only league that requires its cable partner to sell the game to local broadcasters in the cities of the two teams. The NFL would add Turner Network Television, TNT, as a cable broadcast partner in 1990, with that network broadcasting a game on Sunday night during the first eight weeks of the season. On September 9, 1990, the New York Giants hosted the Philadelphia Eagles in the inaugural regular-season game broadcast on TNT.

Rozelle had contended in 1987 that "we [the NFL] believe that our television policies have clearly been in the interest of our fans. The NFL is the only professional sports league that televises every game played by every one of its teams. All of a club's road games are brought back to its home market. In addition, the league has voluntarily adhered to the principles underlying the 1970s legislation requiring local telecasts of all sold out home games, and has televised sold out home games in the home markets." He told a Senate subcommittee in 1987, "Whatever decision we make as to future television arrangements will be a responsible one that fully accounts for the interests of our fans and the views of Congress. In evaluating the league's future plans, we will certainly recognize that we have no interest whatsoever in alienating our fans or losing public support by making it difficult for fans to see NFL football on television."

The use of the television medium helped promote other important aspects of the overall NFL brand. Beyond television and film, Rozelle thought it was important to grow the image and business of every aspect of the NFL. Rozelle was savvy enough to develop and help manage many aspects of the NFL brand. Along with NFL Films capturing the history of the league, Rozelle would be instrumental in developing the Pro Football Hall of Fame. On September 7, 1963, the Pro Football Hall of Fame was dedicated in Canton, Ohio, the site of the first NFL organizational meeting in 1920.

In 1963, NFL Properties was founded to serve as the licensing division of the NFL. Merchandising through NFL Properties became a successful endeavor for the NFL and helped bring further recognition to teams on a national level. For example, a fan in Chicago could now easily obtain a Miami Dolphins jersey. In 1973, NFL Charities was created with a mission of being a nonprofit organization deriving its income from revenues generated from NFL Properties. NFL Charities would support national education and charitable activities as well as supply economic support to players formerly associated with professional football who could no longer support themselves. Rozelle would call the work of NFL Charities one of his most meaningful achievements. And it was Rozelle who came up with the idea in 1974 for the NFL to develop a relationship with the United Way, with its now famous public service announcements featuring NFL stars from various teams, which are broadcast during the games each week.

In all of these ancillary aspects of the NFL business, Rozelle would place a strong emphasis on quality. The NFL logo in association with NFL Properties would only be placed on quality merchandise. The game program that would be sold in all the NFL's stadiums would have the same format, with some national NFL feature articles and some local articles and information as well. David Stern, commissioner of the National Basketball Association, explains the importance of maintaining the quality of the overall league brand, stating "Sports are very much branded entertainment. They are extraordinary content that adapts well to a technological environment and works well globally." Stern claims the NBA was not averse to borrowing the best practices of other sports, especially the NFL and some of its merchandising endeavors through NFL Properties.

All of this growth helped allow Rozelle to internationalize the NFL. In 1976, the NFL would hold the first preseason game outside of North America in Tokyo when the Cardinals defeated the Chargers before 38,000 fans. In 1978, the NFL would play for the first time in Mexico City with the Saints beating the Eagles in a preseason game. In 1986, the American Bowl was created. The 1986 preseason game between the Dallas Cowboys and Chicago Bears in London's Wembley Stadium would draw a sellout crowd of 82,699. Finally, Rozelle's vision of playing games internationally and growing the NFL globally would be truly realized when on October 2, 2005, the Arizona Cardinals and the San Francisco 49ers played a regular-season game for the first time outside of the United States, playing before a crowd of over 103,000 in Mexico City.

CHAPTER 8

A Man of Two Worlds

WHILE PETE ROZELLE was accomplishing some of his most monumental achievements for the NFL, his personal life was going through a tumultuous period. Jane Rozelle was suffering from alcoholism and battling through periods of mental instability. In 1965, Pete and Jane Rozelle would get a divorce. Although he would rarely convey the feeling outwardly, Rozelle was heartbroken by the separation and eventual ending of his marriage. Rozelle would doggedly fight to win full custody of Anne Marie in 1967, something rarely granted to a father in that time period. The divorce was obviously difficult for Anne Marie as well. At first Jane lived only a block away from Rozelle's apartment, but when Anne Marie was thirteen she moved to California. Christmas Day for Anne Marie would sometimes entail waking up in California with her mother, then flying cross-country to have dinner with her father.

Pete Rozelle was absolutely devoted to his daughter, and her care was always his primary concern. Any situation that Anne Marie was dealing with would fall on his shoulders alone. When she was a little girl Anne Marie would often have nightmares and sneak into her father's bed. She explains, "The doctor said the only way I would get over it is for us to set up a system where I could wake him up any time and as often as I needed and he could never get mad or show displeasure and he would come into my room with me and sit until I fell asleep. In the beginning I would wake up six to eight times a night to get him and this went on for weeks until I got used to sleeping on my own. And he never got mad, he just did it."

On one occasion, while attending a Catholic girls' school, Anne Marie was given an assignment to draw something special to her. While other students, coached by their mothers, were drawing pictures of people giving to the poor or feeding the homeless, Anne Marie drew a picture of a black limousine. Rozelle received a call from the school indicating that his daughter's priorities were not correct. In the end, Anne Marie explained that the black limousine simply meant special times between her and her father, as it might often be a limousine taking them to an event or on a special day together. It was her father who would take her sledding in the park and ice skating in Rockefeller Center, or even fishing and camping.

For many years Pete and Anne Marie Rozelle lived in an apartment on Sutton Place near Fifty-seventh Street in Manhattan, a few blocks away from the NFL office, close enough that on nice days Rozelle could walk to the office. He and Anne Marie often spent time walking together in New York City. Some of their walks had a purpose. Anne Marie says that when she was growing up they had an Irish nanny who was a terrible cook. Her father taught her to hide food so as to not hurt the nanny's feelings, then the two of them would tell the nanny they were going for a walk and would stop at PJ Clark's for a hamburger or pizza. Anne Marie describes her father as having unbelievable style and taste and that everything he did was well thought out. She claims that he was not in search of extravagance, but always trying for everything to be perfect, classy, and elegant. She does point out that her father was at times a little bit off in what to get a girl—such as lime green go-go boots instead of white. On one Christmas he used all of his black-market sources to acquire a scarce talking Barbie doll, only to find when Anne Marie pulled the string that the voice spoke Spanish—*"Buenos días. Me llama Barbie. Donde esta Ken?"*

Rozelle was able to keep his situation of being the commissioner of the NFL and a single father in perspective by often taking time at the end of the day to sit down at his desk, think things through, and write long letters to his daughter, or others. Anne Marie explains that even though he might be very busy dealing with some NFL problem, she could always get through to him, or he would immediately call her back. She describes her father as a great listener and problem solver and says she "never made any big decision without him." She recalls even when angry he never yelled, but would sometimes talk sternly or between clenched teeth. She stresses, "He got his message across."

Rozelle would also get some assistance in raising Anne Marie from many of his friends, including his colleagues at the NFL. When traveling to NFL meetings, Anne Marie might be babysat by some of the owners' wives and also spent many Saturdays in the NFL office playing with the staff as they tried to work. Anne Marie recalls playing hide-and-seek with some of the staff, who would let her stay hidden for a little bit while they would sneak off to get some work done before finding her. At the instruction of her father, Anne Marie always sent thank you notes and Christmas and Easter cards to the NFL staff to show appreciation for their spending time with her.

Rozelle was surrounded by friends, many of whom would spend time with Anne Marie when he could not be there. On weekends, Anne Marie would go to museums, the opera, or the ballet with Rozelle's secretary, Thelma Elkjer, if he needed to be out of town. These friends would also help Anne Marie obtain some incredible experiences working summer jobs for NBC Sports; assisting Mary Jo Slater, then casting director for the ABC soap opera *One Life to Live*; working for Roone Arledge at ABC News during a time when workers were striking, so she got to have more extensive responsibilities; interning for Congressman Jack Kemp; or assisting Ethel Kennedy with charity events.

In delivering a eulogy at her father's memorial service in Los Angeles, Anne Marie stated,

> To me, he was the best father, mother, adviser, and friend anyone could have dreamed of. He fought for custody of me back in the '60s when that just wasn't done. He raised me from day one. He looked after me and dedicated himself to me. He never missed a Christmas pageant, father-daughter dance, birthday, or graduation. And he never broke a promise. He raised a daughter completely on his own while doing one of the most visible and demanding jobs—and he did it well.

Pat Summerall speaks to how much he admired Rozelle's love and caring of Anne Marie. Summerall says he had "never seen a father more devoted to a daughter than Rozelle" and he was as "near perfect as a father as one could be." He adds, "The devotion to his daughter is a better indicator of the man he was than anything he did in business." Paul Tagliabue comments on the relationship between Pete and Anne Marie, "Once you got to know him and listen to him talk about when she was a young girl, and the time he spent with her, and the joy that she brought into his life, it was a very moving thing."

Although the job of the commissioner of the NFL is incredibly time consuming and Rozelle was never completely disconnected from the operations of the league, he would make the most of any opportunities he had to relax. Rozelle was mostly a private person, but there were a few people whom he did consider special friends. He would relish spending time with people such as Frank Gifford, Jack Kemp, Jack Landry, Bill MacPhail, David Mahoney, Ed Sabol, Tex Schramm, Herb Siegel, Pat Summerall, and Bob Tisch. Rozelle would often say, "If you are a true friend, you do what you have to do to be there."

Rozelle enjoyed fishing on his boat, the *Triple Eagle,* named after the *Double Eagle,* on which he had served in the Navy. Rozelle also loved to play tennis, so he would often spend vacations in places where he could play tennis and fish. On one fishing trip Rozelle landed a large marlin that he had mounted and placed on a wall in the NFL office. The office with the marlin would soon be dubbed "The Fish Room." Rozelle would also enjoy an occasional rusty nail, scotch and drambuie, but he always smoked.

Another person to whom Rozelle would become devoted came into his life in 1973. At a party leading up to Super Bowl VII in Los Angeles, while having dinner with Pat Summerall and Jack Landry, Rozelle met Carrie Cooke. Carrie was a former television model, having done commercials for Ivory Soap, Oldsmobile, and Carnation Milk. She was familiar with the football business because she previously had been married to Ralph Cooke, son of Washington Redskins owner, Jack Kent Cooke. Rozelle instantly fell in love with Carrie. This unfortunately would cause friction between him and the Redskins owner for the rest of their relationship, and presenting the Super Bowl trophy to Jack Kent Cooke would create a most uncomfortable situation. In fact, Super Bowl XVIII between Al Davis's Raiders and Jack Kent Cooke's Redskins created a definite no-win situation for Rozelle to avoid an awkward moment.

Pete and Carrie shared similar interests and formed a great partnership. Friends would comment that they could see right away how well matched he and Carrie were. Pete and Carrie were married within a year of their meeting in December of 1973. In their early years of marriage Pete and Carrie spent every moment together and vowed never to spend a night apart. Carrie would make every road trip, and Pete would take the good-natured kidding from his friends and office colleagues. Joe Browne says that everyone on the senior staff, including Rozelle, would joke, "If there's Pete, there must be Carrie."

In a 1984 *Boston Globe* interview, Carrie Rozelle described to Marian Christy the characteristics that drew her to her husband. She said, "Pete has a great sense of humor. Without humor, a marriage can take a nosedive. Pete is a generally kind, considerate man. His word is his bond. He doesn't fly off the handle. He thinks things through." She continued, "It was love at first sight" and "from the moment I saw him, I was madly in love with him. Immediately,

I knew he was the man I would soon marry. It was a mutual emotion. Within a week, we spoke to each other about our romantic feelings. Within a few months we spoke of marriage. This has continued to be a true love affair. I love to travel with Pete. He's fun to be with, a man to enjoy. We care for each other. I care very much about him as a human being."

Anne Marie points out that she and her father never kept secrets but recalls noticing something different when Carrie came into his life, initially recognizing that her father was taking more trips. Finally, Rozelle would sit his daughter down and tell her that he had met this women, she too has children, and the next day she was to meet them all.

They bought a new house in Harrison, a town in Westchester County just north of New York City. For Anne Marie the marriage would be a major adjustment. She would now have to move from New York City to Westchester County and switch schools, going from an all-girls Catholic school to a co-ed school. And her time with her father, which was already limited because of the job, would now have to be shared even more. Rozelle would become an active stepfather to Carrie's children.

Generously giving of themselves in both time and money to charitable causes would be something both Pete and Carrie Rozelle would constantly participate in. Carrie Rozelle's three sons suffered from dyslexia, two severely, and Carrie, who was a registered nurse, developed the Foundation for Children with Learning Disabilities, a national volunteer organization designed to raise money for dyslexia research. She would describe the goals of the foundation at a fund-raising event in Boston in 1982: "to bring the public a sense of awareness concerning the problems of the learning disability child . . . that these children have been labeled as stupid, dumb, and lazy, are in need of some specific academic programs tailored for their special needs to bring them to adulthood as productive, balanced, happy citizens." In the interview with Marian Christy Carrie Rozelle said, "I'm a positive person. I like to face a problem head-on. I deal only with the good of any situation. Negativeness deludes the intelligence. Positive means you're dealing with the upside of any situation. That alone implies carrying on in an upward motion."

Carrie was very comfortable with her husband's position of prominence and recognition. She also told Marian Christy, "Pete is the celebrity of the family, not me. When you're the spouse of a celebrity, you have to feel awfully good about your position in the marriage. I'm in the shadow of my husband's celebrity. I could feel unbalanced, unhappy. But I like myself. I like what I do. I have good friends. I'm involved. Pete's celebrity does not touch me in a negative way." Carrie would in fact help make Pete better enjoy the social aspects of the NFL job. At the house in Westchester the two hosted many events, such as a western-themed party where guests would dress up in western clothing or a family day with people from the NFL office. And Thanksgiving would now be spent at home—with the meal coming at halftime of the NFL games being played. Friends would also regularly come over to play tennis at their Westchester home.

After retiring as commissioner of the NFL, Pete Rozelle became a grandfather. Anne Marie recalls that because horse racing was one of her father's real passions she decided to tell him that he was going to become a grandfather while at the Breeders Cup. She would break the news to him in a poem. Rozelle was so excited about the news that he raced over and lifted up Ann Mara, Wellington Mara's wife and the grandmother of forty.

Overall, the quiet times with his family and close friends were what Rozelle most cherished. Anne Marie recalls her father loving to come home from work, putting on a bathrobe and sitting with his family having a drink and just talking. As Anne Marie told NFL Films in its production, *Rozelle: Building America's Game,* "He actually enjoyed having two worlds, the football world and the coming home to another world, the simpler world."

CHAPTER 9

It's Always Something: Players, Coaches, & Owners

A S C O M M I S S I O N E R there are simply so many decisions that need to be made and so many different people who need to be dealt with, primarily the players, coaches, and owners within the league. A critical part of the development of the NFL in Rozelle's estimation was for the players and coaches to promote the values of the league, most notably the integrity of the game. Rozelle had a deep respect for the players and coaches, whom he thought of as the game itself. He would often comment on the abilities of the players and the visual beauty of the game of football. Still, how the people involved in the sport behaved would always be of prime importance to Rozelle in the presentation and image of the league and the NFL brand. He would advocate the players be more than on-the-field superstars, to contribute to their communities. An example of what Rozelle desired from the league's players and coaches was revealed when presenting the championship trophy to Vince Lombardi for the first time after the 1961 championship game. As quoted by David Maraniss in his book *When Pride Still Mattered: A Life of Vince Lombardi*, Rozelle stated, "I'd like to say that as commissioner I'm not concerned with individual records or individual team efforts. I am concerned with the high caliber of players we have in the league, and the owners, and coaches, who have that indefinable something called class. And the gentleman I'm handing this to personifies it—Vince Lombardi." Rozelle had great respect for Lombardi, and he immediately recognized his importance in the growth of the NFL, so much that one

The future commissioner.

Young Rozelle (right) with his father and brother.

Rozelle joined the Navy in 1944 and served aboard a tanker until 1946. He is shown here with his mother on shore leave.

Rozelle with his brother Dick.

Rozelle, first wife Jane, and daughter Anne Marie.

A formal portrait of the NFL commissioner by Fabian Bacharach.

REPORT OF BALLOTS. COMM. ELECTION	1	2	3	4	5	6	7	8	9	10	11	12	13	14	15	16	17	18	19	20	21	22	23	24
BALTIMORE	G	G	G	A	K	K	K	A	K	A	K	K	K	K	K	K	K	G					R	G
BEARS	P	P	P	P	P	P	P	P	P	P	P	P	P	P	P	P	P	P	P	P			P	G
BROWNS	L	L	L	L	L	L	L	L	P	L	L	L	L	L	L	L	L	L					R	G
CARDS	L	L	L	L	L	L	L	L	L	L	L	L	L	L	L	L	L	L					R	G
DETROIT	L	L	L	L	L	L	L	A	A	A	L	A	L	L	L	L	L						R	
GREEN BAY	L	L	L	L	L	L	L	L	L	L	L	L	L	L	L	L	L	L					R	G
L.A.	L	G	L	L	L	L	L	L	L	L	L	L	L	L	L	L	L	L						G
N.Y.	L	L	L	L	L	L	L	L	L	L	L	L	L	L	L	L	L	L					R	G
PHIL	G	G	G	A	K	K	G	K	A	A	K	K	K	K	K	K	G						R	G
PITT	G	L	L	L	K	K	K	A	K	K	K	K	K	K	K	K	G						R	G
S.F.	L	L	L	L	L	L	L	L	L	L	L	L	L	L	L	L	L						L	G
WASH	G	G	G	A	A	K	K	A	A	A	K	K	K	K	K	G							R	G

CODE
G = GUNSEL
L = LEAHY
K = KELLETT
S = SCHISSLER
P = PASSED VOTE
A = ANDERSON
R = ROZELLE

Decided on 23rd Ballot

Note. 24th BALLOT WAS FOR TREASURER

A copy of the election ballot in which Rozelle was selected as the sixth full-time commissioner of the NFL. Note, Rozelle did not receive one vote until the twenty-third ballot.

With Tex Schramm (left) and Lamar Hunt announcing the NFL/AFL merger. Courtesy of the Pro Football Hall of Fame.

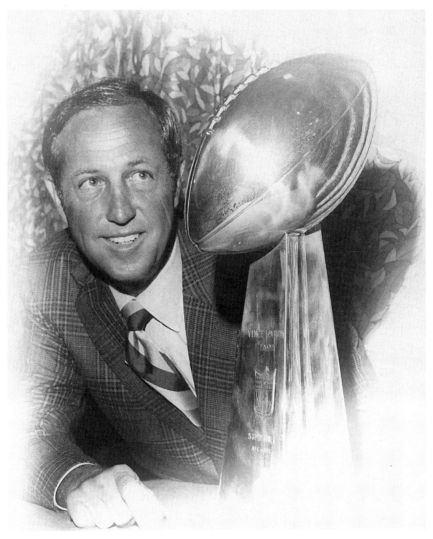

Rozelle and the Super Bowl Trophy, the game he helped cultivate. Today the Most Valuable Player of the Super Bowl receives a trophy named in Rozelle's honor.

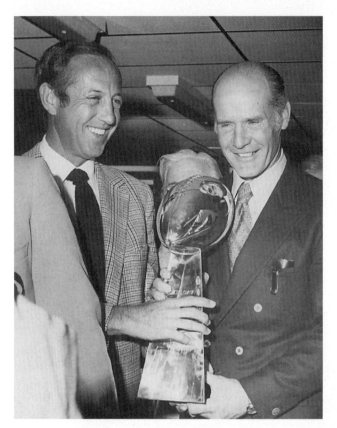

Rozelle presents the Lombardi Trophy to Dallas Cowboys coach Tom Landry following Super Bowl VI in 1972. Bill Mark photo.

Testifying before U.S. Senate committee in 1982. George Halas and Paul Tagliabue are seated to Rozelle's left.

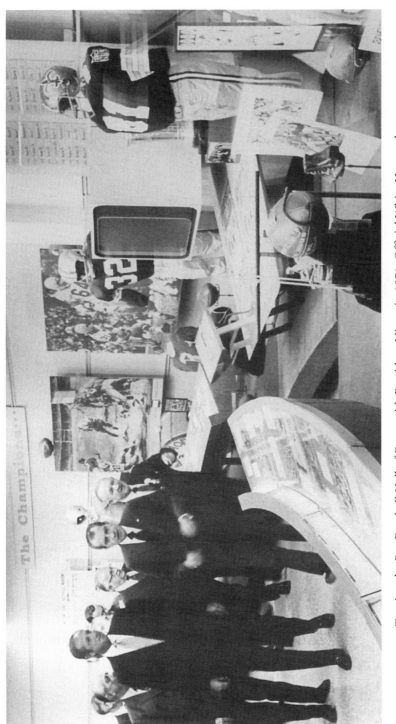

Touring the Pro Football Hall of Fame with President Nixon in 1971. Official White House photo.

Rozelle and daughter Anne
Marie at her college
graduation.

Pete and Carrie Rozelle at
Wimbledon.

With Howard Cosell and Johnny Carson.

Celebrating a birthday among close friends. Standing, left to right, are Jack Landry, Herb Siegel, Bob Tisch, and Frank Gifford. Seated with Rozelle is David Mahoney.

Joking with another legend, Chicago Bears running back Walter Payton.

Rozelle and NFL attorney Frank Rothman celebrate their victory in the USFL trial.

Rozelle was instrumental in making the United Way the official charity partner of the NFL.

THE NATIONAL FOOTBALL LEAGUE

410 PARK AVENUE,   NEW YORK, N.Y. 10022 • 758-1500

22 March 1989

Dear Staff:

I regret this means of communicating with you but, unfortunately, it is the only feasible way of doing it.

Today I am announcing to the club presidents and the media that I intend to retire.

My decision was made last October, but I felt it important to keep it to myself. I did not wish to be a 'lame duck' commissioner during the course of the season.

I simply decided that while I was still in good health Carrie and I should have more stressless time to do many of the leisure activities that holding this position does not permit.

The conscientious efforts of the entire staff, many of you with the league for a considerable period of time, have certainly lessened the day-to-day burden on me. I will be eternally grateful for your constant devotion to the National Football League.

I would think it will be June or July before a transition can be fully implemented and we will be moving to California.

In the meantime, I will be looking forward to seeing all of you on my return.

Best,

PR:te

Rozelle's resignation letter to his staff.

Rozelle's favorite activities, fishing and tennis.

Rozelle following his induction into the Pro Football Hall of Fame. Tex Schramm is at left.

week after Lombardi's death in September 1970, the Super Bowl trophy was renamed the Vince Lombardi trophy.

Dealing with players, coaches, and owners, many of whom were friends, on an individual disciplinary basis was always a challenge. In the NFL Constitution and Bylaws the disciplinary powers of the commissioner are explicitly detailed as "whenever the Commissioner, after notice and hearing, decides that an owner, shareholder, partner or holder of an interest in a member club, or any player, coach, officer, director, or employee thereof, or an officer, employee or official of the League has either violated the Constitution or Bylaws of the League, or has been or is guilty of conduct detrimental to the welfare of the League or professional football, then the Commissioner shall have complete authority to suspend and/or fine such person."

Rozelle gained credibility early on with those in the league when he confronted George Halas for abusing the officials. Rozelle called Halas and asked him to come to New York for a meeting. Halas replied by telling Rozelle that he would meet him at the airport. Rozelle, however, then sternly told Halas that the meeting was to take place in the commissioner's office. Halas acquiesced. Dan Rooney recalls at an NFL meeting one year after Rozelle was elected that George Preston Marshall, Washington Redskins owner, showed up in a bathrobe and slippers, and while Rozelle was giving his report on the league Marshall kept interrupting, "That's not right," "You're wrong here." Rozelle would sternly tell Marshall in front of all the other owners, "Please let me give my report, then you can respond." Rooney says episodes like this showed he could handle the owners. Bill MacPhail also told of a situation involving Marshall, when MacPhail and Rozelle were visiting each of the NFL owners to discuss pooling television rights. MacPhail was quoted in the *NFL GameDay Program* that was issued to commemorate Rozelle's career, saying, "Marshall didn't like the idea of giving up his network, which went deep into the South. Marshall, who was an intimidating man, held his finger an inch away from Pete's nose and screamed at him, 'I've been putting together television packages since you were in diapers.' It was so bad that I could feel myself trembling, but Pete wasn't scared. He stood firm and said, 'Mr. Marshall, I want you to answer my question.' Right there I knew the NFL had hired one tough cookie." Frank Gifford points out that "how Rozelle dealt one-on-one with the owners helped convince people such as Halas, Mara, and the other owners to respect him so much." Rozelle had also been widely praised for his handling of the Paul Hornung and Alex Karras gambling scandals in 1963.

In 1969, much like having to deal with Hornung in 1963, Rozelle was forced to confront another superstar, Joe Namath, the Most Valuable Player of the previous year's Super Bowl. Namath was part owner of a New York City bar and restaurant called Bachelors III that was being investigated by the FBI for gambling and other criminal activity. Rozelle would tell Namath to divest his interests in the restaurant or face suspension for associating with undesirables, known gamblers who had frequently attended Bachelors III. Rozelle was again concerned with any association between players and gamblers damaging the integrity of professional football.

Namath would initially refuse to sell the bar claiming that he did nothing wrong and that he never bet on football games with a bookmaker, never lost a game on purpose, or shaved points. Namath would later joke about the charges in his book written with Dick Schaap, *I Can't Wait Until Tomorrow . . . 'Cause I Get Better-Looking Every Day*, "I admit I had deliberately given information to gamblers to affect their bets: Before the 1969 Super Bowl, I'd guaranteed that we'd win the game and I told everybody—out in the open—to bet on the Jets." Namath felt that the situation of his being asked to sell Bachelors III was "filled with hypocrisy" and a double standard was being applied to him by Rozelle, as other people involved with the NFL had associations with gambling, including the Jets' own team president, Phil Iselin, who was also the president of Monmouth Park race track in New Jersey.

On Tuesday June 3, 1969, Namath, Iselin, and Jets head coach Weeb Ewbank would meet with Jack Danahy, the lead investigator from the NFL and a former FBI agent. At this meeting Danahy warned Namath that a raid on the restaurant was imminent and that he should sell. Namath would meet the next day with Rozelle where he advised Namath of the clause in the standard players contract to not associate with gamblers and that the commissioner had the power to impose disciplinary action against any player who did. Rozelle would concede to Namath that he believed Namath had not done anything illegal, but because of his connection to Bachelors III he did violate the rule and would be suspended if he did not sell. Namath left the meeting without giving Rozelle any decision as to his selling.

By Thursday, through his attorney, Mike Bite, Namath informed Rozelle that he was going to sell. However, still adamant that he had not done anything wrong, Namath would change his mind and once again refuse to sell his interests in Bachelors III. Before any suspension from Rozelle could be implemented, on Friday June 5, Namath conducted a teary-eyed press conference at Bachelors III in which he informed the media of Rozelle's ultimatum and announced he was retiring from professional football. Namath stated, "They said I'm innocent, but I have to sell." He added, "I can't go along with that. It's principle."

In a statement issued reacting to Namath's retirement announcement, Rozelle would begin, "Joe Namath's decision to retire from professional football is a personal one, a decision made by him ultimately. It is the responsibility of this office to advise individuals, both players and other club personnel, whenever any of their associations could possibly cause harm to their individual reputations or the game of professional football." In the statement, Rozelle acknowledged that the NFL had no evidence that Namath was personally involved in any illegal activities and that it is impossible for him to have known the backgrounds of all of the people who came into the bar. Rozelle would, however, say in the statement, "Continuation of such associations after learning of a person's undesirable background and habits is cause for deep concern. Such conduct gives the appearance of evil, whether or not it actually exists, and thereby affects the player's reputation, the reputation of his fellow players, and the integrity of the sport."

While there was a clear disagreement over the situation, there was not any malicious animosity between Rozelle and Namath. Namath wrote in his book, "Rozelle and I respect each other; he thinks I'm a helluva passer and I think he's the best commissioner in pro football." There would be no contact between Rozelle and Namath until June 26, when the two met at Rozelle's apartment. The meeting would surprisingly begin with Rozelle asking Namath to sign autographs for his daughter and her friend. Namath described the meeting in his book: "Rozelle kept insisting that it was important for pro football to have special standards for its players because public faith in the game was essential. I could see his point, but I could also see my own. Personally, I hadn't done anything to violate the public faith." Namath would further explain his position, "I could understand him not wanting me to bet—that's obvious grounds for suspension—but I hadn't bet, on my team or against my team. Rozelle knew that, and I knew that." In their meeting Rozelle would tell Namath, "I'd be a damn fool if I didn't want to see you in football," adding, "you're the biggest name we've got." The meeting ended on a humorous note as described by Rozelle, "As he [Namath] left my apartment, my daughter, who was listening through the door in the den came out. She said, 'Mr. Namath, I just want you to know that everyone in the Rozelle family doesn't hate you.'" Rozelle and Namath would again meet on July 14. That meeting too ended without a resolution and Namath remained the retired quarterback of the Super Bowl champions.

On Thursday July 17, Mike Bite would propose a compromise. Namath was to sell his interests in Bachelors III in New York but have the right to invest in other Bachelors III restaurants that might be opened in other parts of the country. The next day the proposal was presented to Rozelle with the commissioner immediately accepting those terms. Namath would go to Rozelle's office and the two would shake hands on the agreement. Joe Namath's retirement had lasted one month and a half.

Gambling allegations were at the root of another confrontation that Rozelle would have to deal with when he investigated Carroll Rosenbloom. The gambling allegations would only be one of a series of incidents that caused friction between Rosenbloom and Rozelle. Another point of contention was when Rozelle awarded Rams running back Cullen Bryant to the Lions as compensation for the Rams signing free-agent wide receiver Ron Jessie from Detroit. After the Bryant incident Rosenbloom considered himself an enemy of Rozelle and tried to get him fired. At a league meeting in November 1975 Rosenbloom openly and strongly criticized Rozelle, claiming he would not attend another league meeting so long as Rozelle was the commissioner. Rosenbloom then stormed out of the room. Rozelle recalled in the *New York Times* that once Rosenbloom left the room he told the other owners, "Anyone who would like to talk to me privately about the charges you just heard, feel free. But for now, let's continue the meeting." In the same article Art Modell described the scene. He said, "Carroll blasted Pete with a slashing attack. He threatened the league and everybody. I thought it was a totally unjustified attack, but I was impressed with the way Pete handled it, with enormous patience and fortitude." Any movement by Rosenbloom to oust Rozelle would receive no momentum. Jay Moyer describes how in the meeting Rosenbloom, "seeing that he did not have a receptive audience among the owners, stood up, pointed at Pete, and said, 'If I can't get you in here, I'll get you out there.' As it happened, within a few months the NFL office underwent an extensive examination conducted by the fraud division of the IRS. The league came out totally clean, but we always suspected that Rosenbloom had a major hand in catalyzing that examination."

Rosenbloom would continue to criticize Rozelle, including chastising him for what he claimed was a deliberate scheduling of the Rams to play a game beginning at 4:00 p.m. in Miami at the start of Yom Kippur in 1976. Rosenbloom would tell the *Los Angeles Times*, "It's insensitive, arrogant and stupid, but Rozelle has no sensitivity." He added, "Yom Kippur is the one holiday most important to Jewish people. This is a thing that was done with malice afore-thought. They said, 'let's put the Jew in Miami for Yom Kippur and see how he likes it.' I just know Rozelle and the stooges were giggling about it on the day they released the schedule." Rozelle simply denied the charge and offered, "We attempt to avoid scheduling conflicts with all religious holidays. Unfortunately, it is not always possible to do so."

One situation where Rozelle would meet resistance from some NFL owners was on the issue of cross-ownership of an NFL team with a team in another sport. Rozelle did not want an NFL owner to be the majority owner of a franchise in another sport because of potential conflict of interest in that the NFL competes with all other forms of entertainment, including other sports leagues, for fan, sponsor, and television network money, and for attention from the media and the public. Rozelle would advocate a resolution that prohibited cross-ownership. If in violation of the rule the owner could face substantial fines that would be collected by the league through withholding payments from the national television contract. This rule directly impacted Lamar Hunt from Kansas City and Joe Robbie from Miami, who both had connections with teams of the North American Soccer League (NASL), and Jack Kent Cooke from Washington, who also owned the NBA's Los Angeles Lakers and the NHL's Los Angeles Kings. Cooke would sell his interests in the Los Angeles teams and maintain ownership of the Washington Redskins. Hunt and Robbie, however, would partake in a lawsuit that tried to allow for cross-ownership to continue. The federal district court would rule in favor of the NFL, but the decision would be reversed on appeal, allowing them to continue owning their teams in the soccer league. The NFL appealed to the Supreme Court, but it chose not to hear the case.

In another situation, much as he had been asked to do with the Rams when being named the team's general manager in 1957, now as the commissioner, Rozelle would have to intervene to help solve an ownership dispute involving the New York Giants in the late 1970s. The team that was started by Timothy J. Mara in the 1920s was given equally to his two sons, Jack and Wellington, at the time of his death. Wellington Mara at nine years old was with his father at the Giants' first-ever game on October 18, 1925, against the Frankford Yellow Jackets, a Giants loss, 14-0. When Jack Mara died in 1965, his controlling interests in the Giants were to be held by his son, Tim. Tim, who also represented his mother and sister in their controlling interests of the Giants, owned 50 percent of the franchise, with the other 50 percent owned by Wellington, his uncle. The NFL had, in fact, created a rule to avoid such situations by having each team have one owner controlling at least 51 percent of the team's stock. The rule did not apply to the Giants, whose ownership situation had been grand-fathered into the previous rule, allowing for the completely equal ownership scenario.

The Giants of the late 1970s were also going through a low point in the franchise's history on the field. The team had last qualified for the playoffs in 1963, losing the championship game to the Chicago Bears, 14-10. Entering the 1978 season the Giants were trying to break a streak of five consecutive seasons with a losing record, never winning more than five games in any one season and finishing last in their division on three occasions. On November 19, 1978, the team would reach a new level of futility. Leading the Eagles 17-12 and only needing to have the quarterback kneel on the ball one more time to secure the victory, the Giants instead ran a play called "pro 65 up" that was supposed to have Larry Csonka take the handoff and simply plow into the line to run out the clock and end the game. But the handoff exchange between quarterback Joe Pisarcik and Csonka was fumbled and picked up by Eagles defensive back Herman Edwards, who returned it twenty-six yards for a touchdown with twenty seconds left in the game, giving Philadelphia a 19-17 victory. The game became known as the "Miracle in the Meadowlands." John McVay, Giants head coach, would simply comment afterward, "That's the most horrifying ending to a ball game I've ever seen."

The Giants fans would react angrily at the team's home game on December 10 against the Cardinals. The game had 24,374 no-shows, a small group of fans even burned their tickets in the parking lot, and Wellington Mara was hung in effigy in the second quarter. A group of fans calling themselves the Giants Fans Committee also passed out sheets before the game that said there would be a plane flying over the stadium carrying a banner and for fans to react by chanting "We've had enough." When the plane did fly over Giants Stadium with a banner reading, "Fifteen years of lousy football . . . we've had enough," it was greeted with cheers and the Giants fans dutifully chanting as they had been instructed, "We've had enough . . . we've had enough."

Wellington Mara and his nephew Tim had already clashed in the deci-sion making about the team. The first serious disagreement had occurred when, without Tim's approval, Wellington had signed Csonka. In May of 1978 Wellington hired Terry Bledsoe to serve as an assistant director of football operations to Andy Robustelli, the former Giant and Hall of Fame defensive end who was running the team. Tim Mara objected to the hiring of Bledsoe and wrote a letter to Rozelle requesting assistance.

After the 1978 season the relationship between the Maras reached a critical point of conflict as to the future direction of the team. On December 18 Robustelli resigned as director of football operations and John McVay was released as the team's head coach. The Maras even had some disagreement over Robustelli's resignation, with Wellington Mara indicating Robustelli might reconsider. Robustelli's relationship with Wellington went back to 1956 when Mara, learning of a dispute between Robustelli and the Rams, had called Robustelli and asked him if he was interested in playing for the Giants. A trade was then worked out between the Giants and the Rams. But Tim Mara was against Robustelli being retained. According to a *New York Times* article written by Tony Kornheiser, it was reported that Tim told Robustelli, "As far as 50 percent of the stockholders are concerned, your resignation is irrevocable."

The Giants were now trying to decide on a new director of football operations, but Wellington and Tim Mara could not agree. Wellington wanted to elevate Bledsoe, and Tim wanted to try to hire either Gil Brandt from the Cowboys or Don Klosterman from the Rams. In February 1979 Rozelle would ask each of the two owners to submit a list of four acceptable names for the director position. The only name to appear on each list was the NFL's personnel director, Jan Van Duser, who rejected the job. Because no agreement could be reached on a director, Wellington suggested that the team hire its head coach first, then fill the director position. Wellington, maintaining that as president of the Giants he had greater operational authority over the team's decisions, held a press conference claiming that he alone would hire the head coach. The strategy and announcement created yet another disagreement between him and Tim.

Wellington Mara had asked Rozelle to recognize him as the final decision maker, something Rozelle could not do. Rozelle would then take on an even larger role as the mediator in the conflict. Rozelle offered a compromise choice, the Dolphins' director of scouting and the person whom Miami's head coach, Don Shula, referred to as "my right-hand man," George Young. According to Jerry Izenberg in his book, *New York Giants: 75 Years*, Rozelle called Tim Mara and told him, "I want you to choose between George Young and Frank Ryan [former Bears quarterback and at the time the athletic director at Yale]." Rozelle then called Wellington and instructed him to "make sure George Young is somewhere on your list." On Valentine's Day 1979, a deal was reached in the early evening at Rozelle's office that made George Young the new general manager of the New York Giants. With everyone in the NFL office gone home for the day, Rozelle typed up the press release himself.

It would be Young who would make the football decisions that over the next few years included the drafting of Phil Simms in 1979, Lawrence Taylor in 1981, and the hiring of Bill Parcells as head coach in 1983. In Young's eighth season as general manger and Parcells' fourth season as head coach, the Giants defeated the Denver Broncos 39-20, to win their first Super Bowl. Rozelle presented the Super Bowl trophy to Wellington Mara stating, "I'm very pleased to congratulate Wellington Mara, the president of the Giants, and also the president of the National Football Conference. Well, your father, Timothy J. Mara, founded the Giants in 1925. In that first season you were a nine-year-old ball boy and ever since that time I think the Giants have been both the business and the love of the Mara family."

Any problems between a player or coach and a member of the press would also have to be dealt with by Rozelle. For example, as David Maraniss reports, Vince Lombardi banned Ken Hartnett, an Associated Press writer, from the Packer locker room and all pregame and postgame press conferences for writing a story about Green Bay running back Jim Taylor complaining that he was not receiving enough playing time and that other Packer players had received large salary increases. Sportswriters from Wisconsin would write to Rozelle to protest the situation. When Rozelle finally called Lombardi to remind him of the NFL's policy that credentialed reporters could not be banned from the locker room or press boxes Lombardi gave in.

Not all infractions were as serious as some of the gambling or integrity issues of the league, but even things such as being strict about how players wore their uniforms was an issue of importance to Rozelle, as it again represented the image of the entire league. In 1985 as the Chicago Bears were making their run toward winning the Super Bowl, Rozelle would fine the team's management $5,000 for letting the Bears wear too much advertising on their uniforms. Jim McMahon, Bears quarterback, who had previously worn an Adidas headband, would answer the commissioner by wearing a white headband with the name Rozelle in black block letters for the NFC championship game against the Rams. Rozelle's daughter, Anne Marie, recalls how strange it was to be walking the streets of New Orleans prior to Super Bowl XX between the Bears and the Patriots with throngs of people wearing headbands with her last name on it. Pete Rozelle would call the actions of McMahon, "a great gag."

CHAPTER 10

NFL Constitution and Bylaws, Section 4.3

A T T H E end of the 1970s the NFL was absolutely thriving. Television contracts negotiated in 1977 continued the trend of large increases in broadcast-rights fees, including ABC's *Monday Night Football* package, which was now seven times more than the network had first paid. The NFL was performing exceedingly well in the critical television audience demographic of men between the ages of eighteen and forty-nine, the most desirable, but hardest to reach, demographic.

The popularity of the NFL was demonstrated in a 1978 Harris poll that showed that 70 percent of the nations sports fans said they followed football, compared to 54 percent who followed baseball. This growth in popularity allowed for more teams, more games, more playoffs, and overall more NFL product for the fans to consume and the NFL to earn revenues from. The league had expanded to twenty-eight teams when Tampa Bay and Seattle joined the NFL in 1976. In 1978, the NFL expanded its regular season from fourteen to sixteen games and expanded its playoffs from eight teams to ten, adding a second wild-card team from each conference. Also, during this time period a great rivalry between the Pittsburgh Steelers and the Dallas Cowboys had developed and was among the best in sports. All of these developments gave Rozelle great confidence to state at his press conference prior to the 1980 Super Bowl that the 1980s "will be the NFL's greatest decade." The third decade of his being commissioner would, however, be vastly different from the previous two for Rozelle and the late 1970s ended up marking the last peaceful period of his commissionership.

The decade of the 1980s would begin very favorably for the NFL. The league had produced record television ratings in 1981, just as it was finishing up negotiations on a very lucrative television contract. The television networks were also profiting, as a *Time* magazine article estimated that CBS made $25 million from the NFL alone in 1981. In March 1982, the NFL signed a then record $2 billion television deal to remain with ABC, CBS, and NBC over the next five years. Rozelle would begin negotiations with ABC by offering the network the opportunity to broadcast its first Super Bowl in January 1985. Rozelle described his strategy to Marc Gunther and Bill Carter in *Monday Night Mayhem*, saying "I knew Roone. When I offered him in the Olympic year [ABC would televise the 1984 Winter Olympics from Sarajevo, Yugoslavia, and the Summer Olympics from Los Angeles] a chance at the Super Bowl, I knew that would pique his interest. That would create a tremendous year for them." ABC agreed to pay the NFL $650 million for five years of broadcast rights to *Monday Night Football*, including special prime-time games on Thursday or Sunday, and $17 million for the rights to Super Bowl XIX.

Rozelle would then turn to his other broadcast partners, quickly agreeing with NBC for $590 million. The negotiation with CBS would be more complicated, with CBS balking at Rozelle's demand of $720 million. Rozelle would contact Arledge at ABC to see if he and ABC had any interest in broadcasting the NFL on Sunday afternoon as well as on Monday night. When Arledge expressed some interest, Rozelle used that as bargaining leverage against CBS. Afraid to lose the NFL, CBS finally compromised at the price of $665 million. The 1982 contract was a dramatic increase, where each NFL team on average would earn approximately $14.2 million per season, $11.8 million in 1982, up from the $5.8 million per season they had been earning. For some owners, profit was guaranteed before selling a single ticket or collecting any money from parking or concessions.

The in-stadium product also appeared to be stable. The issue of new stadiums had largely been addressed in the late 1960s and early 1970s with many NFL teams moving into new stadiums. In 1970, the Chicago Bears would leave Wrigley Field when Rozelle declared that no team could play its home games in a stadium with an attendance capacity of less than 50,000. Buffalo would open its Rich Stadium in 1973, and Kansas City moved into Arrowhead Stadium in 1972. Dual-purpose ballparks were built for baseball and football in Cincinnati, Philadelphia, Pittsburgh, and St. Louis. In 1968, the Oilers moved into the Astrodome, the first domed stadium in Houston, and it would be shared by major league baseball's Astros. In 1975, the Saints and the Lions would also move into newly constructed domed stadiums. In addition to the newly constructed dual-purpose ballparks, in 1979 NFL franchises in Atlanta, Baltimore, Cleveland, Minnesota, New York (the Jets in Shea Stadium), Oakland, San Diego, San Francisco, and Seattle (although the Kingdome was only a few years old with the Seahawks entering the NFL in 1976) were all sharing their stadium with the baseball team in their city.

Many other owners throughout the NFL who had not been provided a new stadium remained interested in upgrading their existing stadiums, particularly with an eye toward developing luxury boxes that could generate large revenues for their franchise. The construction of new stadiums was encouraged by Rozelle, but teams relocating to another city was not. To Rozelle, the NFL franchise was an invaluable and intricate part of the fabric of a community. As long as the city continued to support its team, Rozelle did not see any reason for a team to relocate. Rozelle prided himself on the fact that no team in the NFL had moved to another city since the owners voted to allow the Cardinals to leave Chicago for St. Louis prior to the 1960 season. With the presentation of the game on television always of paramount importance to Rozelle, part of that equation was the cities where the teams were located. The relocation of the Cardinals from Chicago to St. Louis was applauded by the television networks because the NFL was often forced to black out Bears' road games in Chicago because the Cardinals were playing at home on those dates. Rozelle viewed the fact that no teams had moved since then as an indication of league strength and stability. However, when a city or state government would not build a new stadium or upgrade the existing facility, NFL owners began to explore their options.

Article IV, Section 4.3 of the NFL Constitution and Bylaws dealt with franchise relocation and prior to 1978 outlined that a team can move its franchise to a location within the home territory of any other club *only* if approved by a unanimous vote. A home territory was defined as a seventy-five-mile radius from where a team plays its home games. In this rule a vote by a single owner (presumably the owner that already has the team in that geographic region) could block the move of another team invading the territory. A move of an NFL team to a city that did not have a franchise would require the approval of three-fourths, or twenty-one of the twenty-eight franchises, voting in favor. The NFL's rationale for these rules was that having exclusive territories for clubs contributed to league stability, created geographic regional balance, created rivalries, helped new franchises coming into the league, ensured fair competition on the field, and assisted in developing marketing and television practices. All of which would foster fan loyalty and contribute to ticket sales and television viewing. The NFL, therefore, believed it must be allowed to have some control over the location of its franchises.

The event that would begin to bring the issue of franchise relocation to the forefront of Rozelle and the NFL owners' attention was Carroll Rosenbloom's decision to move the Los Angeles Rams to Anaheim. Since moving to Los Angeles to start the 1946 season, the Rams had played their home games in the Los Angeles Coliseum. Formerly Rosenbloom had been the owner of the Baltimore Colts, acquiring complete ownership of the team in 1964. But with many financial and personal connections to Los Angeles he had developed an interest in owning the Rams. He also wanted out of Baltimore for financial reasons, including his growing displeasure with Baltimore's Memorial Stadium and what had become a contentious relationship with the Baltimore press. Rosenbloom along with Joe Thomas, a man who had been fired as the personnel director of the Dolphins but who had ambitions of becoming the general manager of the Colts, thought that if they could find someone to buy the Rams and agree to trade them for the Colts franchise, both men could get what they desired. Thomas knew Robert Irsay, a man who had started and built up one of the country's largest heating, ventilating, and air-conditioning companies before selling it for a huge profit. When Irsay agreed to purchase the Rams for $19 million, a trade was arranged in July 1972 where Rosenbloom would give Irsay the Colts and $4 million in cash, with Rosenbloom obtaining ownership of the Rams.

With the move to Los Angeles, Rosenbloom inherited a stadium with only two years left on its lease, and he started exploring the possibility of Anaheim as a location for the Rams. Rosenbloom could also use any flirtations with Anaheim as leverage in negotiations with the Los Angeles Memorial Coliseum Commission (LAMCC), which controlled the Coliseum. Rosenbloom asked for numerous improvements to the Coliseum, including the construction of luxury boxes. But in 1973, unsuccessful in his negotiations in Anaheim, he ended up remaining at the Coliseum for double the rent and a three-year lease. Rosenbloom renewed for another three years in 1976, agreeing to a lease that would terminate at the end of the 1979 season. By the time the Rams' lease ended in 1979, Rosenbloom would have already announced his intention to move the team to Anaheim.

A team trying to relocate within their same geographic region for a better stadium, as the Rams were attempting to, had been done before with the Cowboys moving from the Cotton Bowl in Dallas to Texas Stadium in Irving, the Patriots from Boston to Foxboro, the Lions from Tiger Stadium in Detroit to Pontiac, and the Giants moving from Yankee Stadium to the Meadowlands. These locations were often where an attractive stadium could be built at a cheaper land cost and were all well within the geographic region of the previous home stadiums.

Only the New York Giants had chosen to go to an entirely different state, leaving New York for a new location in New Jersey, but the stadium would be built only seven miles from Manhattan. Having shared stadiums with baseball teams by playing in New York's Polo Grounds and Yankee Stadium throughout their existence, in September 1971, Wellington Mara signed a lease that would give the Giants their own football stadium in New Jersey for the start of the 1976 season. John Lindsay, New York City mayor, threatened to bring another team into New York City, but under the NFL Constitution and Bylaws such a move would have to be approved by all NFL owners, and certainly Mara would have objected. Also, the ownership of the Jets would not have approved of having to compete with a third team in the same market. Lindsay's second threat was that if the NFL did block his attempts to bring a team to New York City he would file an antitrust lawsuit against the league, but he would not follow through on either threat.

The situation in Los Angeles, however, was vastly different from the Giants' move to New Jersey. New York still had the Jets, and both New York teams had strong attendance. Despite winning the NFC West every year from 1973 through 1979, attendance was starting to decline for the Rams at the Los Angeles Coliseum. Rumors about Rosenbloom moving the team were heightened by a *Los Angeles Times* story on April 28, 1978, that indicated that the Rams move to Anaheim was imminent. Under a headline that read "Rams to Move to Anaheim Stadium in '80," the article had as its opening sentence, "Carroll Rosenbloom is going to move his Rams to Orange County—lock, stock and shoulder pads." The article left little doubt as to the probable location of the Rams' future home. In the article Rosenbloom denied any final decision was made, but admitted that he had made a lease proposal to officials in Anaheim. Kenneth Hahn, a Los Angeles County Supervisor, stated in the article, "This is just a diversionary tactic. I think Rosenbloom is simply trying to see who will make him the best offer."

In late June, Rosenbloom visited Anaheim Stadium, where major league baseball's California Angels played. The Anaheim proposal would expand the stadium's seating from its 43,250 capacity to approximately 70,000 by placing seats in the vacant area beyond the outfield. Rosenbloom would convey his thoughts, stating in the *Los Angeles Times*, "They [Anaheim] have so much to offer. What really concerns me is that if we don't come here, somebody else will come here. I know it's a great place, and the plan they have to improve the stadium is fabulous. If they go through with it they'll probably have the best dual stadium setup in the country."

Anaheim, with its stadium located approximately thirty-five miles from the Los Angeles Coliseum, had tried to get a professional team and was actually mentioned by Al Davis, then AFL commissioner, for a possible AFL expansion team. The merger between the NFL and the AFL ended that possibility. Anaheim also had a team in the unsuccessful World Football League. Finally the city would get its team when on July 25, 1978, Rosenbloom announced that the Rams would play their home games at Anaheim Stadium beginning in the 1980 season. The Rams signed a thirty-year lease, agreeing to pay 7.5 percent of gate receipts and split parking and concession revenues evenly with the city of Anaheim. Rosenbloom announced at the press conference, "I doubt that anyone can understand what a traumatic experience it has been. It will be with feelings of deep regret that we leave the Coliseum. But we shall look forward to having our playing site, our training facility, our players, our coaches and management together. We believe that this, coupled with a closed, intimate stadium where fans can be more a part of the game, will help us win." Rosenbloom also indicated the team would still be called the Los Angeles Rams, explaining, "The way we feel about it is we have moved across town. They have certainly been most loyal fans. I don't think they are Coliseum fans. I think they are Ram fans."

Although the Coliseum would still be the home of USC's and UCLA's college football teams, Jim Murray would editorialize in the *Los Angeles Times* about the city's loss of professional football. He wrote, "Moving the Rams out of the Coliseum is like moving the opera out of La Scala, moving the Mona Lisa out of the Louvre, moving the pigeons out of St. Mark's, moving the kings out of Westminster Abbey, or Grant out of Grant's Tomb. It'll never be the same. Every cleat mark in the Coliseum has history."

Unlike New York, the city of Los Angeles quickly moved to acquire another NFL team to play in the Coliseum. Rosenbloom indicated his intentions would not be to block another team from moving to Los Angeles. He stated at his press conference announcing his move of the Rams, "If my 27 partners [the other NFL owners] decide they want to put another team in California—or if they want to put one team in Hong Kong—I could not vote against it." However, Kenneth Hahn, Los Angeles County Supervisor, insinuated that Rosenbloom had a "sweetheart agreement" with the other owners, who would raise the necessary objections that would block another team from moving into Los Angeles.

The LAMCC contacted Rozelle about the prospects of another team playing in Los Angeles, but Rozelle responded that the NFL was not yet ready for expansion. In a letter sent to the LAMCC, Rozelle clearly articulated his position, writing, "I cannot in good conscience encourage any existing NFL franchise to leave its present metropolitan market," and on expansion, "I can provide no assurance that Los Angeles will be preferred over other potential franchise sites." He would tell the media at his annual press conference before the Super Bowl in 1979, "I think our clubs should repay the support they have locally. I am not against per se moving a team to Los Angeles. My concern is with the void left. I don't think any of the 28 teams can justify moving." Bill Robertson from the LAMCC would state in the *Los Angeles Times*, "They [Rozelle and the NFL] are certainly treating Los Angeles in a cavalier fashion in dealing with the same question of the void in Los Angeles, a city that has supported professional football over three decades."

On the issue of expansion, Rozelle felt that the timing was key and there must be stability in the league before the owners should agree to expansion. Having just expanded in 1976, Rozelle did not feel the league should once again expand so soon. Rozelle had explained the impact of expansion on the NFL's economic system before a House Select Committee on Professional Sports in 1976:

When the NFL expands, the new franchises come in as equal partners and become entitled to share equally in the league's overall television income. League expansion is therefore, in a purely economic sense, not a profitable operation for existing NFL clubs. The total expansion fees paid by the purchasers of expansion franchises do not offset the permanent reduction in television income which each existing club experiences by reason of TV income sharing.... We do not make money on expansion, as some other sports do, because we share television revenue equally, and in a very short time, if not the first two or three years, the sharing of television negates what we get for the franchise.

The LAMCC would counter the decision of Rozelle with an antitrust lawsuit against the NFL, claiming that Section 4.3 of the NFL Constitution and Bylaws violated the Sherman Antitrust Act and was an illegal restraint of trade. Filed in September 1978, the case would be put on hold in federal district court when the court concluded that no controversy existed, as the LAMCC did not have the standing to bring a lawsuit until a team had actually been prohibited from occupying the Coliseum.

The movements by the city of Los Angeles to acquire a team to replace the Rams began before the Rams had even officially left for Anaheim. A July 6, 1978, article in the *Los Angeles Times*, three weeks prior to Rosenbloom's announcement, would feature the headline, "L.A. May Get Oakland Team If Rams Move." In that article Kenneth Hahn indicated the Raiders might be interested in moving to the Coliseum, an assertion that would not be confirmed or denied by the Raiders. After the Rams officially moved, the intent of the city of Los Angeles became even more clear, as the July 31, 1978, headline in the *Los Angeles Times* read, "Hahn Invites 27 NFL Teams to Move to L.A." In the article, Hahn claimed, "At least three owners can't wait to come here. Their stadiums aren't as good, their fans don't support them."

When the owners convened in October 1978 in Chicago, with a potential lawsuit looming on the horizon, the vacancy of Los Angeles was a prominent issue. Rozelle suggested that the NFL amend its Constitution and Bylaws so that there would only be a requirement of a three-fourths vote for all franchise relocations. A new rule would eliminate the unanimous vote needed for a team to move into another team's home territory, such as would be the case for any team trying to move into Los Angeles, which was still the home territory of the Rams, as it was within the seventy five-mile radius of Anaheim. Sensing a threat from the lawsuit initiated by the LAMCC, Rozelle's thinking was that the amendment to the rule could potentially get the lawsuit dropped, or at least provide the NFL with evidence that would appear favorable in court. At the meeting in October 1978 Al Davis, Oakland Raiders owner, would make several ambiguous statements regarding the issue of franchise relocation including at one point arguing for the complete elimination of the rule, thus allowing any team to move to any location whenever it wished, without league approval. He also called for the league to adopt clear guidelines governing franchise relocations and asked for an independent panel to review the motivations of an owner for making a move, not league officials or the other owners, who might have a clear agenda influencing their vote for or against a franchise moving. It would be this independent panel that would render the verdict on team relocations. Tex Schramm described Davis in Bob St. John's book, *Tex*, stating, "Al can be a charmer. Give him time to study a situation and think about it, and he's outstanding. About the only way you can get him is to pull out something he's not expecting or something new, and he'll back off."

Davis's intentions, if not apparent to all, would crystallize, and he truly raised the stakes of the debate on the relocation issue when during this meeting he hinted that he might consider moving the Raiders to Los Angeles when their lease expired with the Oakland Coliseum after the 1979 season. Rozelle saw a clear distinction between moving a team a few miles into a new stadium and abandoning a home territory completely, especially if the city had vociferously supported its team as was the case of Oakland with the Raiders. Rozelle might have made a miscalculation in viewing the Rams' move to Anaheim in the same vein as the moves of the Cowboys, Giants, Lions, or Patriots. He reasoned that the team's games still would be shown on television in the Los Angeles market and that Anaheim would be closer for many Rams fans than the Coliseum. But the people and government of the city of Los Angeles certainly didn't see the Rams' move to Anaheim as the same as previous franchise moves. The irony, of course, was that Los Angeles had lobbied for the Rams' move from Cleveland in 1946, and the Lakers and Dodgers were successfully recruited by Los Angeles politicians. Finally, Al Davis certainly didn't see Carroll Rosenbloom's moving the Rams any differently than his moving the Raiders out of Oakland.

As debate continued over the two-day meeting in Chicago, votes were finally cast on two matters. The first was to amend Section 4.3, lowering the number of votes required for one team to move into another's home territory. The new rule stated that no team would have the right to move to a different city either within or outside its home territory without a three-fourths majority. The motion passed 27-0, with one abstention coming from Al Davis, who would simply claim that he reserved his rights. The meaning of his statement to "reserve his rights" was ambiguous to the other owners. Davis would later explain his abstaining from the vote when testifying before Congress in 1982, saying "The reason was because I was looking for objective standards. I was looking for guidelines, something that could be fair, that was functional, not based on whim or caprice. After two days of fighting and arguing over the issue, I acquiesced and said I would abstain for the right to move without approval someday down the road."

The second vote would grant Rosenbloom permission to move the Rams to Anaheim. This measure passed 26-0, with two abstentions, Davis and Patriots owner Billy Sullivan. Rozelle would be quoted by David Harris in his book *The Rise and Decline of the NFL*, stating, "Of all the meetings over which I presided, I will never forget that meeting. We must have been awfully dumb not to realize what Al Davis had in mind." The league meeting ended with a city strongly desiring a team and threatening litigation against the NFL and an owner with a stadium whose lease was about to expire having what he viewed as his rights reserved to move his team at his own discretion and without league approval. All Rozelle and the NFL could do was wait for the next card to be played.

The relationship between Pete Rozelle and Al Davis was contentious from the days of the merger. Davis had not been in favor of the AFL joining the senior league, certainly not under some of the circumstances in which it did. Davis then wanted to be the commissioner of the newly merged league, but was rebuffed in favor of Rozelle. In 1976, the two would confront each other over a play concerning Raiders defensive back George Atkinson. In a game against the Pittsburgh Steelers, Atkinson delivered a hit to the head from behind on an unsuspecting Lynn Swann, Steelers wide receiver. Swann suffered a concussion and missed the next two games. No penalty was called on the play during the game, as no official saw Atkinson's hit. The play came under much scrutiny, however. Chuck Noll, the Steelers' head coach, would call for players such as Atkinson to be kicked out of the league and thought that the play was a premeditated act on the part of the Raiders to injure the Steelers' best players. He also claimed Atkinson was part of a "criminal element" that was in all areas of society.

Rozelle would review the play and fine Atkinson for the hit, but he also fined Noll for his comments. Dan Rooney, Pittsburgh Steelers owner, reacted by writing to Rozelle and lodging a complaint on the leniency of Rozelle's ruling. Atkinson, with the alleged support and financial backing of Al Davis, responded by filing a $2 million slander lawsuit against Chuck Noll. The jury would return a verdict within four hours that there was no malice or slander and that George Atkinson was to receive no monetary damages.

Rozelle also removed Davis from the prestigious NFL competition committee that was responsible for rule changes in the game. The removal of Davis was termed a mistake by Tex Schramm and caused a disagreement between Schramm and Rozelle. But these disagreements between Rozelle and Davis would merely serve as preliminary battles compared to the one that was coming on the issue of franchise relocation in the 1980s.

The NFL's disapproval of the Raiders move was based on several reasons. Clearly there was a concern for league stability and that a team moving without a vote and approval of the owners would set an unhealthy precedent and put the viability of the league's constitution in jeopardy. A major concern of Rozelle's was that if the league's Constitution and Bylaws could be circumvented on this issue, there was a possibility of other rules coming into question. Second, the Raiders had sold out twelve straight seasons through 1979 in Oakland, while the Rams were not selling out the cavernous Los Angeles Coliseum. The sentiment was that Oakland didn't deserve to lose its team, and again, Los Angeles was not necessarily even losing a team with the Rams going to Anaheim. Finally, from a leaguewide business perspective, if the Raiders occupied Los Angeles, there would be no chance to cash in on an expansion franchise originating there. The Tampa Bay Buccaneers and Seattle Seahawks had each paid $16 million to join the NFL in 1976. Certainly, placing a team in the second-largest television market would be worth considerably more. Any expansion fee would also be split among all twenty-eight teams, rather than only the Raiders reaping the economic benefit of the Los Angeles market if they relocated there.

Another development that might have changed the situation of a team moving into the Los Angeles Coliseum would occur on April 2, 1979, when Carroll Rosenbloom drowned at the age of seventy-two while swimming in the Atlantic Ocean off Golden Beach, Florida. Rosenbloom, an experienced ocean swimmer but a man who'd had heart bypass surgery in November 1975, was dragged out to sea by a strong undertow. Upon his death Rozelle would comment on Rosenbloom's contributions to the NFL, stating, "He showed great ability in giving coaches opportunities. He made Don Shula a head coach from an assistant and Chuck Knox.... Unlike a lot of owners, Carroll really worked at it. He attended league meetings and took an active part in everything from playing rules to implementation of the AFL-NFL merger."

Rosenbloom's death would not change the Rams' plans to move to Anaheim. A headline in the *Los Angeles Times* on April 3 plainly read "Death Won't Interfere with Rams' Move." The article featured statements from Anaheim and Los Angeles officials confirming the Rams' move to Anaheim would still occur. After seven years of fighting to move out of the Los Angeles Coliseum and now finally having it be a reality, Rosenbloom would never see his Rams play in Anaheim. Many owners in the league believed at the time that if Rosenbloom were still alive, Davis would never have moved to Los Angeles due to concerns of creating an enemy in Rosenbloom.

Meanwhile Davis was involved in negotiations with both Oakland and Los Angeles. In Oakland he was demanding stadium renovations that would include luxury boxes. Davis was also not crazy about sharing the Oakland Coliseum with major league baseball's Athletics, and the appeal of the second-largest television market was obviously of interest. Rozelle was hopeful that Davis was simply using Los Angeles as leverage to get a better stadium deal in Oakland and thought that Davis would ultimately be more successful in the smaller market.

The Raiders were not the only possibility for Los Angeles, as Minnesota also held talks with city officials and overtures were made to and from the Baltimore and San Diego franchises. Joe Robbie, owner of the Miami Dolphins, would also meet with officials from the LAMCC on several occasions, even as late as November 1979.

While Rozelle might have underestimated Davis's intentions to move, the real difference between Rozelle and Davis emerged over whether the Raiders' move to Los Angeles could actually be executed. Rozelle claimed that any move would have to go before a vote of the owners and obtain the three-fourths majority. Davis felt no vote was necessary based on the position that he believed he articulated in the Chicago meeting of 1978. The realization that Davis would not win any vote to move the Raiders was probably not lost on either man. Rozelle and Davis met alone on January 7, 1980, but remained in disagreement as to the need for a vote.

In January 1980 Rozelle would also send a letter to Davis threatening not to include the Raiders in the 1980 schedule if they moved without the approval of the NFL owners. The letter to Davis read, "Unless the clubs approve a transfer, the Constitution and Bylaws of the NFL will not permit this office to prepare a schedule calling for the Oakland Raiders to play their home games in a location other than Oakland." Rozelle would argue to Davis that the NFL's rule regarding team movement "is in the interest of every member of the league" and that "franchise transfers can affect league television practices, the television income of all clubs, the overall reputation and goodwill of the league, and visiting team gate receipts." In the letter Rozelle reasoned, "If an informed and considered case for the transfer can be made, and the Raiders can establish [it] will not negatively affect the interest of the clubs generally, then I know of no reason why any significant number of the clubs should object." Finally, Rozelle explicitly stated that if Davis tried to move without twenty-one votes, "it would be my obligation to take whatever steps appropriate" in enforcing the NFL Constitution and Bylaws.

Davis felt entitled to the same approval that Rosenbloom had been given to move the Rams, and even despite the dissimilarities that were visible to the league, he didn't want to seek the same league approval as Rosenbloom. Rozelle feared that the Raiders' move could trigger other clubs moving without the approval of the league. He stated, "Playing field competitive balance, fan good will, and community support are at the core of the popular appeal of professional football." He would testify before Congress in 1982 that if a team's lease is up and clubs can go wherever they want, "I assure you that you will have auctioning of franchises. You will have an owner going to a city and saying, 'come in governors, come in mayors; who wants my club? What will you offer in the way of inducements for my club to move from where it is to another city?' We do not think that is in the interests of sports, the fans, or the public."

Rozelle's hope was not simply for Davis to agree to a vote approving the Raiders' move, but rather for Davis to keep the Raiders in Oakland to maintain the league's stability and not abandon its fans. Rozelle felt so strongly about teams not relocating that he intervened on behalf of team owners by talking to politicians from city and state governments to try to get stadiums constructed or renovated. He was successful in this endeavor in helping get the Metrodome built in Minnesota. Max Winter, Vikings owner, had flirted with Los Angeles and was quoted in the *Los Angeles Times* in March 1979 admitting, "I have met with the stadium commission of Los Angeles and they make it very attractive for a team to move in there. I still want to work out my problems in the state of Minnesota . . . I am not asking to move."

The question of whether Davis ever did seek Rozelle's assistance in speaking to government officials from Oakland would be a point of dispute between the two men. Rozelle would testify before the United States Senate on August 16, 1982, claiming, "I was advised by the people of Oakland that they were told by Al Davis that if they saw me, then they could no longer negotiate and he was going to go. That was during the period when he was negotiating in Los Angeles secretly and in Oakland, and he did not come to me for help with the authorities. He told them if they attempted to come to me, then he was through negotiating with them." Davis countered in his testimony to the same committee on September 20, 1982, stating, "I talked to him [Rozelle] and I said to him, 'I want you to do one favor for me. Give me the same treatment you gave Minnesota,' because I was having trouble with the people in the Bay Area in getting any commitment from them on the things that I thought were necessary to be competitive in the eighties."

Jay Moyer recalls that on the issue of meeting with officials from Oakland, "Pete and I were in the Bay Area, scheduled to meet with the Oakland Alameda County Coliseum Commission at their request. When I met Pete in the lobby of our hotel at the time we were supposed to leave for the meeting, he told me he had gotten a call from an Oakland representative saying that they'd better not have the meeting because they didn't want to give Davis an excuse to break off negotiations."

In addition to the threats of Davis moving the Raiders from Oakland, the LAMCC had no intentions of dropping its lawsuit. On Friday, January 18, 1980, claiming that the Oakland Raiders "are on the verge of transferring to Los Angeles," the antitrust lawsuit originally filed on September 13, 1978, against the NFL was activated in federal court. The LAMCC specifically requested the court not allow the NFL to implement its rule requiring the approval of twenty-one franchises for a team to move.

After months of negotiating with both Oakland and Los Angeles, Davis would finally make his decision on March 1, 1980, when he signed a memorandum agreement to unilaterally move the Raiders from Oakland to Los Angeles. Davis would state in the *Los Angeles Times*, "I've had many years of glory sprinkled with a few days of defeat. This is a day of glory, to embark on a new challenge, to come to Los Angeles." In the deal Los Angeles promised to provide $18.5 million to the Raiders, including ninety-nine luxury boxes, new locker rooms, and a press box for the Coliseum. Davis would get most of the money raised from tickets as well as concessions, parking, and stadium advertising. The Raiders would also receive a new practice facility and relocation expenses. Rozelle reacted to the news in the *Los Angeles Times*, claiming "the greater issue is anarchy."

The NFL owners, with an already scheduled league meeting for March 10, would meet at the behest of Rozelle even earlier. When the NFL owners convened in Dallas on March 3, the topic was the Raiders' impending move to Los Angeles and Rozelle's fear of the Raiders' move leading to "anarchy" in the NFL. At this meeting Davis reiterated his intentions to relocate the Raiders and that he was not going to ask the league for approval to do so. According to Charles Maher and Henry Weinstein in the *Los Angeles Times*, Davis explicitly told the other owners that although he did have "a traumatic feeling about leaving the fans in Oakland, he was committed to Los Angeles." Davis would indicate that he was in a compromising position in negotiations with representatives from the Oakland Coliseum and that was why a deal could not be made to keep the Raiders in Oakland.

Rozelle requested more information be gathered before making any permanent decision on the matter. He appointed a five-person committee consisting of Bill Bidwill, from the Cardinals, George Halas, Wellington Mara, Art Modell, and Herman Sarkowsky, from the Seattle Seahawks, to talk with Davis, officials from the LAMCC, representatives from the Oakland Coliseum, and the three television networks to gather facts and report back to the group at the league's already scheduled meeting on March 10. Rozelle explained the purpose of the committee in an article in the *Los Angeles Times*, commenting, "This committee will not come in with any sort of recommendations. What it will do will be to develop all information possible between now and our meeting next week."

With Davis making his decision to move to Los Angeles, and the committee set to report back to Rozelle and the owners in one week, the NFL also immediately countered with a legal tactic of its own. On March 4, only three days after Davis had signed the memorandum agreement to move the Raiders, the NFL filed a lawsuit in Oakland's superior court asking Davis to be restrained from moving the Raiders, charging him with a breach of the NFL's contract. The argument of a breach stemmed from when the AFL teams entered the NFL as part of the merger and they agreed to comply with the NFL Constitution and Bylaws. On March 6, a temporary restraining order banning the Raiders from moving to Los Angeles was granted. Davis would claim that the team had already moved. Litigation was also beginning against Davis by the city of Oakland, which was suing the Raiders under the rule of eminent domain, arguing that the Raiders were a public necessity and the property of the city.

By the time the NFL owners convened again for their annual league meetings on March 10, Davis felt that Rozelle was working to galvanize the support of the owners against him. He was quoted by Paul Zimmerman in *Sports Illustrated* stating, "Pete's managed to polarize those owners pretty good." Davis would argue, "I'm not for anarchy. I love the NFL. But I'll be damned if I'm going to let those Oakland Coliseum people hold me hostage." Rozelle countered in the same article, "Al says he's not for anarchy, and I'm sure he wants a stable league. He just wants anarchy for himself. I don't know why he didn't seek league support when he was having trouble over his lease with the politicians in Oakland, and I know his trouble was very legitimate then. I don't know why he didn't let the other owners know what was happening."

Davis might have made a miscalculation thinking that the NFL would give in and not vigorously fight the Raiders' move to Los Angeles. He challenged the NFL owners commenting, "We'll see what happens when this thing gets into punitive damages. You'll see how many guys will back down rather than fight." Dan Rooney defied Davis's position, claiming, "I think he'll find that we're committed to go all the way on this thing. Our constitution, our whole league is at stake."

At the league meeting, without Davis asking and without his agreement, a vote was taken on the question: Should the move of the Raiders from Oakland to Los Angeles be approved? Davis referred to the vote as "a business conspiracy." The result was a resounding show of togetherness on the part of the league's owners, with a vote of 22-0 against the move, with five abstentions and Davis not being present for the vote. The abstentions came from Paul Brown from Cincinnati, Ed DeBartolo Jr. from San Francisco, Don Klosterman representing Rams owner Georgia Rosenbloom, Mike Robbie representing his father from Miami, and Leonard Tose from Philadelphia. It was DeBartolo and Georgia Rosenbloom who were the most geographically affected and who had the most at stake economically in the Raiders' move. If the Raiders did move, DeBartolo would have the entire Bay Area market to himself for the 49ers. On the other side of the equation, the Rams would now have direct competition imposed by the Raiders in Los Angeles. After the vote, Davis would tell reporters, "I just want to make it clear that I no more believe in anarchy than Pete Rozelle does, and he knows it. I just want to receive the same treatment others had."

On March 17, the league would take its legal action against Davis a step further by asking the court that he be removed from control of the Raiders and the franchise placed in receivership. The grounds for the NFL motion were that nothing had been done to sell tickets for games scheduled in Oakland for the upcoming 1980 season. With the outcome of the owners' vote, Rozelle was clear that the league intended to schedule the Raiders games in Oakland for the 1980 season and that the NFL would not schedule any games to be played in Los Angeles. The NFL would get its temporary victory on March 25 when the court ruled that the Raiders could not solicit any ticket action for games other than in Oakland or take any final action to move the franchise.

In this latest chess move, Davis did not sit idle, and on that same day he went to court to join up with the LAMCC lawsuit, asking for $160 million in damages from the NFL for violating the Sherman Antitrust Act. Davis also named Gene Klein, San Diego Chargers owner, Georgia Rosenbloom, and Pete Rozelle directly as individual defendants in the lawsuit, claiming they had conspired to keep the Raiders out of Los Angeles. The contentions of Davis were that Section 4.3 of the NFL Constitution and Bylaws was illegal because it restricted teams from moving and was anticompetitive because it did not allow stadiums to compete for NFL teams. Davis also felt the rule did not apply in this case because in his judgment he had been granted an oral waiver from the league's owners at the 1978 meeting that a vote of approval for him to move the team was not necessary. The position of the NFL was simply that Section 4.3 was legal and necessary for league stability and that any franchise movement must be approved in accordance with the NFL's Constitution and Bylaws.

CHAPTER 11

The Raiders v. The NFL

T HE ACTUAL trial for the future home of the Raiders would not begin until May 1981. In the interim, Al Davis would have the satisfaction of beating teams owned by two staunch critics of his in the AFC playoffs, the Browns of Art Modell in the divisional playoff in Cleveland and the Chargers of Gene Klein in the AFC Championship game in San Diego. After the AFC Championship Game, Gene Upshaw, Raiders all-pro guard, would be quoted by Paul Zimmerman in *Sports Illustrated*, stating, "One thing that gave me great pleasure was coming down here and sticking it to Gene Klein." Upshaw added, "The only thing that's left is to win the Super Bowl, to stick it to our commissioner. I'm waiting for him to come into our locker room to present the trophy to us and find out what it's like to be booed." In the next week's issue of the magazine Upshaw would also comment, "The league has taken shots at Al whenever it could, and its taken shots at us, too. It makes you want to play harder—to stick it to the whole bunch of them." At a press conference prior to the game Rozelle commented on the possibility of presenting the Super Bowl trophy to Davis, stating, "If I give that trophy to Al Davis on Sunday, I will be giving it to Al as a tribute to the job he's done in putting this team together and I'll be giving it to the Raider players." Davis's Raiders did defeat the Philadelphia Eagles, 27-10 in Super Bowl XV, and he did have the Vince Lombardi trophy presented to him by Pete Rozelle. To avoid a potentially awkward moment of extending his hand to Davis and Davis not shaking his hand, Rozelle presented Davis the trophy with both hands.

The first decisive victory of the trial would occur two months before any testimony was taken when in March 1981 Judge Harry Pregerson, who was born in close proximity to the Los Angeles Coliseum, ruled that the trial would be conducted in Los Angeles and not moved to another venue as the NFL had petitioned. Rozelle would later explain the importance of this ruling during testimony before Congress, stating, "The local court and jury seem to view the antitrust laws as designed to serve their own community's position. You can perhaps appreciate these tendencies yourself by asking whether, if the Los Angeles-Oakland dispute were tried in Oakland, an Oakland court and jury would likely have the same reaction to the Raiders' effort to abandon Oakland as a court and jury in Los Angeles." Joe Browne, NFL executive, says, "With a Los Angeles–based judge, a Los Angeles jury, and being in a downtown Los Angeles courtroom, we unfortunately realized that this was the ultimate home field advantage. The only good thing about having the trial there were the restaurants on the weekends." Jay Moyer, former NFL counsel to the commissioner and executive vice president, also points out that the Los Angles jury had been "bombarded by the media on a daily basis for several months with a 'bring the Raiders here' message."

Rozelle was closely involved in every planning discussion concerning the NFL's legal strategy. He was helpful in recommending people who would make valuable witnesses. For example, Paul Tagliabue explains that Rozelle would point out that an advertising executive or a television executive could make the argument why the league's economic structure is important and needed from a completely different perspective than that of a league official. Jay Moyer describes the NFL strategy in court as relying on the fact that the owners had voted against the Raiders' move to Los Angeles and was based on two principle reasons. The first was the fact that the Raiders had agreed to be bound by the league's Constitution and Bylaws, something, Moyer contends, "we knew would not appeal to a Los Angeles jury." And, second, the reason most heavily argued by the NFL, according to Moyer, "rested on Pete's conviction, shared by most of the owners, that the league's greatest asset was fan loyalty, and that no team should be ripped out of a community because the owner thought he could make even more money somewhere else."

The trial would begin on May 11, with both Rozelle and Davis testifying for more than a week. Rozelle addressed the important dissimilarity of the Raiders' move to that of the Rams and other teams such as the Cowboys, Giants, Lions, or Patriots, pointing out that the Raiders moved hundreds of miles to a city outside of their home territory and into a home territory occupied by another team. In his testimony Rozelle did concede that the NFL probably would not suffer economically if the Raiders moved to Los Angeles, but that by abandoning Oakland after years of that city's support, the league's reputation would be harmed. The league would have many witnesses testify that during the league meeting of October 1978 Davis was not granted a right to move without league approval and that he never clearly explained what was meant by the comment "I reserve my rights," or which rights he was referring to.

One week after Davis's testimony ended, he and the LAMCC would rest their case. The NFL responded with a motion to drop all charges. The league received a partial victory on June 26 when the charges against Klein, Georgia Frontiere (her new married name), and Rozelle individually were dropped. On July 29 the case was given to the jury, but it would never render a verdict. After twelve and a half days of deliberation, on August 13, a mistrial was declared, with the jury deadlocked at 8 to 2 in favor of the Raiders and the Coliseum after Judge Pregerson contended that the jury could not reach a unanimous verdict. According the Joe Browne, "the deadlock, given the circumstances, was like a victory for the league. However, we knew that we would have to undertake another trial in Los Angeles and that was particularly difficult for Pete."

In the trial an essential legal question was whether the NFL was a single business entity and therefore not capable of combining or conspiring in a restraint of trade. The NFL had argued it was a single entity. That aspect of the case would, however, never reach the jury. One ruling by Judge Pregerson given in the trial was that the NFL was not a single entity as it had contended and that the twenty-eight teams are separate entities. Jay Moyer explains that "at least half of our evidence was aimed at persuading the jury that they should regard the NFL as, effectively, a single unitary business for purposes of making decisions about where the NFL's jointly-produced product would be presented—and if the jury had agreed, the Raiders' antitrust claim would have collapsed. But the jury never got that chance."

In the interim between the mistrial and the second trial commencing, Rozelle appeared before the House Judiciary Committee's hearings on antitrust policy and professional sports. He explicitly addressed the position of the NFL being a single entity, testifying in December 1981, "The most basic antitrust law, section one of the Sherman Act, is directed at trade-restraining agreements among independent parties. But the clubs of a sports league are incapable of operating independently. Their business operations are necessarily dependent and joint. The business of league sports requires co-production, and member clubs can only engage in producing league sports entertainment through league agreements, through the cooperation of the teams they play, the other clubs."

In testimony trying to get Congress to clear the ambiguity surrounding the antitrust issue of the NFL as a single entity, Rozelle explained that different courts had provided various rulings. He pointed out that a federal district court in Philadelphia found the NFL is "a unique type of business" and its clubs "must not compete too well with each other in [a] business way." A federal court of appeals in St. Louis would offer a similar assessment that the NFL is "unique" and as a business organization has "some of the characteristics of a joint venture." A federal district court in New York even explicitly stated, the NFL is a "single economic entity." Rozelle would also describe completely contradictory court rulings, such as when a federal district court in Minnesota ruled the NFL is like any other business and there must be "unfettered competition" among its franchises. A federal district court in Los Angeles explicitly stated the NFL is not "a single business entity" and that the teams are business competitors.

Dan Rooney, Pittsburgh Steelers owner, in testimony before Congress in 1982 would further illustrate the ambiguity of antitrust laws and the difficulty of their application to the NFL's activities, claiming that whatever decision the league might make could come under scrutiny and the threat of antitrust liability. Rooney would provide an example, explaining that the World Football League "advised us that they would sue the NFL in an antitrust suit if we selected Memphis as one of our two expansion cities. The NFL carefully avoided any interference with the World Football League. Tampa and Seattle were selected as the new expansion sites. When the World Football League collapsed in 1975, the WFL interests which formerly contended that it was a violation of the antitrust laws if the NFL expanded to Memphis then demanded that the NFL must expand to Memphis." Rooney added, "Thus it was contended in 1974 that an NFL decision to expand to Memphis was an antitrust violation. However, that decision not to expand to Memphis in 1976 is now claimed to be an antitrust violation."

Rozelle would point out another example of the difficulty of the antitrust laws in relation to the NFL's business practices in testimony in 1985: "The Raiders had not received one affirmative vote to move when a vote was taken, if we had approved the move the city of Oakland had a suit drawn up on the same general basis of the Raider case, that we were leaving the San Francisco

Bay market to the 49ers, that is why we were permitting the move, and they would sue us, and we were damned if we did and damned if we did not."

As evidence that the NFL was a single entity, Rozelle would often point to its revenue-sharing practices. Rozelle explained that the business of professional football is a unique relationship and partnership in producing public entertainment among its franchises that is different from any other American business. He would state in testimony before the House of Representatives in December 1981, "On the playing field, the teams are clearly competitors. But in producing and marketing the NFL product, the clubs are co-producers and co-sellers, not competitors. They are partners acting together in a common enterprise. Because of this unique relationship, the patterns of sports league operations and the financial aspects of these operations are distinct from any other type of business." Rozelle also explained to Congress that in 1982, approximately 97 percent of all income was shared, with television and marketing income shared equally among all teams and gate receipts shared 60 percent for the home team and 40 percent for the visiting team, with the design of encouraging effective team and business operations locally. He stated, "We say that we are a partnership off the field. We work together from a business standpoint. On the field, of course, they fight like hell. They try to win. But we say we are, more or less, a joint venture off the field."

The LAMCC and the Raiders simply held the opposite position, that the league is composed of twenty-eight separate entities that act independently. In testimony before the U.S. Senate in 1982 Al Davis stated, "I think that the National Football League is twenty-eight individual owners who are individual competitors and I would go a little further and say vicious competitors to be number one on the football field. We do have common rules. We have common scheduling, but we do not share profits and losses. We do not share them at all. And to make us a single entity is totally unfair because that is what we are not." Davis would even indicate that he was in favor of complete revenue sharing, stating, "I would like to share all revenue equally, the box revenue, the concessions and the parking revenue equally, and then let us go out on the field and compete equally on the football field and not worry about the financial money that comes into each club."

A new trial would not commence until March 30, 1982, meaning the Raiders would also play the 1981 season in Oakland. In the opening statement of the second trial, Joseph Alioto, the Raiders' lead attorney, would refer to the NFL's position as "monopolistic practices to shackle a competitor and to shut off the lifeline of the Los Angeles Coliseum." He added the motivation of the

NFL was to force the Raiders to play in "an inferior city with an inferior sports stadium," calling the Oakland Coliseum, "the lousiest stadium in the league."

In the second trial Rozelle would again testify. He reiterated several points from the first trial, including that the Raiders' move should have been approved by a vote of the NFL owners and that the analogous arguments of the Raiders' move to Los Angeles and the Rams' move to Anaheim were invalid. Rozelle, who grew up in the Los Angeles area and considered himself an L.A. guy, felt Anaheim was a suburb of Los Angeles and therefore the city still had a home team. Rozelle would also point out that with the Rams' games sold out in Anaheim, the city of Los Angeles was now able to see the Rams' home games on television. He stated, "The biggest winners were the followers of professional football in Southern California."

In his four-day testimony beginning on April 1, 1982, Rozelle would make one statement about the fact that Los Angeles presented an economic opportunity for the entire league through expansion. He testified, "The league had a right to derive benefits of an expansion franchise in Los Angeles." Rozelle continued, "It is a corporate right of all 28 clubs if all have contributed to the growth of the NFL. They're entitled to share the benefits." This gave Davis's attorneys an opening—that the motivation of the NFL's restricting the Raiders' move to Los Angeles was more for economic concerns than the reasons of Oakland being abandoned, league stability, and the threat to the NFL's Constitution and Bylaws that had been previously articulated and emphasized. Maxwell Blecher, attorney for the Los Angeles Coliseum, would even get Rozelle to agree that the expansion policy, by definition, could mean that a team might potentially be forced to stay in a location where the franchise was worth less money.

Davis later explained his thoughts on the Rozelle admission to Congress, stating, "Pete Rozelle admitted, under oath, that the reason they did not want me to move to Los Angeles was that the Los Angeles franchise was worth a lot more money than the Oakland franchise, and that by my moving to Los Angeles, I would get a valuable piece of property that the other owners thought they should have and they should divvy up amongst themselves." Rozelle did point out in his testimony during the trial, however, that Davis would also share in any revenue derived from a new expansion franchise in Los Angeles. Davis later criticized Rozelle's performance as a witness in the trial in the *New York Times*, commenting, "He's good at a press conference when he's got control of the situation. But when he was on the witness stand I wasn't impressed with the way he handled himself under pressure."

Davis, too, would testify in the second trial. He claimed that his objection to the inclusion of the clause in the NFL's Constitution and Bylaws that the exclusive territory of teams be protected went as far back as the merger. Davis argued that he felt it was "unfair" that the Rams made $5 million more than the Raiders did in 1980 because he was forced to keep the team in Oakland. He stated, "I don't begrudge the Rams or any other team for what they want to do," adding "I want personally to be competitive with them." His simple position continued to be that it was unreasonable to allow the Rams to move to a better stadium, but not the Raiders.

As for the question of his needing a vote of the NFL owners to move the team, Davis claimed that at the October 1978 meeting he had argued that the rule, even with its reduction to only three-fourths needed for passage, could not be defended, that the rule should be eliminated, and that team movement not be subject to any vote at all. He testified that at the October 1978 meeting he told the owners, "If you fellows want to bind yourself, I'll change my 'no' vote to 'abstain,' but I reserve the right to move as I see fit." None of the other owners at that particular league meeting recalled Davis stating that idea.

There had been the usual attempts to reach a settlement, with the judge in the case making different proposals, but none were plausible. On the possibility of Davis being permitted to move to Los Angeles and an expansion team simply filling the location in Oakland, Rozelle didn't see that as being equal for the fans of Oakland. He stated, "I think that after a 22-year romance with a football team, the community of Oakland . . . wants the Raiders." He added, "They don't want to start from scratch with an expansion club and build. They want the Oakland Raiders, and they feel that the Raiders made commitments to stay in Oakland as long as they were well supported." Other preliminary proposal discussions included the exploration of the Raiders staying in Oakland with Davis leaving to take over an expansion team in Los Angeles. An option Davis had no interest in entertaining. A final idea was advanced by Tex Schramm, who went to Los Angeles to try to negotiate with LAMCC executives to try to convince them that if they gave up on trying to obtain the Raiders, there would be a guarantee that Los Angeles would soon get an expansion franchise. Rozelle would again reject this idea, holding steadfast to the idea that Los Angeles and the Raiders should adhere to going through the proper league channels before allowing such a move. Any settlement that could satisfy the Coliseum, the Raiders, and the NFL simply became an impossibility.

It was a much shorter trial than the first. On May 7, 1982, the case would be handed over to the jury of six women. The jury deliberated for six hours and delivered a resounding victory for Davis and the LAMCC. "We called it the Mother's Day Massacre," Joe Browne recalls. He states, "Mother's Day was two days away and there was no way that the female jury wanted to be sequestered and away from their families. When we received the call that the jury had reached a verdict so quickly, we knew it was not good news."

The verdict held that Section 4.3 did violate the Sherman Antitrust Act and that the NFL had breached a contractual duty of good faith and fair dealing with Davis. The judgment was that rule 4.3 was an agreement to control, if not prevent, competition among the NFL teams through territorial divisions. The rationale was also that stadiums do compete with one another for NFL tenants and that competition was limited because of the implementation of rule 4.3. Finally, the NFL was not able to prove that the transfer of the Raiders from Oakland to Los Angeles would have any harmful effect on the league, including any adverse effect on regional balance by a move from Northern to Southern California, and no loss of future television revenue was foreseen, especially since the NFL had just signed its five-year television contracts in March 1982.

Davis would call the verdict "an injustice that has been rectified." He stated, "I'm not emotionally elated. I wish I could say it's a victory, but I can't look at it that way." Davis would also state in a *Sport* magazine interview, "The trial showed unequivocally that the main reason the other owners wanted to keep me in Oakland was that they wanted the territory for themselves. First Rozelle established that the L.A. territory was worth much more than the Oakland territory. They wanted it for expansion so they could make a lot of money. They were the greedy ones." In the same interview he added, "I love professional football; it's been my life and it always will be. I just felt that I was right, and the NFL was dealing unfairly with me, in bad faith, that this one fellow [Rozelle] with all the power was wrong. And the jury agreed with me."

Rozelle would be quoted in the *Los Angeles Times* after the verdict stating, "If the jury's verdict and related rulings of the court are sustained, sports leagues will have been told that league objectives and community commitments are of no legal consequence in antitrust cases." He added, "The long-range effects could include a serious erosion in the competitive balance that makes sports entertaining. The final result could be a loss of both fan support and public good will."

With the verdict, the NFL immediately dissolved the temporary restraining order it had won in court in Oakland. Within a month the NFL would include the Los Angeles Raiders on its 1982 game schedule. More than two years and two months after signing the memorandum agreement to move the Raiders to Los Angeles, Al Davis was finally able to do so.

The league would still have to wait for damages to be awarded the following year, with the knowledge that antitrust damages are automatically trebled under federal law. In the meantime, Rozelle and the NFL would fight the LAMCC/Davis verdict on two fronts: an appeal in court and once again lobbying Congress for additional antitrust protection. At this point a real concern of Rozelle was that if Davis could unilaterally move his team, could he unilaterally cherry-pick the other rules, for example, create his own television deal solely for the Raiders and completely break the league-first philosophy? Although the Sports Broadcasting Act was law, the fear was that it was not protective enough and that it might have some legal loopholes. After the Raiders first announced the move to Los Angeles without a vote, Rozelle had expressed concern about a slippery slope, with the NFL's rules being eroded. He was quoted in the *Los Angeles Times*, saying, "The next step a team could take contrary to league rules could be to enter a pay-TV contract . . . or they could sell their team to General Motors or Caesar's Palace." The latter would be a violation of the policy that disallows corporate ownership of an NFL team.

Two bills would be introduced before Congress prompted by the situation between the NFL and the Raiders. On May 21, the House of Representatives would introduce The Major League Sports Community Protection Act of 1982. The second bill was the Professional Football Stabilization Act of 1982. If the bills passed, the new laws would prohibit a franchise from using antitrust laws to attack a sports league and would restrict the ability of professional football teams to relocate by requiring that franchises have league approval before moving to another city. They would exempt professional sports leagues from antitrust laws for restrictions on team relocations, specifically allowing owners to band together to prevent franchise shifts and upholding the league's right to share television revenue, thus eliminating the possibility of teams making their own individual television deals. The Senate Judiciary Committee would even hold hearings in August and September 1982 with both Rozelle and Davis testifying.

Paul Tagliabue describes Rozelle as a strong witness in court but more comfortable testifying before Congress because he could explain his positions in detail and not be subject to questions where statements from years ago could be presented out of context. Rozelle appeared before the Senate Judiciary Committee on August 16, 1982. In his testimony, speaking to the league's position on the Raiders case, Rozelle argued, "We are charged with an antitrust violation because we tried to stop an NFL member club from gouging the consumers and taxpayers of the Oakland area—a community that had built and financed a stadium for the Raiders, and supported the team in extraordinary fashion." He pointed out that the Raiders had sold out every home game for twelve consecutive seasons and "that the Raiders had not made a case for leaving Oakland and should remain there. We voted, in other words, that the Raiders should continue to have sellout crowds in Oakland, that they should continue to serve the Oakland consumers, that they should continue to have high revenues." Rozelle would add that the NFL had been applauded by Congress in the merger hearings for the league's effort in keeping all of its franchises in their same locations. He stated, "I have always been a proponent of teams staying in their present locations as long as they are well supported."

When asked by Pennsylvania senator Arlen Specter, "What do you think Mr. Davis is ultimately after on his move to Los Angeles?" Rozelle responded, "I think he likes to live in Los Angeles, Beverly Hills, and Palm Springs more than he likes to live in Jack London Square in Oakland. And I think that he envisions, with the arrangement he has made with the Los Angeles Coliseum for gates and for improvement to the stadium—he envisions the possibility of pay or cable television, and he thinks that he has the opportunity for enhanced revenues over what he could make in Oakland, even though in Oakland he was the fifth highest grosser in the league."

However, Davis appeared to feel that Rozelle was going against him for personal reasons more than to protect league stability, the city of Oakland, or the Rams' territory. Davis would attack with scathing criticisms of Rozelle in the press. He was quoted by Ira Berkow in the *New York Times*, saying, "Rozelle had become the most powerful man in sports. The league probably has the most massive media control of any organization in America other than the President. I admit, he's been brilliant at public relations. But he has used what he could to gain personal power, to secure his job." Davis was also quoted in a 1985 column in the *Los Angeles Times* by Rick Reilly stating, "Rozelle needs to get out of the courtroom, get out of Congress, get off the tennis court, get out of the race tracks, get out of the social circles, get out of his vendettas, and be the commissioner again for the league."

Rozelle would counter in the same *Los Angeles Times* article, "I've become pretty immune to all that. I think this feud between Al and myself is one-sided." He added, "Rather than to say 'I'm having a fight with my 27 partners. I'm suing my 27 partners.' It's much easier to create an image that there's a fight between the two of us than to say that." Rozelle did, however, acknowledge, "It's been tough the lies they've told about me." Years later, Rozelle would tell Michael Janofsky of the *New York Times*, "I will match my circle of friends against Al's anytime he wants." Whatever the feelings of Rozelle toward Al Davis, it seems that Rozelle was once again holding true to his philosophy of doing what he thought was best for the league as a whole. Joe Browne, NFL executive, stated in the NFL Films production, *Rozelle: Building America's Game*, "Pete had been preaching for twenty years as commissioner if we all stick together, if we all think as one there's no one outside who can defeat us and that was true, but it was someone from the inside, who attacked from the inside, that's what really got Pete upset."

More than a personal vendetta with Davis, it was clear that Rozelle greatly was concerned with any franchise violating the NFL's Constitution and Bylaws. Another plausible explanation for Rozelle's strongly contesting the Raiders' move was that he had a deep belief that teams should not leave a community if fans are strongly supporting the team, as he knew was happening in Oakland. "Pete never underestimated or took for granted the loyalty and passion of the Raiders fans," says Joe Browne, adding, "unfortunately, the same could not be said for Raiders ownership at that time." It can also easily be concluded that Rozelle was not motivated by protecting the Rams' home territory. If that was his motivation, he would have been as interested in moving the Raiders to help protect the 49ers' home territory, or argue for moving the Jets to protect the Giants' home territory. The personal comments by Davis toward Rozelle would continue. He was quoted in the January 14, 1985, *Los Angeles Times*, stating, "Rozelle will destroy the whole league if we're not careful. Rome burned. He is a phony and a fraud and he is scurrilous. The dirty tricks he's pulled to try to defeat our organization are just unbelievable." But Dan Rooney, owner of the Pittsburgh Steelers, would address Congress in September 1982, stating, "As one of the 27 club presidents who have been deeply involved in this suit, I can tell you, this committee, that Al Davis's fight is not with the NFL commissioner. It is with league rules, to which the Raiders once fully and voluntarily agreed. Mr. Davis' own club has contract commitments to all the other clubs in the NFL, and its partners do not believe that the antitrust laws should be used to permit a successful, well-sponsored team's abandonment of the community where it grew and prospered." Davis could not even garner any support from his friend Tex Schramm. Bob St. John explained in his book, *Tex*, that "Schramm strongly believed those in the league must adhere to its policies if the NFL is to remain strong and not stumble over the pitfalls that have befallen other professional sports. He believes that all arguments must be hashed out within the league, that it must be the all-powerful ruling body in order for all its franchises to remain viable and successful."

With legislation still pending in Congress about franchise relocation, Davis, too, would testify before Congress. He explained his rationale for the Raiders' move as, "We had the best record in professional football. The (Oakland) Coliseum was selling out. But the Raiders did not have certain of the things that I thought were necessary to be competitive in the 1980s, the things that other stadiums were getting that were being built." He continued, "We have certain teams that have individual contracts based on what we call luxury boxes where they get the money and they keep it. They do not share it with us." Davis's testimony, however, occurred on the same day, September 20, 1982, that the NFL players called their strike. The NFL lost any momentum it had in Congress, with the politicians not wanting to get in the middle of a labor dispute. The proposed legislation regarding franchise location would quietly end. Joe Browne recalls, "The labor strife hurt our chances in Congress, but Pete also felt betrayed by many of our allies on Capitol Hill." He adds, "When we first went to Congress seeking legislation to prevent franchise free agency, we were told that Congress could not act because the Raiders had not yet moved. In 1982, we were told that the Congress could not act because the courts already had determined the Raiders could move. It was very frustrating to Pete." The only hope that the NFL had was now in its appeal.

On April 13, 1983, the NFL finally learned of the verdict regarding damages to be paid. The jury awarded $11.5 million to Davis and $4.9 million to the LAMCC for delaying the move to Los Angeles by two years. With the ruling trebled, the total penalty to the NFL was close to $50 million. The NFL would also have to pay $10 million in plaintiff legal fees. The NFL would appeal the damages verdict too.

Once again Davis's Raiders, now the Los Angeles Raiders, would achieve the ultimate success when on January 22, 1984, the Los Angeles Raiders defeated the Washington Redskins to win Super Bowl XVIII. Rozelle, never confident and always concerned about what Al Davis might do or say, especially on live television, admitted, "One of the toughest trophy presentations I had to make was to Al Davis after the Raiders' 38-9 rout of Washington." He would, however, have one light moment when leaving the locker room he was tapped on the shoulder by Mickey Marvin, Raiders guard, who would tell him, "Not everyone here hates you." Thirty-five days after the Super Bowl victory, the Ninth Circuit Court of Appeals would rule two to one in favor of Davis and the LAMCC. The league would appeal to the Supreme Court of the United States, but the Court declined to hear the case. Al Davis had apparently beaten the NFL and Pete Rozelle as decisively as his Raiders had won their two Super Bowls.

Rozelle and the NFL would, however, receive one late victory in its dealings with Al Davis and the Raiders. In June 1986, the U.S. Ninth Circuit Court of Appeals would affirm the award ruled to the LAMCC, but would reverse the award given directly to Davis and the Raiders. The ruling of the appellate court was that the Los Angeles market was an expansion opportunity and that the Raiders broke a fiduciary duty to the league by seizing that asset, one that belonged to the league as a whole. The reasoning of the appellate court was that the lower court gave the Raiders "double the compensatory relief to which they were entitled." The Raiders had not only gained the injunctive relief of $11.5 million, but also the monetary benefits of moving from Oakland to Los Angeles. Davis would not receive an economic windfall because the reasoning of the court was that Davis was not really damaged in that he had already received a huge economic payment from the city of Los Angeles to move the Raiders there in the first place. As explained by Michael Janofsky in the *New York Times*, "The appeals court said, in effect, that Davis couldn't have it both ways—that the relief must be offset by the gains." The financial settlement reached years later between the NFL and Davis barely covered the Raiders' legal fees during the lengthy process.

The impact of the Raiders' court victory in being allowed to move a team would be the next situation for Rozelle and the NFL owners to closely monitor in the future of the league. After losing in court, the league was not willing to fight as hard against franchises relocating. Pat Bowlen, Broncos owner, explains that "there was not enthusiasm for teams relocating, and Rozelle was certainly not in favor of that at all and dead set against it if the community was supporting the team, but it was hard for the league to prevent." In a *Sport* magazine interview, Davis dismissed the idea of other franchises now relocating and deserting their respective cities as "totally ridiculous." He explained, "First of all, a lot of teams are on long-term leases. And now the communities in which they are in will give them the things they need. They'll work together because the community won't feel that they've got the team locked in. I know a lot of owners wanted to come out of this thing with some stability. Yet they also wanted to come out with an option, to do something that they thought was best for their franchise and not be locked into a community." However, Rozelle's fear of franchises relocating would quickly prove prophetic.

On more than one occasion Robert Irsay, owner of the Baltimore Colts, had raised the issue of moving his team to gain strategic leverage in negotiations with Maryland officials about upgrades to Baltimore's Memorial Stadium. As early as 1976 Irsay talked of moving the Colts to Phoenix, claiming Memorial Stadium didn't have the luxury boxes that other stadiums had. Rozelle and the league had acted as a mediator when these stadium differences arose in Baltimore. When the Davis verdict was announced, Irsay would comment, according to Jon Morgan's book *Glory for Sale*, "I don't think the implication is that every team is a free agent. As for myself, I'm happy in Baltimore." In 1979, however, Irsay had escalated shopping the Colts by talking to Jacksonville, Memphis, Los Angeles, and, soon after, Phoenix and Indianapolis. A couple of years later, Irsay would even have brief discussions with New York City when the Jets decided to also play their home game at Giants Stadium in New Jersey.

In 1980, the state of Maryland agreed to pass a $23 million renovation bond if the Colts would sign a fifteen-year lease to stay in Baltimore. However, in 1981, the Colts would only agree to a two-year lease. Pressure on Irsay was beginning to mount. When the press learned of a scheduled meeting between Irsay and Bruce Babbitt, governor of Arizona, the meeting was cancelled and Irsay would return to Baltimore and hold a press conference with Baltimore mayor William Donald Schaefer to dismiss any rumors of the Colts moving to Phoenix.

In the early 1980s the Colts continued to deteriorate on the field. The team didn't have a winning record from 1978 to 1983, including a strike-shortened winless season in 1982, 0-8-1. The constant talk of moving the Colts created a lack of enthusiasm for the team in Baltimore, and attendance had dropped to an average of 41,000 in 1983. The team would also be spurned by quarterback John Elway, who refused to play in Baltimore when selected by the Colts as the first pick in the 1983 draft. Ernie Accorsi, then general manager of the Colts, would ask for three first-round picks in exchange for Elway, who was threatening to play baseball instead of joining the Colts. Accorsi would tell *Sports Illustrated* in 1986, "Elway wasn't going to give up a chance at the Hall of Fame to play in Greensboro, North Carolina, which is exactly where he would have been sent. If we'd been patient we could have signed him." Without consulting Accorsi or Colts head coach Frank Kush, Irsay traded Elway to the Broncos for Denver's number-one pick in 1983 (offensive lineman Chris Hinton), a first-round pick in 1984, and quarterback Mark Herrmann. Denver would also agree to host the Colts in preseason games for two years, which Irsay would admit in *Sports Illustrated* was attractive because "Denver preseason games are one of the richest games you can get." The Colts would earn approximately a half-million dollars for each preseason visit to Denver.

Baltimore, Phoenix, and Indianapolis were still negotiating with the Colts in March 1984. The NFL, after losing its lawsuit with the Raiders and still awaiting the outcome of its appeal on damages, took the position that it would not stop Irsay from moving the Colts. The league did, however, ask for a decision by April 1, in order to make a schedule for the 1984 season. Rozelle would state in a *Washington Post* article on March 3, "With a $49 million judgment standing as of now against them for attempting to stop the Raider move to Los Angeles, they [the NFL owners] thought it would be prudent not to take any action concerning Mr. Irsay should he move." Rozelle added that the owners "probably will continue to give free agency to franchises. As of now, they think that is good business judgment." (It is important to note that these quotes were prior to the appellate court's ruling in 1986 reversing the monetary damages to Al Davis.)

Baltimore's final offer to Irsay was for a $15 million loan at 6.5 percent, a guarantee of at least 43,000 tickets sold per game for six years, and the purchase of a training facility for $4 million. On March 27, however, the state of Maryland passed legislation that enabled the state to seize the Colts on the grounds of eminent domain. Irsay learned of the decision on the morning of March 28, 1984. His response would be to call William Hadnut, Mayor of Indianapolis, to inform him that the Colts were moving.

On a rainy evening of March 28, 1984, just a little more than a month after the NFL's appeal to the U.S. Supreme Court on the merits in the Raiders case was denied, in large Mayflower moving trucks, Irsay and the Colts left Baltimore for Indianapolis. Instead of playing in Baltimore's aging Memorial Stadium, the Colts would now call the newly constructed Indianapolis Hoosier Dome home. Indianapolis guaranteed Irsay $7 million in ticket and preseason radio and television money for each of the first twelve years, the first $500,000 of luxury box revenue, and the construction of a new $4.4 million training facility for the Colts, which would be sold to Irsay for one dollar.

Even after the Raiders and Colts had moved, Rozelle would continue to selectively fight the relocation issue. For example, a lawsuit was filed to prevent the Philadelphia Eagles from relocating to Phoenix. In testimony before the U.S. Senate in 1985 Rozelle pointed out that over half the teams would have their stadium lease expire in the next fifteen years. He commented, "In the absence of league controls, individual clubs may be willing and able to walk away from existing leases in favor of a more lucrative offer from another community." He also added that guidelines for moving were proposed where teams would have to give reasons for their move.

With no feeling of an obligation to stay in their present city due to the court verdicts in the Raider case, over the next decade there would be four other NFL relocations: the Cardinals from St. Louis to Arizona for the 1988 season (still while Rozelle was commissioner), the Rams from Anaheim to St. Louis for the 1995 season, the Browns from Cleveland to Baltimore for the 1996 season, and the Oilers from Houston to Tennessee for the 1997 season. All of these franchise relocations were approved by the league's owners. The league looked more favorably on franchise relocation if the team was in a bad market and had a legitimate reason to move. Such was the case with the Cardinals leaving St. Louis. Even before all of these team movements, but after the Colts had moved, Rozelle was quoted in January 1985 in the *Los Angeles Times* saying, "I said that when the trial ended that this would cause franchise free agency. Now, I'd have to say, while I made a lot of mistakes in estimates, I was certainly right about that one."

One other franchise relocation would occur—the Raiders moving from Los Angeles back to Oakland for the 1995 season after thirteen seasons in Los Angeles. Although winning Super Bowl XVIII while there, the stay in Los Angeles would not deliver to Davis all of the treasures he had hoped. Davis would not get the luxury boxes or renovations to move seats closer to the field completed at the Los Angeles Coliseum. Rozelle had also been proven right that Davis and the Raiders were better off in Oakland. After a couple of seasons in the Coliseum, Davis accepted a $10 million nonreturnable fee and had talks about constructing a new 65,000-seat stadium in Irwindale, California, approximately twenty-five miles east of Los Angeles. The Raiders would also have a tough time averaging more than 70,000 fans in the over 92,000 seats of the Coliseum. Davis was quoted in *Sports Illustrated* in a 1987 article by Rick Reilly, saying, "The stadium [Los Angeles Coliseum] is a concern to me because it affects the team. Players need to hear the roar of the crowd. That place just swallows up the noise." Lester Hayes, Raiders all-pro defensive back, stated in the same article, "I remember when teams used to hate to play us in Oakland. It was the old silver-and-black mystique of intimidation. Now teams actually like to play us in L.A." If opposing players liked to play in Los Angeles, opposing fans did not, and there were numerous incidents of fan violence in the Coliseum, with visiting fans often the target. The Coliseum on Raiders' game days gained a national reputation for unruly fan behavior.

From the league standpoint, the lack of sellouts in Los Angeles also meant the television blackout of many Raider games in the Los Angeles market, which affected the NFL's relationship with the television networks. On a Sunday afternoon, another game could be televised in Los Angeles, but the NFL had to adjust its *Monday Night Football* schedule so as not to have the second-largest television market in the country unable to see the game. October 28, 1985, would be the last *Monday Night Football* game played in Los Angeles, before a crowd of only 72,022. With the Raiders being a huge draw on Monday night, their next nineteen Monday-night games would all be on the road. The Raiders would not host a *Monday Night Football* game again until November 4, 1996, when they were back in Oakland.

Overall, Rozelle was right in that franchises would relocate, which one could argue did create some instability, not to mention some anguish in cities such as Baltimore, Cleveland, Houston, and Oakland. The league, however, remained strong under his direction, and the fan loyalty and support in those cities when the NFL did return was markedly evident. In many ways the fact that the movement of franchises didn't ruin the league was a testament to the strength of the league and the sport that Rozelle had been so instrumental in building.

CHAPTER 12

The Rozelle Rule

ALEAGUE-FIRST economic philosophy, with owners equally sharing television money and striving for competitive balance, has a dramatic impact on the players and their salaries. Economic rules that eliminate distinctions between larger-market and smaller-market owners by not allowing wealthier owners to pay whatever they would like to acquire players do help create competitive balance, but they could also place inherent restrictions on player salaries. If player movement is restricted and there is no bidding on players by multiple teams with a player's rights held by only one team, salaries will not grow. The balance between competitive equality and the economics of the sports industry is obviously linked to the various revenue streams that the league and its individual teams can acquire, but this balance also must take into consideration other factors, such as players wanting more money and some owners wanting to spend more money to win. Once the system was established in the early 1960s Rozelle, for the most part, didn't have to deal with any owners trying to dramatically alter the economic structure of the league. He was, however, constantly forced to confront the players on economic matters.

Rozelle would argue in 1985 before the U.S. Senate about how the NFL's economic system of revenue sharing and competitive balance was beneficial for the players. He stated, "The salary, pension, and other benefits currently available to NFL players are dependent on the league's ability to maintain its current financial structure, including the guarantee that each club will have adequate revenues to operate its franchise. The NFL's inability to share revenues would have a substantial and adverse effect on player interests." Rozelle added, "An inability to share revenues would result in sharply increased disparities in the earnings of NFL clubs. This would not only threaten the athletic competitive balance within the league, diminishing the appeal of the league's entertainment product and the earning power of its clubs. It would also force the clubs at the lower end of the economic spectrum sharply to reduce the salaries and benefits that they would be able to offer their players."

In trying to increase the income provided to its members, sports unions are different from unions in other industries. Sports unions do not negotiate the salaries of their individual members. There are large disparities among player salaries based on a player's individual ability and his longevity in the league, and salaries are usually negotiated by agents. The players also work under a different and unique economic system in which in most aspects their employers are partners with each other—as the league continuously argued in the Raiders lawsuit—but in others, certainly on the field, are competitors. The union membership in a sport such as football is also very transient. There are a limited number of jobs in a sports league, and for the NFL the average length of a player's career is approximately four years. Other unions can collectively bargain for longer-term gains, knowing its current members will probably be able to receive some of those benefits in the future. With such a short playing career in sports, any long-term benefits that might be negotiated for are usually not obtained by the current membership.

Bert Bell had received criticism from Congress that the NFL was a nonunion employer, and he helped convince owners to recognize the players' union. In speaking before the House Antitrust Subcommittee in August 1957, Bell granted recognition to the NFL Players Association, acting unilaterally "on behalf of the league." Rozelle, then general manager of the Rams, commented, "If Bell has made the announcement I feel the league will undoubtedly abide by his recognition. The league certainly has done very well in the past with Bell as commissioner." In 1968 the National Labor Review Board (NLRB) recognized the National Football League Players Association (NFLPA) as a labor organization, defining it as the exclusive bargaining representative for all NFL players.

On the issue of collective bargaining negotiations between the owners and the players, Rozelle always tried to remain a neutral party. His thinking was that the commissioner represented the entirety of the game and the interests of both owners and players. A management council comprised of all NFL clubs with an executive committee of a few selected owners was designed as an independent organization separate from that of the commissioner's office.

The management council would act as the main negotiating arm with the Players Association. At most Rozelle would only make suggestions to move along negotiations or try to get the parties back to the bargaining table. With a strike threatening regular-season games in August 1970, and with players already boycotting training camps, Rozelle did, however, intervene. He helped bring owners and players together and convened a meeting at 12:30 p.m., on August 2, 1970, with a mandate that they would not leave until a deal was made. An agreement was reached at 7:00 a.m., the next morning. John Mackey, Baltimore Colts tight end and leader of the Players Association, would comment on the outcome, "They gave us what they wanted to give us, made us smile and say 'thank you.' But from that day forward, we decided to build a legitimate union."

Traditionally, one of the most contentious issues between the owners and the players in all sports has been free agency. Rozelle did have strong feelings against complete, unrestricted player free agency. The motivation for his position was once again competitive balance, league stability, and not alienating fans in a particular city. The NFL was operating under a reserve system, with every player bound to play for the team that he signed a contract with for the term of the contract, plus one additional year at the option of the club. A player who played out the option year of his contract was subject to a 10 percent salary reduction during the option year. With a potential pay cut looming, the player was more apt to agree to a contract extension with his current team before entering into the option year. If the player did play out the option year of his contract, when the season ended the player finally had the opportunity to become a free agent.

Prior to 1963 there was a gentlemen's agreement among all of the NFL owners not to sign free agents away from other teams. Carroll Rosenbloom, then owner of the Baltimore Colts, would violate this agreement by signing free-agent wide receiver R. C. Owens from the 49ers after Owens had played out the option year of his contract at the end of the 1961 season, a year in which Owens had fifty-five catches for 1,032 yards and five touchdowns. The signing of Owens would be done without any compensation going to his former team, the San Francisco 49ers. Owens would be the only free agent signed where the former team would not be compensated. With the Owens signing, the league moved to unilaterally adopt what would become known as the "Rozelle Rule."

The Rozelle Rule established a compensation system whereby when a player's contract to one team expired and he played out his option year, if he signed with a different team, the team that signed the player had to provide compensation back to the player's former team. The rule also stated that "if the two clubs are unable to conclude mutually satisfactory agreements, the *commissioner* [emphasis added] may award compensation in the form of one or more players and/or draft choices as he deems fair and equitable." The design of the rule was to strongly discourage franchises from signing other teams' free agents. Teams would simply be less apt to sign free agents if they would have to heavily compensate another team in the form of high draft choices or even another player. The rule would also hold down players' salaries by limiting the number of teams bidding on a player.

In 1968, the New Orleans Saints signed tight end Dave Parks away from the San Francisco 49ers. When no agreement could be worked out between the two teams Rozelle stepped in and declared that the Saints must give up Kevin Hardy, a defensive end who was the New Orleans first-round draft choice in 1968, and an additional number-one draft choice as compensation. This level of compensation would certainly curtail teams from actively pursuing other free agents. From 1963 to 1974, 176 players would play out the option year on their contracts. Thirty-four free agents signed with other teams, and in three of those cases the former team waived compensation. In twenty-seven cases the two teams reached a mutual agreement on compensation. In fact it was often the practice that a team would sign a free agent only when it had already been able to reach a compensation agreement with the player's former team. In the four remaining cases Rozelle would award the compensation. In addition to the award given to San Francisco for New Orleans signing Dave Parks, Rozelle ordered the Rams to give the New England Patriots a first- and third-round selection for the signing of Phil Olsen in 1971. The Rams were also forced to give the Bears a first-round draft choice for their signing of Dick Gordon in 1972. The Washington Redskins had to give the Cardinals second- and third-round picks for their signing of Pat Fischer in 1968.

Players were obviously disgruntled with this free-agent system that was limiting their options of where to play and limiting their salary potential. In 1972, John Mackey brought suit against the NFL. The goal of the lawsuit was to eliminate the Rozelle Rule and allow players to sign with another team without the penalty of compensation when their contract expired. The lawsuit claimed the Rozelle Rule violated the Sherman Antitrust Act by restricting player movement and that player salaries were being held down because there wasn't competition between the teams for talent. Closely aligned with Mackey in his lawsuit against the NFL was Ed Garvey. Garvey became involved in the NFL in the 1970 bargaining sessions, when the labor contract between the NFL owners and players was being negotiated. At the time, Garvey was working with a labor law firm in Minneapolis that was helping to write the actual contract that was being negotiated. It was during this time that Mackey and Garvey would meet and begin a working relationship. Pleased with Garvey's performance, in May 1971 Mackey hired Garvey to become the executive director of the NFLPA. With the addition of Garvey in the collective bargaining process the players would have a more forceful and unifying voice.

Garvey, with only an ancillary role in the 1970 negotiations, felt there was a lack of unity among the players, and when he became executive director of the union in 1971 he immediately worked to bring them together. Garvey created an organizational structure, with each team selecting a union player representative and those representatives choosing a six-man executive committee. When the collective bargaining agreement was about to once again expire in 1974, the Garvey-led union appeared more prepared and unified. Garvey had created a more defiant tone against ownership, and there was clear animosity toward Garvey from the owners over the Mackey lawsuit, with many owners referring to the impending work stoppage as "Garvey's strike." Garvey felt that the animosity directed at him for being the catalyst of the players' ideas was unfounded. He had stated in *Sports Illustrated* in 1974, "They [the owners] can't come to grips with the idea that the players are the ones who are challenging them and I'm just a conduit. They have to believe that I'm responsible. It's another example of how insensitive they are to what the players are thinking." Garvey thought the lawsuit gave him tremendous leverage in negotiations and that it would force the owners to bargain in good faith. Garvey also had a simple issue to rally the players: low, stagnant salaries. In 1974, the average NFL player salary of $25,000 had not increased since 1968. The bringing of the Mackey lawsuit would give the players a unifying cause, as there was an understanding that obtaining free agency was their best vehicle to escalate salaries. In the first negotiation session between the players and owners on March 16, 1974, Garvey articulated fifty-eight demands, including the elimination of the Rozelle Rule, the creation of total free agency, and the elimination of the commissioner's authority to discipline players. The union would add another thirty-three demands in May, but there would be little progress on a new collective bargaining agreement. The Rozelle Rule remained the top issue throughout the summer of 1974. Bill Curry, veteran offensive lineman and president of the NFLPA, stated in *Sports Illustrated*, "The basic issue is the right of a player to move freely from one team to another when his contract has expired. We think he should have that right, just as everyone else has."

The position of the NFL was that without the Rozelle Rule star players would move to cities with natural advantages based on either economics, winning opportunities, or media opportunities, resulting in the destruction of the league's economic and competitive balance structure. The NFL also contended that player movement would create a lack of continuity among team rosters and the quality of play would suffer. All of these reasons would contribute to diminishing spectator interest and potentially franchise failures. Rozelle and the NFL maintained the league could not survive without the rule restricting free agency. To Rozelle, complete, unrestricted free agency would undo much of his extensive efforts in developing the league-first philosophy. He was quoted as saying, "If NFL players are given total freedom to negotiate their services, the league would be dominated by a few rich teams and would eventually lose both fan interest and revenue." Rozelle also cautioned that complete, unrestricted free agency could potentially force some teams in smaller markets to fold, an idea that caused concern for some players, but not Ed Garvey, who stated, "Let those teams go out of business if they can't run a profitable enterprise. That's what happens in American industry."

On July 1, 1974, the union announced its players would not report to training camp on July 3. Following through on the threat on July 3, Garvey would lead a picket line of players in San Diego, all wearing T-shirts featuring a clenched fist and the slogan "NO FREEDOM, NO FOOTBALL." While Garvey had achieved some unity among the players, it was far from complete. As training camp continued, the fragility of the union began to surface. The NFL reported that by July 29 approximately 20 percent of the NFLPA had defected. In the August 5, 1974, issue of *Sports Illustrated* Mike Curtis, Colts linebacker, stated, "Ed Garvey is a left-wing opportunist who is trying to make a name for himself at the players' expense. They're talking about freedom issues because it's a catchy phrase. You can't be any freer than we are." On August 7 the NFL released another report showing that over one hundred more players had returned to training camp. NFL management, sensing an impending victory over a fractured union, asked Garvey to drop the Mackey lawsuit. Garvey realizing the strike was not working convinced the players to return to work, but the strategy was to continue to fight in court with the Mackey case. On August 11, Garvey announced his plan and the forty-one-day strike ended with all players returning to training camp. The union was now completely reliant on the outcome of the Mackey lawsuit.

With the case pending, limited negotiations between the two parties occurred, with management's insistence that any agreement include the Rozelle

Rule. This insistence would quickly end any negotiations with Garvey and result in the union holding firm in waiting until the Mackey verdict. The case of *Mackey v. NFL* finally began on February 3, 1975, in a Minneapolis federal district court, with both sides agreeing the case would be decided by a judge and not by a jury. The trial would consume fifty-five days in court with sixty-three witnesses providing testimony.

With the verdict in the Mackey case pending, Rozelle would have to deal with another significant test on the player free-agent issue. Again it would be Carroll Rosenbloom at the center of the controversy. Now owning the Los Angeles Rams, but still without a victory in the Super Bowl with that team, Rosenbloom felt the perennially contending Rams were just one player away. After the 1974 season, and after testifying in the Mackey lawsuit that the Rozelle Rule was essential to maintain the competitive balance of the NFL, Rosenbloom signed Ron Jessie, a wide receiver coming off of a 54-catch, 761-yard season in the option year of his contract with the Detroit Lions. Not wanting to enforce his own rule at this precarious time in the legal question of free agency, Rozelle asked the Rams and the Lions to negotiate the compensation that the Lions would receive from the Rams for their signing of Jessie. When no amicable solution could be reached by the two teams, Rozelle was forced to intervene.

On the four previous occasions when Rozelle had to rule on a free-agent signing, only once had his ruling included a player. The other compensation rulings were all future draft choices. On the matter of the Rams signing Ron Jessie, Rozelle would hand down his most severe ruling, awarding the Lions Cullen Bryant, a promising running back who had been the Rams' second-round draft choice in 1973. Rosenbloom adamantly opposed the ruling. Claiming a violation of the Sherman Antitrust Act and hoping to void Rozelle's decision, at the encouragement of Rosenbloom, Cullen Bryant filed a lawsuit against the NFL on July 29, 1975. The next day, a preliminary hearing was conducted in a Los Angeles federal district court with the judge temporarily stopping Rozelle's awarding of Bryant to the Lions. The judge also commented that the Rozelle Rule was in violation of the Sherman Antitrust Act. With a second hearing set for August 12, but clearly not wanting to fight the league's free-agent policy on another legal front, on August 2 the NFL announced the ruling of Bryant to the Lions would be voided and replaced by the Lions receiving first- and second-round draft choices from the Rams. Ron Jessie would belong to the Rams.

During the Mackey trial, several witnesses testified that absent the Rozelle Rule there would be increased player movement. Rosenbloom indicated in his testimony that without the Rozelle Rule he would have signed more free agents. Charles De Kaedo, a player agent, testified that the New Orleans Saints were interested in signing one of his clients, Dick Gordon, but could not reach a compensation agreement with Gordon's former team, the Chicago Bears. Jim McFarland, an end for the St. Louis Cardinals, testified that when he played out his option he tried to sign with the Kansas City Chiefs but was unable to do so because of the compensation being asked for by the Cardinals. Hank Stram, Chiefs general manager and head coach, corroborated McFarland's testimony by indicating he would have given McFarland an opportunity to make the Chiefs team if they had not been required to compensate the Cardinals. There was also testimony by two economists that the elimination of the Rozelle Rule would lead to a substantial increase in player salaries. Alan Page, defensive end of the Vikings, testified that the Rozelle Rule was a hindrance on player movement, but its principle effect was on players' salaries.

After fifty-five days of testimony, on December 29, 1975, the ruling in *Mackey v. NFL* was finally handed down with the court concluding that the Rozelle Rule was unreasonably restrictive and in violation of the Sherman Antitrust Act. The court found that the NFL's argument that the Rozelle Rule was necessary for the successful operation of the league was insufficient to justify its restrictive nature of suppressing player movement and player salaries. The court held that the rule deterred teams from negotiating with and signing free agents and was a substantial deterrent to players playing out their option year and even becoming free agents. Therefore, the players' bargaining power in contract negotiations was significantly decreased, with players denied the right to sell their services in a free and open market. All of these restrictions resulted in salaries lower than if competitive bidding among teams were allowed.

The court also concluded that the elimination of the Rozelle Rule would not have significant short-term or long-term disruptive effects on the NFL. Judge Earl Larson argued that the "quality of play in the NFL will not decrease." He rejected the NFL's principle claim of needing the rule to ensure competitive balance, stating, "The court finds the existence of the Rozelle Rule and other restrictive devices on players have not had any material effect on competitive balance in the National Football League." Judge Larson would also argue that even if the quality of play and competitive balance in the NFL were negatively impacted, "the fact does not justify the rule's anticompetitive nature." Finally, in determining the Rozelle Rule invalid, the court rejected the NFL's claim that the rule was protected because it had been collectively bargained. The court actually contended that even if the NFL and the union could come to a collectively bargained agreement about the implementation of the Rozelle Rule in some form, it would still be illegal.

The verdict was a major victory for Ed Garvey and the NFLPA. Garvey would state the union was "tremendously gratified by the court's decision. The NFL has said that the Mackey case was the test because it was the first fully litigated case on the reserve clause in the history of professional sports." Garvey added, "In 1974, the NFL players struck for freedom. Today, the federal courts said they deserve the right guaranteed other citizens in our country. Professional football will flourish under this ruling."

Rozelle's position on the need for restricting free agency to protect competitive balance would not waver. After the verdict he maintained, "We had hoped that the court would find the antitrust laws to be sufficiently flexible to accommodate the unique and special needs of a professional football league." He added, "Such leagues depend on competitive balance and the quality of their teams for fan interest in each season's schedule. We continue to believe that team equalization rules have served and will continue to serve the interests of fans, players and clubs alike."

The NFL appealed the district court verdict. In the interim, some players who had played out the option year on their contracts became free agents on May 1, 1976, and did sign with other teams. Some of the notable signings included John Riggins, the Jets' team MVP, who was earning less than $100,000 in 1975, going from New York to the Washington Redskins. Also returning from the defunct World Football League, Paul Warfield joined the Cleveland Browns, and Larry Csonka joined the Giants signing a four-year contract with a value totaling over $1 million. Although not obliged to do so, both Art Modell and Wellington Mara agreed to voluntary compensate the Dolphins for their signings. Miami received the Giants' third-round selections in 1978 and 1979 as compensation for signing Csonka and received the Browns' fourth- and seventh-round draft choices in 1978 as compensation for signing Warfield. The Jets did not receive any compensation from the Redskins for their signing of Riggins.

The NFL would lose its appeal of the Mackey case in a ruling on October 18, 1976. The appellate court did, however, make an important adjustment to the district court's ruling, claiming that the Rozelle Rule would be legal and exempt from Sherman Antitrust Act liability if free agency were accepted through collective bargaining. The appellate court concluded that the Rozelle Rule was unilaterally imposed by the owners in 1963 and had not been the result of collective bargaining, but it pointed out that any agreement as to a compensation system reached through good faith collective bargaining might very well be immune from antitrust liability. It seemed apparent that the decision of the appellate court in the Mackey lawsuit was designed to force the parties back to collective bargaining and that the rules governing player movement should be resolved through the negotiation process rather than by the court. The court also came to the conclusion that some reasonable restrictions relating to player movement are necessary for the successful operation of the NFL.

The aiming for collective bargaining to solve the issue of player free agency was a result that Rozelle and the NFL could live with. Three months before the appellate court decision, on July 21, 1976, Rozelle had testified before the House Select Committee on Professional Sports, stating "If there is one single legal principle which I think should be applicable to all sports leagues, it is that labor and management should be permitted to resolve their differences without outside interference." In pointing out that neither Congress nor the federal courts could resolve the variety of issues between ownership and the players, Rozelle added, "So long as either party to the collective bargaining relationship pursues its objectives elsewhere, outside of the collective bargaining process, the give-and-take of the bargaining process is never going to function effectively."

The league and Rozelle viewed the appellate court decision as an opportunity to still invoke some form of limitation on player free agency. With the new ruling, Garvey was forced to once again bargain with the NFL owners. On February 16, 1977, marking the first time in two and a half years, the two sides would finally come to terms on a collective bargaining agreement. Among the concessions given to the players in the new five-year agreement was an absolute recognition of the union such that players would have to pay dues even if they didn't join, a limitation of Rozelle's authority on player grievances, $107 million in benefit payments over the length of the contract, and $13.65 million over ten years in damages emanating from the Mackey lawsuit. However, the result of collective bargaining would not grant the players complete, unrestricted free agency. The agreement instead created a first refusal/compensation system governing free agency, where the price of at least a first-round draft choice would be the compensation for signing another team's free agent.

Significantly, the NFL owners won the reinstatement of the Rozelle Rule, with it now being legally protected from any antitrust violation, having been collectively bargained. With this concession the players had essentially forfeited what they had won in the Minneapolis courtroom in December 1975. Thus,

Rozelle had averted the most serious threat to the stability of the economic system and practices of the NFL. Ernie Accorsi calls the period of the Mackey lawsuit, with its potential for instituting complete, unrestricted free agency, a pivotal one for the league because it presented the possibility of a sudden change to the entire economic structure of the NFL.

Each labor deal is to some extent an incremental build up to the next collective bargaining session. The agreement in 1977 in many aspects set the tone for the negotiations of 1982. Like all labor negotiations, the root of the problem was money. For the NFLPA the real question was how to increase and then divvy up the NFL's revenues to the players. In the beginning of negotiations in 1982 Ed Garvey had convinced the players to try to attain an economic system where they would essentially become partners with the owners and receive a set percentage of the NFL's gross revenues. The players had initially asked for 55 percent of the league's gross revenues. The players also initially insisted on a pay scale based on years in the league with incentive and performance bonuses.

Garvey would explain his proposal in David Harris's book *The League: The Rise and Decline of the NFL*, stating, "We [the NFLPA] want fifty-five percent of all revenues put into a fund from which all players would be paid. Of that fund, seventy percent would go to base wages. You'd start with about a $90,000 base for rookies and work on up, on a basis of seniority, to about $450,000 base pay for a player with, say, fourteen years of experience." NFL ownership through management council negotiator Jack Donlan would argue that the 55 percent proposal, "would turn over control of the business to the players. The owners believe pro football is the most successful of all sports entertainment businesses because of the business decisions made by the owners over the years, and the owners don't want to give up the right to make those decisions." According to Donlan and the owners, players were already earning 48 percent of the NFL's gross revenues in salaries and other benefits. Garvey wanted the 55 percent to be allocated to only salaries.

On the issue of players' salaries, the average salary for an NFL player was well below that of major league baseball or the NBA in 1982. Baseball players had an average salary of $240,000, the NBA players $215,000, but the NFL players only $95,000. In fact the combined salaries of three major league baseball players, Reggie Jackson of the California Angels, Mike Schmidt of the Philadelphia Phillies, and Dave Winfield of the New York Yankees, was more than the entire Dallas Cowboys roster. Ed Garvey would have little problem achieving a strong consensus with the players on this point.

While the salary arguments certainly helped provide a uniting initiative, one person also responsible for the coming together of the Players Association was its new president, Gene Upshaw of the Raiders. Upshaw was the first-round draft choice of Oakland in the inaugural combined NFL-AFL draft in 1967. As a player, Upshaw commanded the utmost respect. After winning the left guard position as a rookie, Upshaw held that spot for fifteen seasons, starting in 207 consecutive regular-season games. Upshaw would play his last game in 1981, as an injury sidelined him prior to the 1982 season. He was elected to the Hall of Fame in 1987. Upshaw contentiously argued the position of the union in *Sports Illustrated*, stating, "They [management] want us to think we're animals. They want to tell us what time to go to bed, what to eat, what to wear. What we're going to show them now is not just a matter of economics, it's a matter of dignity." It would be Upshaw's idea to have the players engage in solidarity handshakes at midfield prior to exhibition games played in 1982.

Management had made it clear that it rejected the concept of 55 percent for the players because that would essentially make the union and the owners partners. On Friday, September 17, in what would be the final negotiating session prior to the strike deadline, the union revised its proposal to 50 percent of television revenues, approximately $1.6 billion over four years, which the league was to deposit in a newly created players compensation fund. The union continued to claim that its insistence on a wage scale based on longevity and supported with incentives and performance bonuses was etched in stone. Management viewed that proposal as the implementation of an unfair minimum-salary structure. Donlan and management also claimed that their offer was not far from the union, proposing $1.6 billion over five years. To demonstrate the contentiousness that had formed between the union and management, Garvey would comment, "I am convinced they're offering $1.6 billion about as much as I'm convinced there is a tooth fairy."

CHAPTER 13

The Unthinkable Happens

T HE HEADLINE in the *Newark Star-Ledger* on Saturday September 18, 1982, read "NFL Talks Break Off; Strike Looms." In the article, Mark Murphy, player representative for the Redskins and now the athletic director at Northwestern University, described the previous day's negotiation session. He stated, "In essence what they are saying is it's the current system or nothing. It is apparent the owners want a strike. It scares me how close we are to the baseball situation from last year. Management's objective seems to be whether the union can be broken." Gene Upshaw would comment, "We do not want a strike," but added, "We will not play under the current system until it is repaired."

At 4:30 p.m., on Monday September 20, Ed Garvey and Gene Upshaw at a press conference at the Halloran House, a New York City hotel, announced that the NFL players would go on strike at the conclusion of that evening's *Monday Night Football* game at the Meadowlands between the New York Giants and the Green Bay Packers. Upshaw stated, "There will be no practices, workouts, or training. No games will be played until management abandons its unlawful course and engages in good-faith bargaining and executes a fair and equitable agreement. We are prepared to withhold our services, however long it takes. We have a solid front." When the players did announce their strike, Upshaw estimated that 94 percent of the players were in agreement with the union position. Coincidental, but certainly reflective of the mood and condition of the NFL, the Giants/Packers game would be played in a driving rain storm, twice delayed by power outages at Giants Stadium. The players on both teams would be repeatedly booed throughout the game. The strike of 1982 became the first work stoppage by the NFLPA that resulted in the cancellation of regular-season games.

Even with a strike called, Rozelle remained relatively silent, still trying to maintain the role of impartiality. If anything, he continued to mediate or ignite negotiations between the two sides. But Rozelle was mostly powerless. Often the extent of his role in the negotiations would be to attend meetings of the management council and occasionally help them modify a position. He might also on occasion meet with the leaders of the Players Association. For example, in one meeting with Garvey and Upshaw, Rozelle expressed his doubt that ownership would ever agree to an economic system that reflected a percentage of the gross. Years later in the *Washington Post*, Rozelle would explain how he saw his role on the labor issue: "Other commissioners have different roles. In football, we have the management council, a separate staff which handles negotiations between management and the players. I attempted to be a liaison once in a while, but it was not my function." In 1982, Rozelle would be called to intervene in the strike by many of those involved, including Al Davis. In an article in the *Newark Star-Ledger*, Davis was quoted as saying, "We have a commissioner who refuses to get involved in it, at least at this stage. Why, I don't know." The players, however, for the most part still viewed Rozelle as aligned with ownership. Ed Garvey was quoted in the *New York Times*, contentiously stating, "His whole history of dealing with players has never been evenhanded but confrontational, and always on the side of management. They pay him, and so he is simply a hired hand for them."

Pressure to settle the strike would emerge from many outlets. Certainly the fans wanted to see the return of their sport. Pressure was also emanating from the television networks, which had just signed five-year contracts with the NFL beginning in 1982. The game between the Pittsburgh Steelers and the Dallas Cowboys on the opening week of *Monday Night Football* in 1982 had produced a television rating of 24.9 and an audience share of 42 percent for ABC. In showing movies to replace football, ABC was only receiving a rating of 14.3 and an audience share of 22 percent. NBC would try televising games from the Canadian Football League. Garvey and Upshaw were faced with pressure to keep the union together once the players stopped getting paid. The union would hold two all-star games that were televised by maverick Ted Turner's cable superstation, but both games were sparsely attended, with reported crowds of only 8,760 in Washington, D.C., and 5,331 in Los Angeles.

As negotiations slowly moved along, the management council made a concession to the union, proposing $1.28 billion over four years on October 31, the sixth week with no games. After an immediate rejection by the union, the league countered by increasing the offer to $1.313 billion on November 4. This offer also included $60 million in immediate bonuses paid to the players upon the conclusion of the strike. When that offer was too rejected, the owners decided not to conduct any meetings with the players and froze out Garvey by not returning any of his telephone calls. Rozelle would join in on boycotting Garvey's calls. In addition to the freezing out of Garvey, the owners circumvented the union leadership and hierarchical communication system by mailing out copies of their latest proposal directly to all of the players. Not long after receiving the owners' proposal, the Cincinnati Bengals, Houston Oilers, Los Angeles Rams, and New Orleans Saints all voted by large margins to accept management's offer.

Finally, on November 17, a new collective bargaining agreement was reached and ratified by the NFL owners. The eight-week strike lasted fifty-seven days and cost the owners an estimated $450 million. The new contract would run through the end of the 1986 season. In the settlement, the owners guaranteed to pay the players $1.6 billion over four years, including $60 million in immediate bonus money. The players also gained victories in that a minimum salary schedule for years of experience was established and that training camp, postseason pay, medical insurance, and retirement benefits were all increased. A first for sports was also agreed to when a severance-pay system was introduced to aid in career transition.

For the owners, their biggest victory clearly came in that there again would be no complete, unrestricted free-agency system. The players also conceded that there would not be a percentage of the gross revenues forming the players' salary structure and there would be no central fund as the players had demanded. Upon its settlement, Keith Fahnhorst, San Francisco 49ers player representative, stated, "Nobody's excited with the contract we ended up with." In assessing winners and losers from the strike in a *Sports Illustrated* column written by Paul Zimmerman, Rozelle would be portrayed as coming out on the losing end. Zimmerman wrote of Rozelle, "His image has suffered. He stayed out of negotiations because he wanted to keep the Commissioner's office separate from the bargaining table, but the world had come to look on him as some kind of savior. He wasn't."

To repair the 1982 season, Rozelle devised a nine-game schedule that commenced on the weekend of November 21–22. The NFL would also have sixteen teams qualify for the playoffs. In the week that the NFL players returned to action, the average attendance dropped 8,390 from the same week of the previous year and there were no-shows totaling 115,586. The following weeks of the strike produced average no-shows of 14 percent of ticket sales. Rozelle explained in the *New York Times,* "My greatest concern is that the no-shows become no-buyers. It is important that the owners and the players use the off-season to promote the game and get the public back any way we can." Television ratings for the NFL also declined in comparison to the previous season.

At the annual pre–Super Bowl press conference Rozelle described the 1982 season as "a very distasteful year for the players, coaches and owners of the National Football League." Overall in 1982, however, despite the strike, the average attendance for the NFL was 58,472, which at that point was the fifth-highest in league history. Any potential negative lingering effects were dismissed after the Super Bowl between the Washington Redskins and the Miami Dolphins, which was at the time the second-highest-rated live television program of all time, with the game being viewed in more than forty million homes.

In June 1983, Ed Garvey resigned as the executive director of the NFLPA. Gene Upshaw, now officially retired as a player, was elevated from president to become the executive director of the union. The resignation of Garvey would not, however, lead to a more harmonious relationship between the Players Association and the owners' management council, particularly its two leaders, Hugh Culverhouse, chairman of the management council and owner of the Tampa Bay Buccaneers, and Tex Schramm. It would be Schramm who would be the more outspoken leader. For example, at one point in the bargaining process Schramm would state, as quoted in Bob St. John's book, *Tex,* "The union doesn't have what you might call adult leadership in its executive committee."

The accord that was reached between the owners and players in 1982 expired on August 31, 1987. Similar to 1982, the NFL had just renegotiated its new television contracts. Three-year agreements were reached with ABC, CBS, and NBC to broadcast games for the 1987–1989 seasons. The NFL had also introduced its movement into cable with ESPN becoming the first cable network televising games. Many of the same issues from 1982 would be revisited: player salaries, free agency, guaranteed contracts, a wage scale, drug testing, and pension benefits. The issue of pension benefits, particularly to include players who retired from the NFL prior to 1959, was a point of agreement between the union and Rozelle, who was clearly in favor of helping the older players. A new program was created for players who spent at least five years in the league and played all or part of their career prior to 1959. The program called for each player to receive sixty dollars per month for each year of service in the league. In 1986, the NFLPA claimed the career of the average player was 3.2 years, short of the 4 years needed to be vested in the NFL pension system. The initial stance of the union on this issue was that because an injury can occur at any time, players should immediately be vested after only one game.

The issue of developing a tougher drug policy was also gaining more prominence. The league had proposed random testing in 1982, but it was not implemented. The climate on the drug issue in 1987 had dramatically changed following the tragic deaths of University of Maryland basketball star and Boston Celtics draftee Len Bias and the less publicized death of Don Rogers, a defensive back with the Cleveland Browns. Rozelle thought the timing was right and that it was necessary for the league to implement a strong drug program. He announced unilateral implementation of a plan that called for a preseason test and two random tests during the season. For first-time offenders the remedy would be removal from the roster for thirty days and a fine of a half-month's pay. The player would also be sent to a rehabilitation center. Players in violation for a second time would again be removed from the roster for thirty days, but fined the full month's salary. Rozelle also pushed for a potential lifetime suspension for players who failed a drug test for a third time.

The NFLPA did not approve the unilateral approach of Rozelle and feared that acceptance of this policy could create a slippery slope of Rozelle unilaterally implementing other initiatives. The NFLPA also contended that random drug testing was an invasion of privacy on the Fourth Amendment grounds of unreasonable search and seizures. The NFLPA thought any drug policy should be collectively bargained. Rozelle, knowing that the input of the Players Association was needed to be a part of any decision, agreed to binding arbitration on the matter. The policy eventually called for only mandatory preseason testing with the clubs having the ability to test in the regular season if they deemed there was a "reasonable cause."

Free agency, long the most volatile issue between the two sides, would be a more prominent issue in 1987 than it had been in 1982. Still having never achieved the free-agency status in collective bargaining that they had won in court in the initial Mackey verdict in December 1975, the players would once again ask for complete, unrestricted free agency. But they quickly moved off that stance and proposed free agency for players after serving four years in the league. Management continued to maintain that any form of free agency would kill the economic system that the players had benefited from. In *Tex*, Bob St. John quoted Schramm: "Sports are different, unique, unlike any other business, and so the same rules can't be applied. You're partners on one hand and competing on the other. You can't run around signing free agents and upping salaries like baseball, because you'll run your competition out of business. The only way you're successful over the long haul is if the league is strong from top to bottom." Gene Upshaw would state his position on free agency in the *Newark Star-Ledger*, claiming, "It cannot be summed up in terms of dollars. It's not about the money, it's about dignity and freedom. It's about who you want to work for."

The tactics of the owners would also be different in 1987. With the players threatening to strike, the owners were planning to field teams with replacement players to compete in NFL games that would count in the standings until the regular players returned. This was not the first time that the idea of replacement players was thought of, but would be the first time it was executed. In 1974 Gene Klein and Wellington Mara had indicated they wanted to play the games with whoever was available. Exhibition games in the summer of 1974 were played with rookies, who were not yet part of the union, and the ever growing number of union defectors.

The possibility of using replacement players to play in NFL games had also been raised by Lamar Hunt during the 1982 strike. The headline in the *Newark Star-Ledger* on September 22, 1982, read, "Garvey Scoffs at Threat to Stage Games; Owners Considering Options during NFL Strike." In that newspaper on the previous day in 1982, several prominent coaches had expressed their disagreement with the idea of playing games with replacement players. Joe Gibbs, head coach of the Redskins, stated, "Grabbing a bunch of people and trying to pull a team together is not a viable solution." Mike Ditka, head coach of the Bears, asked, "Would you pay to see free agents play? I can't imagine it." Dick Vermeil, head coach of the Eagles, even commented, "I have no intention of coaching a scab football team. Maybe Rozelle can force me."

Jack Donlan, head of the owners' management council, and Gene Upshaw, leader of the NFLPA, met in Washington, D.C., on September 18, but when no agreement was reached a strike was called. The strike would commence on Tuesday, September 22, 1987, after week two of the NFL season, at the conclusion of the *Monday Night Football* game in Giants Stadium just as it had in 1982, with this time the Jets defeating the New England Patriots 43-24 before a crowd of 70,047. Week three of the NFL season was cancelled, but the NFL would resume in week four with its replacement player teams.

The management council, consisting of Mike Brown, Culverhouse, Joe Robbie, Dan Rooney, and Schramm (Billy Sullivan from the Patriots would not be an active participant of the council during the strike) would vote 5-0 for games with replacement players. Pat Bowlen, Denver Broncos owner, contends that using replacement players was an idea embraced by a number of owners as a practical solution, claiming, "The idea of shutting down football did not make sense and bringing in replacement players did." The owners would honor requests for ticket refunds or give credit toward season tickets for the following season.

The idea of using replacement players in 1987 was roundly criticized. Paul Zimmerman commented in *Sports Illustrated*, "Regrettably all the results will count. Which teams get playoff berths may well be determined by a bunch of guys the NFL euphemistically calls replacement players. Franchises that didn't hustle for scab ball talent because they thought they had better things to do, like getting real NFL teams ready for the season, or because of loyalty to their regulars are going to be patsies of the SFL (Strike Football League or Scab Football League)."

Always concerned with the image of the NFL, Rozelle, too, feared that using replacement players could hurt the league and was against the idea. On the topic of the NFL's image, Zimmerman wrote, "The NFL's image has been badly damaged by the strike, and scab ball will only make it worse. The reason that the owners kept camps closed during the last players' strike, in 1982, when each club lost seven games, is that they feared subpar games would hurt the league. Some owners wanted to play with pickups back then, but commissioner Pete Rozelle convinced them that was a bad idea. Privately, he's still opposed to playing games during the strike, but he hasn't tried to stop them." Rozelle maintained his position against the idea of replacement players. Bob St. John quoted him as saying, "I wasn't thrilled, but I understood why they did it. This was the fifth strike, and they wanted a new approach. By the time I had consulted with them, they were going ahead with the games." In 1987, Rozelle would once again not be active in negotiations, continuing to maintain his position of neutrality. On occasion, he didn't even know when the management council, which had its office in a separate location from the NFL office, was holding a meeting.

The team executives responsible for putting together the replacement squads still did not know if a strike was definitely going to be called even on the Sunday prior to the walkout. Charley Casserly was in the front office of the Washington Redskins and explains that when players were released during training camp they could be signed to a contract that would bind them to that team if replacement games were played. He claims the Redskins did take some advantage of that rule, but that "it was a touchy situation because you did not want to offend any of the current players." According to Casserly, it was not until the Wednesday before the final regular-season game before the strike that the Redskins really began to get a replacement squad together. He remembers Jack Kent Cooke, Redskins owner, asking him on the morning of the game, one day prior to the strike being officially called, how many replacement players the Redskins had lined up? Casserly recalls telling him that the number changed by the hour.

Resentment between the NFL regular players and replacement players was immediately apparent. The Redskins replacement team had their first meeting on the Tuesday after the strike was announced, fifty-five players showing up at a hotel, with extra security present. At the first practice at Redskin park, Washington's regular players were picketing and greeted the replacement players' bus by smashing its front window. The first week of replacement games featured picket lines at many of the NFL stadiums hosting games. Worried about security and its own union troubles, United Airlines even had the Raiders board their charter flight to Denver not at the terminal but in an area across the airport near the United Airlines hangar. The team traveled with extra security guards and was also bused into Mile High Stadium earlier than usual, at 3:30 p.m., for their Monday-night game, to avoid any potential confrontations with picket lines.

The idea of replacement players created an easy divide in the Players Association, which had never been overly unified. Casserly explains that Joe Gibbs told the Redskins regular team to stick together and that if they go out on strike together he wanted them to come in together. The Redskins replacement team would win all of their three games, and nobody from the regular team crossed the picket line and played in a replacement game. The Redskins would eventually go on to win the Super Bowl that season, defeating the Denver Broncos 42-10.

Ernie Accorsi, then general manager of the Cleveland Browns, recalls that team executives were told by the league before training camp to prepare replacement teams. He said he worked hard to field the Browns' replacement squad and that the replacement team won a critical road game in Cincinnati, a place where the Browns had not had much success, losing in four of the previous five years, to help Cleveland win its division in 1987. In addition to Washington and Cleveland, some other teams, including Houston, Indianapolis, and Tampa Bay, were proactive in fielding their replacement teams, telling some of the players they released in training camp to make themselves available. Tampa Bay would have two of its four wins of the 1987 season in replacement games. Houston and Indianapolis would each go two and one in their replacement games, helping each team qualify for the NFL playoffs. It marked the first time Houston had qualified for the playoffs since 1980 and the Colts the first time reaching the playoffs since 1977. The Giants, the defending Super Bowl champions, would be one of the franchises that did not go to great lengths to field their replacement team and lost all three of their replacement games, dropping their record at that point of the season to 0-5.

The team unity displayed by the Redskins would be the exception. Prominent players, such as Mark Gastineau, Jets all-pro defensive end, and Randy White, Cowboys all-pro defensive tackle, immediately crossed the picket line. Gastineau indicated that he would cross the picket line on the day of the Jets' final Monday-night game before the strike. He stated, "Right now, I feel like I've put a lot of work in the off-season. To give up on it now is against my judgment. I want to play. That's why I reported to camp." Gastineau added, "I have a different opinion, and I hope everyone respects it. As far as not getting along with my teammates, I hope everyone understands and respects how I feel." Three days later, on the first day that replacement players practiced and NFL players actually had to cross the picket line, Gastineau elaborated on his decision, "I'm here out of loyalty to Mr. Hess [Jets owner Leon Hess]. He's always been fair to me. He's always done the things he said he would do." He added, "Because of the contract he gave me [a contract worth $725,000 signed in 1984], he had to change the pay scale for the entire team. I'm talking about loyalty to someone who has been loyal to me for eight years." Gastineau would receive much criticism from players around the league. Neil Olkewicz, Redskins linebacker, stated in a television interview, "Gastineau's a jerk and all his teammates know he's a jerk." Dan Hampton, Bears defensive lineman and future Hall of Famer, would also comment, "Gastineau's got an IQ about room temperature."

Randy White explained in *Sports Illustrated*, "When I decided to cross the picket line, it was not to make a statement against the union or to show I'm one hundred percent behind the owners. I made my decision based on what was best for me, my family and my future." White commented, "I'm 34 years old. I'm at the end of my career. I only have one year left on my contract. I'm paid $31,000 a game because I busted my butt. And money I lose, I'll never make up." Danny White, Cowboys quarterback, would also quickly cross the picket line, stating, "I had a hard time looking myself in the mirror, making

$725,000 a year and being on strike. My opinion of striking is something you do when you think you're being treated unfairly."

The Cowboys would, in fact, provide one of the more interesting team situations during the strike. The Cowboy players were already in a precarious situation with Tex Schramm being one of the main negotiators, and often the spokesperson with the press for the management council. Schramm would even on occasion walk out to the Cowboys' picket line and speak with the players about the issues. Several of the Cowboys prominent players, including Doug Cosbie, Tony Dorsett, Ed Jones, Everson Walls, Danny White, and Randy White, were also signed to contracts that included annuities that were threatened to be lost if they did not play. Dorsett was at risk to possibly lose over $3 million in annuity payments if he did not cross. He stated in the *New York Times*, "I had no choice but to come in because of my financial situation. I am still one hundred percent behind my teammates and the cause of the strike." Dorsett would, however, practically beg head coach Tom Landry not to play him in the replacement games. Twenty-one Cowboy players crossed the picket line, with only Cosbie and Walls signed to annuity contracts not crossing. Cosbie, the team player representative, stated, "We stayed together for all of fifteen minutes."

The replacement games would be received in very different fashions, although most were not positive. Only 12,370 people witnessed the Jets hosting the Cowboys in their first replacement game. In the *New York Times* Dave Anderson described a game where "imposters in Dallas Cowboy uniforms grounded the wingless Jets." He pointed out in the article that Tex Schramm had promised competitive, exciting games, but described the Cowboys/Jets replacement game as "more compost than competitive." The union would, however, be dealt a blow during the second week of replacement games when a crowd of 61,230 would show up in Denver for the Broncos Monday-night game against the Raiders. The crowd was by far the largest to watch a replacement game, attracting approximately 20,000 more fans than the next-largest crowd. Mark Heisler would write in the *Los Angeles Times* that the game "was played in a din that suggested that maybe the locals haven't even figured out there is a strike." Fans would have signs at the game that read "Elway, K-Mart is Hiring," and "We STILL Hate the Raiders."

Defections across the picket line continued throughout the strike. Ten days into the strike forty-nine players had crossed. The rule established by the owners was that if a player was back in camp by Wednesday, he would be eligible to play in Sunday's game and receive his paycheck. After losing over

$56,000 a week, Lawrence Taylor eventually crossed the picket line to play in the Giants' final game with replacement players, a 6-3 loss at Buffalo. Taylor explained in the *New York Times,* "I feel the real reason is that the Giants are losing and I'm losing a lot of money." He added, "Each guy has to do basically what he wants to do. It was very frustrating watching instead of playing." All total, more than 260 players would cross the picket line.

The regular NFL players would finally return to work after a twenty-four-day holdout on Thursday October 15, 1987, without a new collective bargaining agreement. Even though the strike ended in time for the games on Sunday, the owners would argue that the players were retuning after the Wednesday deadline and instead chose to use the replacement players for a third weekend of games. For example, after two weeks of replacement games, the entire Washington Redskins team had voted to return to work. The players did not report by the Wednesday 1:00 deadline, however, and did not play in the final replacement *Monday Night Football* game against the Cowboys, a game that featured the Dallas crowd actually cheering for the replacement players and booing the regular Cowboys players who had defected.

Management's decision of not having the regular players be allowed to play and having replacement players still be used in games for a third week would be a major disappointment for Rozelle. Upon hearing that the regular players were not going to be allowed to play, Paul Tagliabue, at the time the league's primary outside counsel, recalls receiving a call from Rozelle, who asked him if he thought the owners' refusal to allow the players to return would ultimately lead to them being held libel to pay damages for keeping them out. Tagliabue indicated to Rozelle that he thought the owners would be held libel, a different legal opinion than what the attorneys for the management council had been telling the owners. After a long administrative trial by the National Labor Relations Board five years later, the NFL teams had to pay approximately $30 million to the players in lost salary plus interest for that weekend. The league also provided approximately $60 million in reimbursements to the television networks.

On the same day that the players agreed to return, the Players Association filed an antitrust lawsuit against the league in federal court in Minnesota challenging the college draft and the first refusal/compensation system restricting free agency for veteran players. The union also filed a grievance with the National Labor Relations Board, claiming that the owners did not bargain in good faith. Upshaw stated, "We started the bargaining process on April 20 and on April 23 the owners sent out a memo about getting a scab season ready." Rozelle would comment on the end of the strike, stating, "Obviously I would have much preferred to see a bargaining agreement. That would have eliminated more litigation, but everyone realized litigation was always possible."

With lawsuits pending to try to end the stalemate on free agency, the union was presented with three proposals, but would reject them all resulting in yet another bargaining impasse. The NFL owners would eventually unilaterally institute a limited free-agency system called "Plan B" where teams could "protect" or "restrict" thirty-seven players, but players not on that list were free to sign with other teams without any compensation being awarded. The Players Association would continue its free-agency battle in court by filing an additional lawsuit that the Plan B system was also too restrictive and in violation of antitrust law.

Rozelle would try to bring both parties together to come to an agreement on a deal prior to his retirement in 1989, but none would be reached. Upon taking over as commissioner, Rozelle would express to Paul Tagliabue that a priority needing to be addressed was the league's governance and committee structure in relation to labor. Tagliabue indicates that Rozelle conceded that as commissioner he had been too hands-off and in reality the commissioner could not be neutral. Tagliabue recalls Rozelle telling him "it would be better to shape yourself, than have the courts [do it]." Tagliabue would make it a priority to bring about labor peace between the owners and players when he became the commissioner in 1989.

In September 1992 the players would win a verdict in a Minneapolis federal court on the Plan B issue, with the jury finding that the system was a violation of antitrust law and more restrictive than it needed to be to achieve competitive balance. It would not be until January 1993 that a settlement of the many other lawsuits would be reached and the players and owners would reach an agreement on a new seven-year collective bargaining agreement. The settlement was a compromise, with the owners agreeing to free agency, but the players agreeing to a salary cap. On June 29, 1993, the new collective bargaining agreement was officially signed, the first agreement between the NFL's owners and the Players Association since the strike ended in 1982.

Overall, not having any law background, Rozelle had trouble in dealing with the labor issue and was not as comfortable in that environment as he was with the concepts of marketing, public relations, and television. In having the management council handle negotiations with the Players Association, his lack of involvement created a vacuum of strong, credible leadership on the labor issue. Rozelle tried to stay out of the labor issue because he thought the commissioner's role was as the steward of the game and that he was the commissioner of the players as much as the owners, even though he was elected by the owners. With the management council bargaining on behalf of the owners and his hands being tied, it was clearly one of the more frustrating parts of his tenure as commissioner.

CHAPTER 14

Another Rival League: The USFL

To complicate matters for Rozelle and the league, coinciding with the NFL players' strike of 1982 and the Raiders relocation to Los Angeles was the formation of the United States Football League (USFL). This was not the first time that a labor problem and the emergence of a new league occurred simultaneously. While the work action of the NFL players was taking place in 1974, the World Football League (WFL) was planning its existence. Super Bowl IV between the Kansas City Chiefs and the Minnesota Vikings had been the last game played between the NFL and AFL, but the merged NFL would have only three complete seasons unchallenged before October 1973 when the WFL officially announced that it would begin play in the summer of 1974.

The architect of the WFL was Gary Davidson, an attorney from California who had already been instrumental in challenging more established sports leagues by forming the American Basketball Association (ABA) and the World Hockey Association (WHA). As described in David Harris's book *The League: The Rise and Decline of the NFL*, Davidson, in forming the ABA and WHA, had "subscribed all the new franchises, saving one for himself, and established the league with a public relations coup, usually a raid on the existing league for celebrated players. Then Davidson sold his own franchise on the inflated bull market and headed for his next venture. In the case of the World Football League, Davidson peddled his Philadelphia Bell in late 1973, making some $600,000 profit without spending a dime."

The WFL began play in 1974 with twelve teams. Its original goal was to expand in five years to twelve other cities throughout the world, creating a twenty-four-team league with twelve teams in one American division, and twelve international teams comprising another division. With the NFL also engaged in talks of expansion, Davidson had threatened to sue the NFL if it decided to expand into any of the WFL cities. To not directly compete with the NFL, the WFL season would begin in late July and culminate with the "World Bowl" being played prior to the beginning of the NFL playoffs. WFL games were also to be played during the week on Wednesday and Thursday nights.

The WFL would have a very tumultuous inaugural season. Attendance for the first week of the season in July 1974 averaged 43,000. A *Sports Illustrated* article, however, exposed that the attendance figure was misleading because many free tickets were given out. The article, by Joe Marshall, who later became the WFL's public relations director in 1975, stated, "The Philadelphia Bell, which the league admits is its weakest franchise, attracted 55,000 people to JFK Stadium for a game with the Portland Storm. That figure included about 10,000 freebies and many others had tickets on some kind of discount deal." The quality of play was also an issue, with only two of the twelve teams scoring more than seventeen points in the opening week. By the autumn, the WFL was in financial difficulty. Franchises in Detroit and Jacksonville folded after fourteen games, teams originating in New York and Houston moved in midseason to Charlotte and Shreveport respectively, and the Chicago team forfeited its final game of the season. Davidson was replaced after one year as commissioner.

One man who would emerge as the most serious threat to the NFL was John Bassett, the wealthiest of the WFL owners. Bassett was familiar with the sports business, having owned teams in the Canadian Football League (CFL) and the WHA, and had initially desired to place a team in his hometown of Toronto but was blocked by the Canadian government. Bassett chose Memphis as the location for his franchise, merely changing the name of the team from the Northmen to the Southmen. Bassett would follow through on Davidson's original idea of raiding NFL players when, after completing the 1974 season for the Miami Dolphins, Larry Csonka, Jim Kiick, and Paul Warfield would all sign to play with Memphis for the 1975 WFL season.

The three perennial all-stars and pivotal components of the Dolphins' Super Bowl VII and VIII championship teams would not be able to save the fledgling league. Even after the development of a revised economic plan by new commissioner Chris Hemmeter, the second WFL season continued with its financial troubles. The season started with eleven teams, but after five games the Chicago Wind would fold. The entire league soon did the same, and on October 22, 1975, the WFL officially ended without completing the season.

In a press statement when the league folded, Hemmeter was very conciliatory toward the NFL, commenting, "We have the highest regard for the National Football League, and their success in promoting the game of professional football made the formation of our league possible."

From its inception and before playing one game the USFL posed a much more serious threat to the NFL than the WFL ever did. The timing aspect of the USFL's launch was advantageous, as the NFL had its players disgruntled about their salary structure and they would now have an alternative league to play in. The timing also coincided with the emergence of cable television and a need for programming to be put on these newly operating sports networks. David Dixon was the man behind the formation of the new league. Dixon's idea for the USFL to some extent grew out of the same thinking of Lamar Hunt when he began the AFL more than twenty years earlier, a love of football and a desire to capitalize on its ever-growing popularity. What made Dixon's vision unique was that this brand of football would be played in the spring. His simple logic being, if professional football is enjoyed by so many, why wouldn't these same fans want to enjoy the game throughout the year? Dixon, a New Orleans entrepreneur, had some familiarity with professional football, having helped in the construction of the Louisiana Superdome and in bringing the Saints to New Orleans.

Dixon had studied the successes of the AFL and the failures of the WFL. He immediately understood the new league needed a national television contract for revenue and exposure, something the AFL did have from the beginning but the WFL did not with network television. The WFL had only a modest syndicated cable television deal. His thinking was that in the spring there would be less competition and there were unique opportunities to receive a television contract, including cable television, something the NFL at that time had not yet acquired. Finally, Dixon knew he needed owners with the financial ability to withstand the startup and potential early years of instability. According to Jim Byrne in his book *The $1 League: The Rise and Fall of the USFL,* franchises were required to provide a $1.5 million letter of credit and pledge $6 million for operating costs over the initial three seasons.

With investors secure on May 11, 1982, the USFL announced the formation of its league, which would begin with twelve teams in the spring of 1983. Dixon worked intensely on securing a television deal and had reached out to Chet Simmons, then president and COO of ESPN, about the possibility of the network broadcasting the USFL's games. Simmons had worked for both ABC and NBC as a producer when each network had covered the AFL, and he was closely monitoring the USFL's development. With the USFL's investors so impressed by his knowledge and credibility, they soon entertained the thought of Simmons being named commissioner.

The USFL was talking to both ABC and NBC about airing a package of games on network television, while continuing to negotiate with ESPN and Turner Broadcasting about a cable package. On May 24, 1982, an agreement was reached with ABC Sports where ABC would pay the USFL $9 million for the broadcast rights to twenty-one games in the 1983 season. The contract also gave ABC the rights to the 1984 season at $9 million and network options for 1985 at $14 million and 1986 at $18 million. The ABC contract required that the USFL field teams in the three largest television markets (New York, Los Angeles, and Chicago) and in at least four of the five other top-ten television markets. The USFL would indeed begin with eight of its twelve teams in the nation's top ten television markets. On June 17, a broadcast contract with ESPN was finalized giving ESPN the rights to televise thirty-four games on Saturday and Monday nights for $4 million dollars. ESPN would pay $7 million for broadcast rights for 1984. These television contracts yielded approximately $1.2 million per team in the first year. In the interim, on June 14, Simmons was officially announced as commissioner of the USFL.

Clearly Pete Rozelle and the NFL owners could recognize the instant economic stability attained through the USFL's two television contracts causing the actions of the new league to be closely monitored. The NFL could also recognize that the cost of being in the professional football business was about to rise, much as it had when there was intense competition with the AFL. It was a situation that many of the NFL owners had experienced. Steve Ehrhart, former assistant counsel and executive director of the USFL, claims the relationship between the leagues started as "an uneasy truce, but the leagues were quickly forced to be competitors." With the USFL offering new jobs and opportunities, some assistant coaches would be hired away from the NFL.

With some of the economic stability objectives secure, the league still feared games being played in empty stadiums, which would look bad on television. From the outset, David Dixon knew that the USFL had to have quality players and coaches and games played in legitimate, major league stadiums in order to appear credible. Playing in the same stadiums as many of their NFL counterparts would also cause some friction. For example, Jack Kent Cooke, owner of the Washington Redskins, was not pleased when an announcement advertising season tickets for the USFL's Washington Federals was made during a Redskins game at RFK Stadium. The USFL would attract two former NFL head coaches who had led their teams to the Super Bowl, George Allen, head coach of the Redskins in Super Bowl VII, and Red Miller, head coach of the Broncos in Super Bowl XII. Obtaining players would be more difficult, and more expensive.

On the issue of acquiring players, Dixon felt there was an ample supply of talented players available. One idea of Dixon to arouse fan interest was to have a territorial allocation system of players, where teams filled their rosters with players who had played college football in that geographic region. Dixon's philosophy for the USFL in terms of acquiring players was explained to William Oscar Johnson in *Sports Illustrated*. He commented, "I've said from the very start that the best way for us to operate is *not* to go after the NFL's veterans and superstars. We will not try to sign a Bradshaw, a Campbell, a Payton. The price is too high. The risk is too high. Our first-year payroll is going to be full of first-year players or their equivalent. No retreads. No rejects. We are going to create our own stars." Carl Peterson left working for the Philadelphia Eagles to become the general manger for the USFL's Philadelphia Stars. He claims the early philosophy for the USFL was "not to go head-to-head with the NFL, but build the league through its own future stars."

The USFL would claim a quick victory when in August 1982, still months before playing its first game and before many teams had hired their head coaches, the Chicago Blitz signed Tim Wrightman, the third-round pick of the Chicago Bears, to officially became the first player to sign with the USFL. The battle for players began to escalate on January 4, 1983, when the USFL held its first draft. The timing of the draft was four months ahead of the NFL's annual draft, allowing the drafted players to immediately begin getting paid if they signed contracts with the USFL. The first pick of the USFL draft was Dan Marino, taken by the Los Angeles Express. While Marino would later sign with the Miami Dolphins, other prominent college players including the number-two pick of the USFL draft, Tim Spencer, a running back from Ohio State selected by the Chicago Blitz, and the fourth pick, Craig James, a running back from SMU selected by the Washington Federals, signed with the USFL. Spencer was the first USFL-drafted player to sign, agreeing to a contract only three days after being selected on January 7. James would sign on January 11. The league also signed Anthony Carter, wide receiver from Michigan, and Kelvin Bryant, running back from North Carolina, players that were expected to be high-round picks in the NFL Draft that spring.

The credibility of the USFL in terms of its players would increase and tensions with the NFL about player recruitment escalate when Steve Ehrhart received a telephone call on January 5, 1983, from Jack Manton, calling on behalf of junior running back Herschel Walker. Manton indicated that the 1982 Heisman Trophy winner was ready to leave the University of Georgia. Still desiring a marquee name, the USFL actively pursued the star running back. The USFL owners were so excited about the possibility of Walker joining their league that they were prepared to waive the rule against underclassmen being eligible to play professional football. Walker himself would soon after speak with Ehrhart, who counseled Walker about the possibility of him losing his final year of eligibility at Georgia, as the NCAA rules prohibited a player from even negotiating a professional contract.

With regard to the Walker situation, the USFL was also aware that a year earlier Walker had talked about the possibility of initiating an antitrust lawsuit against the NFL because of the NFL's policy that did not allow the league to sign undergraduates. The case would never be brought, but the possibility of a lawsuit against a league that had not played a game was of great concern to the USFL. Chet Simmons, USFL commissioner, stated in the *New York Times*, "Our position by then was that we would not want to take a court challenge on this issue."

The USFL had initially planned to follow the same rule as the NFL of not permitting underclassmen. Simmons, however, defined Walker as a "special case" in the USFL, circumventing the rule against signing underclassmen. Simmons stated, "We felt it would be fruitless to maintain our rules if we were living in the real world." George Vecsey would editorialize in the *New York Times* that the USFL changed its policy "because it does not have time to be nice. Economics, not ethics, are in control here." The league even allowed Walker to choose the team that he would play for. Walker expressed his interest in playing in the New York market where the commercial endorsement potential was at its greatest. The USFL owners voted unanimously to waive any eligibility rules and assign Walker's rights to the New Jersey Generals. The Generals would simply forfeit their first-round pick in 1984. On February 23, 1983, Herschel Walker signed with the Generals for a total of $3.9 million over three years with incentive bonuses that could have pushed the deal to $4.5 million. The Generals would sell approximately 7,000 season tickets in the seventy-two hours after signing Walker.

Although it was clear that he preferred the USFL did not exist, initially Rozelle was not so concerned because the NFL had been through the challenges of rival leagues before and, more important, he was extremely confident in the NFL product. But if Rozelle and the NFL had previously ignored the

USFL, between the television contracts and now the Walker signing, that was clearly changing. With the Walker signing the USFL created enemies not only in the NFL, but also on college campuses all across the country because of fears that players would leave their universities early. Several universities were threatening to not allow USFL scouts to their campuses. The NFL policy had been that college players were eligible for the draft when they had graduated, finished their undergraduate football eligibility, or five years from the entry of their class in college. From the NFL perspective, Rozelle indicated that he had no plans to change the league's policy toward underclassmen and that no NFL owners had urged him to do so. Rozelle was quoted by George Vecsey, stating, "I care about our relationship (with the universities). It works well for us not to draft juniors and sophomores. We get cooperation from them. I would not want to change it."

Rozelle's fear was once again not only the singular act of Walker signing, but much like his concern with Davis moving the Raiders, what else that act might lead to. In the case of the Walker signing it was a concern that signing underclassmen would become the USFL's permanent policy. Rozelle testified before the United States Senate in hearings about collegiate players being eligible to become professional athletes. He explained that if signing underclassmen became a consistent behavior for the USFL, "it would create a situation for the National Football League, if all of the name players were going into another league, that would cause pressures to change our policy." He would also point out that there were certainly historical periods where the NFL would have benefited from making popular underclassmen eligible to play. For example, at the height of its battle with the AFL in 1965, the NFL had pledged not to sign college seniors until the completion of all of their games, including bowl games. Rozelle was empowered to discipline any team up to as much as the loss of an entire draft for violation of this pledge.

Even with the signing of Walker and some other notable players, and having some coaches with credible experience, there was still much skepticism about the USFL succeeding. Paul Zimmerman of *Sports Illustrated* wrote not only of the new league, but the new concept, spring football. He asked, "Is America really ready for this? Are we a nation of football junkies, ready to be hooked by one superstar, a few notables of lesser magnitude and 500 guys named Marvin?"

Walker and the Generals would debut on March 6, 1983, against the Los Angeles Express on ABC in the Los Angeles Coliseum, the site of so many historic NFL moments, including Super Bowl I, the culmination of the Dolphins' perfect season in Super Bowl VII, and on a personal level where Rozelle had seen his first professional football game and worked as general manager of the Rams. The opening weekend would be a success, with an average attendance of 39,170 and crowds of over 45,000 in Arizona and Denver. The USFL also received strong television ratings on ABC for week one, earning a 14.2 rating which was comparable to NFL regular-season ratings. While ratings would decline to an average of 6.2 on ABC and 3.2 on ESPN, and attendance numbers would decrease throughout the year, there were other moments of success that the USFL could point to, such as the Michigan Panthers attracting over 60,000 for a playoff game at the Pontiac Silverdome. Overall, the inaugural USFL season was one to build on, with an average attendance of just under 25,000 per game, and Denver averaging over 41,000.

The USFL would quickly expand from twelve to eighteen teams for the 1984 season, adding franchises in: Houston, Jacksonville, Memphis, Oklahoma, Pittsburgh, and San Antonio. The interesting aspect of the Pittsburgh franchise was that it represented a family competition with the NFL, as the owner of the Maulers was Edward Debartolo Sr., father of the San Francisco 49ers owner. To some degree the expansion would dilute the product; the USFL received exposure on television, but on some occasions didn't have many quality matchups to broadcast. The second season would bring other big-name signings, as established players were now leaving the NFL for the USFL. For the 1984 season, notable NFL stars including Doug Williams, quarterback of the Tampa Bay Buccaneers, and Joe Cribbs, running back of the Buffalo Bills, would jump to the USFL. Doug Williams would explain in his autobiography, "Playing in the USFL was just an opportunity to continue my football career. I would have played for any team or any league that was willing to pay me what I was worth." He added, "What I liked best about the USFL was that it created more jobs in professional football. More opportunities for players, more for coaches."

The USFL also had some success signing prominent players even after they were drafted by the NFL in 1983. Gary Anderson, first-round pick of the San Diego Chargers, and Jim Kelly, first-round pick of the Buffalo Bills, would both sign to play in the USFL. The league also added Steve Young for an astonishing forty-three-year $36 million deal and Oklahoma-dropout running back Marcus Dupree for $6 million. Mike Rozier, 1983 Heisman Trophy–winning running back from Nebraska signed with the USFL's expansion Pittsburgh Maulers for $3 million. From the beginning the thought was for fiscal discipline on the part of the USFL owners so that player salaries would not escalate faster than revenues. The original design called for a salary structure total-ing $1.6 million per club for players. This presented a contradiction in some respects, as the USFL also knew it needed top talent to appear credible and the plan was that each team by 1984 was to have four star players. The com-petitiveness between the owners to win would soon begin to escalate salaries far quicker than originally planned. Carl Peterson explains that when some owners in the USFL started signing star players, other teams were forced to compete and the signing of NFL players rapidly increased. Herschel Walker had brought credibility but also escalated spending on players' salaries. Steve Ehrhart speaks about the difficulties that emerged from the dichotomy be-tween having fiscal discipline and also trying to attract star players. He says, "Once you are in the arena you have to compete or you can't survive as a triple A kind of league." Ehrhart does admit there were some different philosophies of different owners, but in his estimation, not competing for prominent players was unrealistic.

In fact, some of the USFL's modest successes would only fuel more spending and a more competitive edge on the part of people associated with the league. Ehrhart claims that the USFL would be bolstered by some newspaper reports that compared the USFL team favorably to the NFL team in a given city. For example, he points out that after the Michigan Panthers won the USFL title, a newspaper comparison of each team's players would argue that the Panthers were better than the Lions. Ehrhart contends, "The USFL was so good so quickly the threat [to the NFL] was faster than they thought." Others, however, pointed out the difficulty of trying to grow to quickly. John Bassett, owner of the Tampa Bay Bandits and former owner of the WFL's Memphis franchise that signed the Dolphins' superstars Csonka, Kiick, and Warfield from the NFL, was now a proponent of economic discipline and opposed the extravagant spending of the USFL owners, claiming in Sports Illustrated that "[owners] went to the hip too quickly." He expressed it as "crawling before we walked, walking before we ran, running before we flew."

The second year of the USFL provided more enthusiasm and extra media attention, but not from players; it would be from the Generals' new owner, Donald Trump, the successful New York real estate tycoon and owner of casi-nos in Atlantic City. Trump bought the Generals for $7 million but quickly spent another $9 million on player salaries, acquiring six NFL stars including Chiefs all-pro safety Gary Barbaro and Browns quarterback Brian Sipe. The USFL owners were often able to get great publicity from signing star play-ers. For example, Donald Trump would gain more national notoriety and press coverage from signing a prominent NFL quarterback such as Sipe than he would from opening a new building in New York City. Trump also tried signing a number of NFL players still under contract with the NFL to future contracts to play with the Generals, including Giants all-pro linebacker Lawrence Taylor. Trump offered Taylor $1 million a year to join the Generals. But Taylor, scheduled to earn $190,000 from the Giants in 1984, would instead sign a new six-year deal with the NFL team that would pay him more than $6 million, including jumping his 1984 salary to $650,000. In addition to signing its own players to longer-term contracts, the NFL would counter the USFL by holding a supplemental draft of the USFL players still under contract and increasing its roster size from forty-five to forty-nine.

The second season of the USFL would have some highlights, with an opening-day crowd in Birmingham of over 62,000 to see the Stallions face the Generals, but the average attendance for opening day would be just short of 33,000, a decrease from the previous year. The second year also saw a decline in ratings to 5.7 on ABC and 2.8 on ESPN. Still, ABC exercised its option to broadcast the league in the spring of 1985 and even offered a $175 million contract for four additional years beginning in the spring of 1986. ESPN also offered a contract worth $70 million over three years to continue broadcasting the spring league.

Trump, however, had a very clear idea of where he thought the USFL needed to go. Perhaps realizing the USFL in the spring would eventually be a failing business venture, a move to the fall had been one of Trump's objectives since his entering the league, and he raised that possibility at the first owners meeting he attended. He and many others within the USFL realized after two seasons that the league revenues could not match the escalating players' salaries. To try to increase revenues, Trump had two strategies: a new television deal and the more controversial idea of shifting the USFL to begin playing in the fall of 1986. He thought that the USFL salary battle for players was taking its toll on the NFL owners and that in direct competition with the NFL, the USFL could steal some of its television viewers and revenues as well. According to Jim Byrne in his book *The $1 League: The Rise and Fall of the USFL*, Trump thought the NFL would eventually not want to escalate the cost of the professional football business and would in fact merge some teams in the NFL, just as had been done with the AFL almost two decades earlier, with his Generals obviously being one of the teams.

On August 27, 1984, the USFL owners voted unanimously on the second ballot to move to the fall after the 1985 spring season and begin play in the fall of 1986. The USFL was now straying from its original mission of fiscally responsible, year-round football. Rozelle welcomed the USFL's move to the fall, claiming that it would remove the football saturation that might have been occurring. He was also confident that fans would simply choose the NFL over the USFL. Finally, Rozelle pointed out that any merger with the USFL was highly unlikely. He stated, "When we expand, we'd want to pick our own cities and our own owners."

To increase revenue to better compete with the NFL, Trump and the USFL also raised the issue of antitrust violations on the part of the NFL. Chet Simmons would even write Rozelle a letter, dated September 13, 1984, and copied to all of the USFL and NFL team owners, about the USFL's intentions to move to the fall and warning the NFL not to interfere. In the letter Simmons wrote, "Because of the present dominant competitive position of the NFL in professional football, the reaction of the NFL and its teams to this competition will be of great importance to the USFL and its owners." Simmons outlined five areas of concern that the USFL owners had regarding the NFL behavior toward the league: network television, stadium facilities, game schedules, player contracts, and media relations. The prominent concern was the issue of television, with Simmons writing, "Due to the present dominant position of the NFL as the provider of professional football product to television networks in the fall, any conduct by the NFL or its team owners which threatens the position of these networks with the NFL for present or future NFL broadcast rights would almost certainly deny the USFL access to this essential revenue source and irreparably damage the USFL and its member teams." Simmons's letter concluded, "The position of the USFL as a new sports enterprise and the market position of the NFL make it essential to the survival of the USFL that the NFL and the NFL owners operate within the bounds of the laws and regulation which govern the conduct of business having a dominant market position."

Rozelle responded to Simmons in writing in a letter dated October 4, 1984, and copied to all of the NFL club presidents. In this letter Rozelle declared, "The USFL has experienced nothing from the NFL other than the normal aspects of interleague competition." He continued, "If the USFL does adopt a Fall format, the NFL will simply continue to do what it is fully entitled to do: attempt to remain a successful entertainment producer in a broad public entertainment market. In that market, the USFL would be just one factor along with major league baseball, college football, and other forms of entertainment." Rozelle directly addressed the issue of the USFL acquiring a television contract, writing, "The television networks will be guided, as they have always been guided, by their own interests. The NFL has neither the ability nor the desire to determine their decisions." In the last paragraph, Rozelle wrote, "as with all entertainment enterprises, the USFL's failure or success will be determined by the soundness of its business judgment." The letter concluded, "It is also becoming clearer and clearer that a treble-damage lawsuit features at least as strongly in USFL plans as does making your league a business and entertainment success." Rozelle obviously knew that the USFL was gearing up for an antitrust lawsuit should the league fail in its move to the fall, essentially blaming the NFL for its demise.

On October 16, 1984, the USFL owners would vote sixteen to one to approve an antitrust suit, with Los Angeles not allowed to vote and only Ed Debartolo Sr. of Pittsburgh, not wanting to be a part of a lawsuit against his own son, voting no. One day later, the USFL filed suit in the United States District Court in New York against the NFL for antitrust violation. Their lawsuit focused on the USFL's inability to negotiate a television contract for a fall season, claiming that the NFL was monopolizing the television revenues by being broadcast on all three major networks. The lawsuit asked the NFL be associated with no more than two networks and sought damages of $1.7 billion. The USFL would also charge the NFL with conspiring to keep the league out of Oakland and New York City.

Ernie Accorsi comments that you could see the USFL building like a mushroom cloud and a potential lawsuit coming early on. Accorsi states that the league had directed general managers to be prepared and efficient in dealing with players and that everything had to be well documented. He says the NFL was also now more prepared for litigation and adds that by this point lawyers were becoming a more prominent voice and function in league operations as a result of the Raiders litigation. Rozelle had in fact stated in the *New York Times* that he had told the clubs early on that the USFL would eventually sue the NFL. Rozelle was obviously not hoping for any potentially damaging litigation against the NFL, preferring the USFL succeed or fail on the merits of the league and not being dependent on the success of any lawsuit.

With its lawsuit against the NFL pending, the USFL would have a tumultuous third year. Despite no new additional revenue source, the recruitment of top players continued for the 1985 season, the USFL's final spring campaign. Trump signed Doug Flutie to play for the Generals, giving the USFL its third Heisman Trophy winner. Several teams were being forced to relocate, with the Washington franchise moving to Orlando and the successful-on-the-field Philadelphia franchise moving to Baltimore, no longer the home of the NFL's

Colts. The Breakers franchise would be playing in their third city in three years, playing the 1985 season in Portland after having failed in Boston and New Orleans. Rick Telander wrote in *Sports Illustrated*, "NFL teams may switch towns to make more money, but in the USFL you switch towns to keep breathing." In some cases a team would merge with another. The league had been reduced to fourteen teams for its third season, with Oakland merging with Michigan and Oklahoma with Arizona. The television ratings for the "lameduck" spring season of 1985 declined to 4.1 on ABC and 2.0 on ESPN. After the third season concluded and still awaiting commencement of the trial in 1986, there would be more mergers and franchises folding, and the league would be reduced to only eight teams. Houston would merge with New Jersey, and Denver with Jacksonville. Los Angeles, Oakland, Portland, and San Antonio would all fold. In three years the league had played in twenty-two cities with thirty-nine different principal owners. The existence of the USFL now rested solely on its antitrust lawsuit against the NFL.

CHAPTER 15

Back in Court—Again

THE GENERAL argument of the USFL at trial was that the NFL had acquired and maintained a monopoly in the professional football market. The USFL lead attorney, Harvey Myerson, explained in the *New York Times* on May 11, 1986, "We charge that they devised a plan with the specific intent to preclude competition and they implemented it." A court document filed by the NFL would argue that the "only conclusion supported by the facts and the law is that the USFL's 'damages' are the result of its own actions, and that the antitrust laws are not a balm for self-inflicted injuries." In the same *New York Times* article Rozelle would be quoted saying "Our position is that we have not done anything wrong, and that has been our position from the start." The intensity of the trial and what was at stake for the NFL could not be minimized. Jay Moyer, former NFL counsel to the commissioner and executive vice president, explains that in the lawsuit, "there was no affirmative upside for the NFL. The best we could do was stave off the challenge, and avoid encouraging other 'entrepreneurs' to repeat the exercise and try to force their way into the NFL."

One of the critical allegations of the USFL was that the NFL was blocking it from acquiring a television contract in the fall. The contention of the USFL was that the NFL had pressured the three networks by threatening to not renew its television contracts with them. Thus, the argument maintains that the USFL was prevented by the NFL—and not because of its own football product—from successfully acquiring a television contract for the fall season. The USFL was pushing for the NFL to be limited to only two networks and claimed the Sports Broadcasting Act, which granted the NFL its antitrust exemption to pool broadcast rights contracts, was limited to only allow the NFL a single contract with one network.

The arguments of the NFL were that its television contracts with the three networks were not exclusionary, that there was no pressure exerted on the networks to not sign the USFL, and that the USFL's failure to secure a television contract was the independent decision of the networks themselves. After all, the NFL had signed television deals in 1982 that were scheduled to last through 1987, and the league had been with each major network since ABC started broadcasting *Monday Night Football* in 1970. The league had not sought to obtain the third network suddenly when the USFL announced its formation. It could be argued that the NFL wanted multiple broadcast partners for maximum revenue and exposure, but that strategy had become a reality in 1970 and was not designed with the intention to prevent a football league that would not exist until thirteen years later from having a television partner.

Four other points should be noted on the television argument. The first point being that Rozelle had approached both CBS and NBC about the *Monday Night Football* package prior to having ABC agree to televise the games. CBS and NBC refused simply because of their business calculation that they had other, better programming. The second point is that all three television networks wanted to broadcast the NFL as much as the NFL wanted to be on their networks. Third, at this point in its history the USFL was trying to attain a television contract in the fall for a league that was now without teams in major markets such as Chicago, Detroit, Philadelphia, Los Angeles, and Washington, D.C. The USFL's scheduled eight teams for the fall 1986 season only featured one team from a top-ten television market (New Jersey), one other team in a top-twenty market (Tampa Bay), and only one team west of the Mississippi River (Phoenix). Finally, ABC had agreed to extend its agreement with the USFL if the league continued playing in the spring, offering the USFL a four-year, $175 million contract for spring football beginning in 1986. ESPN had also agreed to extend its contract with the USFL if the league continued playing in the spring.

Al Davis and the Raiders were excluded from being named as defendants in the lawsuit. Harvey Myerson explained at a press conference on May 30, 1985, along with new USFL commissioner Harry Usher: "Al Davis and the L.A. Raiders have been victims in the past of the very violations in this lawsuit." Davis would actually testify for the USFL in the suit.

On May 14, 1986, opening arguments in the USFL lawsuit against the NFL were presented. Both lawyers delivered opening arguments that lasted close to an hour and a half. In his opening arguments for the USFL, Myerson, a showman in the courtroom, told the jury that he would produce documents that demonstrated a conspiracy on the part of the NFL to destroy the USFL. Myerson also claimed the NFL's actions were "one of the greatest wrongs perpetrated under the antitrust laws of this country." Frank Rothman, the NFL's quiet lead attorney, countered that the evidence would show that the USFL destroyed itself. He also pointed out that on the issue of television contracts there were other time slots besides Sunday afternoon or Monday night that the USFL might have tried to use to play their games in during the fall and have a network interested.

The trial would have twelve weeks of testimony and feature forty-three witnesses. One strategy of the USFL at trial was to attack Rozelle both professionally and personally. The feeling by the USFL attorneys was that if they could discredit Rozelle, they could win the lawsuit. Myerson would even refer to Rozelle as "Alvin Peter Rozelle" during the trial in some effort to speak to Rozelle's honesty. Rozelle would be questioned by Myerson for three days with the issue of television contracts being a primary line of questioning. Jay Moyer contends that the pressure on Rozelle's testimony in the case was enormous. Moyer explains that Rozelle was "given four or five extremely thick notebooks of information to study, on dozens of business situations that had occurred over nearly five decades in the NFL, and he had to be ready to handle anything that might come out of left field on cross-examination."

On the claim that the NFL had monopolized the networks, the USFL pointed out that during Rozelle's testimony before Congress in 1961 on hearings about the Sport Broadcasting Act he had claimed that if all of the networks were involved with the NFL any competitive league would "possibly be at a major disadvantage." During that same testimony in 1961 Rozelle had, however, on two separate occasions explicitly stated the proposed legislation would allow the NFL to use multiple networks if it so desired. He also testified in 1961 that at the time the NFL was only interested in one network, but that in the future a "single network may no longer be desirable, and it may become much better for the public and the league to use more than one network."

In appearing before Congress in 1966 seeking approval for the merger with the AFL, Rozelle had offered the same position by clearly testifying that the league would continue to broadcast on two networks. His rationale for the plans to have two networks televise the league had been that "because of the logistics of handling perhaps thirteen or fourteen games on a Sunday afternoon, it [the NFL] would require at least two networks." Rozelle pointed out that there would probably be a need for two networks to assure that each of the teams had all of their road games televised in their home city. On each occasion the statute that was approved by Congress did not explicitly call for a limitation on the number of television networks that the NFL could be involved with.

Myerson would try to demonstrate that Rozelle and the NFL had exerted pressure on television network executives not to sign the USFL. Rozelle stated in his first day of testimony that the USFL was never mentioned in negotiations with the networks when signing the 1982 broadcast rights contracts. He also pointed out that those contracts were agreed to before the USFL was officially announced. Rozelle did acknowledge that pressure had been applied to CBS by telling the network's executives that if they did not agree to the price suggested by the NFL that ABC and NBC would have an interest in acquiring those games. Rozelle testified, "I negotiated the best deal I could. Sometimes there is pressure in negotiations. Other times the network puts big pressure on us."

Neal Pilson, president of CBS Sports, testified in the trial that he feared losing the NFL if the network did not agree to pay the NFL's price. Pilson would acknowledge that there was pressure put on him from Rozelle and the NFL, but he clearly indicated that those negotiations had nothing to do with the USFL. Pilson also testified that CBS would consider televising the USFL in the fall only if another network was involved. The rationale was that two networks would increase the USFL's value and not leave CBS in a position where it was the sole network opposing the NFL, perhaps with some fear that the NFL might then treat its other broadcast partners more favorably. Pilson testified, "After we applied production costs and if we deducted the rights fees and took what we felt was a reasonable profit margin, I didn't think there was enough money available for USFL demands."

Harry Usher, USFL commissioner, would testify that he was told by ABC Sports president Roone Arledge, that Arledge had received a "negative reaction from the NFL for putting the USFL on initially." In his testimony Arledge would deny that he or ABC was ever pressured by the NFL with respect to the USFL. Arledge claimed that ABC's having no interest in broadcasting the USFL in the fall was due to the league's "deteriorating image." The only admission on the point of the NFL pressuring the networks that Myerson could get was from Jim Spence, a former ABC executive, who testified that the NFL indicated to him that the league was "less than enamored" with ABC when it signed the USFL for its spring seasons. Spence would, however, add he did not recall that any NFL official had directly expressed displeasure to him. In the trial the USFL even charged that the NFL had given ABC unattractive games for its *Monday Night Football* telecasts because of its association with the USFL.

In conjunction with the arguments claiming the intentional monopolizing of television networks by the NFL, Myerson and the USFL also claimed that the NFL intentionally tried to learn of ways to destroy the USFL. Myerson described a two-hour seminar conducted on February 29, 1984, by Harvard Business School professor Michael E. Porter that was attended by sixty-five NFL executives. The seminar had been arranged by Sargent Karch, an attorney for the NFL owners' management council. Jack Donlan, executive director of the management council, testified that the real purpose of the seminar was not to devise ways to damage the USFL, but to review tactics and help NFL executives better negotiate player contracts with salaries escalating because of the USFL. Only one portion of the entire seminar was the infamous "Porter Presentation." Tex Schramm offered similar testimony that the Harvard meeting was for middle-management executives with the topic of strategies for dealing with player agents. He claimed that Porter's presentation was not significant, that his ideas could not be used, and that "he paid no attention to the Porter report." Rozelle would tell the court that he had nothing to do with the planning of the seminar, that he didn't know of Porter's presentation until a week after it occurred, and that upon learning of it he became "physically ill." The NFL would also introduce a memo from Jay Moyer that the league was not interested in pursuing the suggestions provided by Porter. While some of Porter's suggestions were things the NFL was already aware of and would do, such as signing its current players to contract extensions, other ideas such as secretly moving up the NFL draft to a week after the USFL and sending undesirable players to the USFL would be deemed by most in the NFL as "largely impractical or legally impermissible."

Discrediting Rozelle was the USFL strategy from the beginning of the trial, although when being questioned by the NFL's own attorney, Rozelle explained that he had actually been offered the job of commissioner by the USFL. The USFL brought in people who had had a tumultuous history with Rozelle to testify, including Ed Garvey, who disputed that the management council and the commissioner's office were separate entities. Garvey testified, "My oft-stated position is that the management council worked for the commissioner of the NFL." Garvey would also testify that he thought three proposals made to him during the strike of 1982 were designed with the USFL in mind: moving the draft from April to January or February, having NFL teams retain the rights of players they drafted who signed in the NFL for four years, and expanding the roster from forty-five to forty-nine anytime it desired. Rothman addressed each point when questioning Garvey, getting him to confirm that the NFL had not moved up its draft date and to reveal that he had agreed to the two proposals regarding player eligibility and had signed the agreement.

Also testifying on the USFL's behalf would be Donald Trump (the only USFL owner to do so), Howard Cosell, and Al Davis. Trump testified that Rozelle had promised him an NFL franchise if the USFL remained playing in the spring and did not file an antitrust suit. Trump stated under oath, "The thing that Mr. Rozelle specifically did not want was a lawsuit on antitrust grounds." He also claimed that Rozelle told him the USFL was "doomed to failure" and that he (Trump) "should be in the NFL, not the USFL." In his testimony Rozelle did acknowledge having conversations with Trump but would explicitly deny that he told Trump he was a potential NFL owner or that the USFL would fail. Cosell, then retired from ABC Sports but writing a regular column in the *New York Daily News*, testified that Arledge had told him that ABC had been pressured by the NFL concerning its broadcasting the USFL, a charge that Arledge had previously denied during his testimony. Davis's testimony dealt with team relocation strategies and an NFL meeting that had occurred where the NFL owners reached an understanding that no team would move to New York City after the Jets joined the Giants in New Jersey. According to Tex Schramm, Davis also advanced the idea of a settlement to the NFL owners with the USFL that included the Oakland Invaders becoming a part of the NFL, which from Davis's perspective might mean that if the team succeeded the city of Oakland would drop its eminent domain lawsuit against him and the Raiders.

Rozelle later described the weekend before Davis testified as the most worried he had been during the trial about its outcome. Both Davis and Cosell had met with the attorneys for the NFL. In his meeting, Davis indicated that if he was going to be cross-examined hard he would hurt the NFL even more. He also made his pitch for a merger settlement with the USFL, calling for the NFL to absorb two teams immediately and two teams later on. Davis thought the NFL could earn approximately $40 or $50 million for each incoming franchise. Rozelle explained the events in the *New York Times*, saying, "The attorneys [for the NFL] and maybe a half-dozen of our owners were in my room at The Regency, and the attorneys were really shaken up. They told us what Davis said, and they were worried about how it would possibly affect the jury. Same thing with Howard. The owners were shaken, but they decided to hold firm. They said, 'no, don't do it. No merger.' And that was the last big push for a merger settlement." Jay Moyer explains that Rozelle had made a strong recommendation to the owners not to settle the case. He states, "Pete knew two things: that the NFL hadn't done anything wrong, and that settlement would just encourage others in the future to replicate the USFL's force-their-way-in strategy. He also had to buck up some of the owners during the roughly three months the trial lasted to stay the course. Given what these men had at stake financially, and his personal fondness for many of them, that was a lot of responsibility to shoulder, but he persevered with the courage of his convictions."

Rozelle was the final witness to testify in the trial and claimed that Trump offered to abandon the USFL if Rozelle would promise him an NFL expansion franchise in New York. Rozelle said the two men had met on March 12, 1984, at the Pierre Hotel in New York shortly after Trump had called him to have a meeting. Trump had earlier testified that the meeting was initiated by Rozelle. Rozelle would contend that at the meeting Trump informed him that he was instructed by the USFL to develop an antitrust suit against the NFL. Rozelle testified about the meeting, stating, "He [Trump] said, 'I don't want to do these things, I want an expansion team in New York for the NFL.' And he said and I'm quoting him exactly, 'I would get some stiff to buy the New York Generals.'"

On July 29, 1986, after five days of deliberation, the federal court jury of five women and one man rendered its verdict that the NFL was guilty of only one of the minor counts of antitrust violation. The jury found that the NFL's unlawful monopolization of the professional football market had injured the USFL. The jury, however, also found that the NFL's achieving of this monopoly status was not its own fault and that the USFL had engaged in behavior that largely contributed to its demise. The jury rejected the USFL's television claims, concluding that the NFL had not monopolized the television market nor attempted to do so. In doing so it found the NFL's television contracts were not an unreasonable restraint of trade and that the NFL did not interfere with the USFL's ability to obtain a fall television contract by exerting pressure on networks executives. Finally, the jury found that Pete Rozelle was not personally liable in the USFL's monopolization claim. Rozelle would state in the *New York Times*, "I am pleased with the overall result, and I am particularly happy that I was dismissed as a defendant. I feel totally vindicated." He was particularly pleased that the jury had taken his word over Trump's on the issues.

In contending that there was mismanagement by the USFL, the jury found ample evidence that the USFL failed because it did not make the necessary investments and demonstrate the patience required to bring stability, credibility, and public recognition of a professional sports league. These failures included abandoning the initial strategy of building loyalty through playing in the spring and quickly escalating the cost of business by signing prominent players. The USFL's failures culminated in a hasty move to a fall schedule with the hope of merging some of its teams into the NFL. Having many teams fold or relocate turned television networks against the league, as they would not be broadcasting games in large markets. The jury thus concluded that the networks freely chose not to purchase the USFL and that the league was trying to achieve through the courts what it could not achieve in the marketplace.

Because its demise was due to its own failures rather than intentional behavior on the part of the NFL, the USFL would be awarded damages of only $1, trebled to $3 because it was an antitrust violation. The jury was initially divided on the award, with three jurors leaning toward the USFL and three siding with the NFL. One juror, Miriam Sanchez, described the award verdict as a compromise. She said, "One dollar was all we could do, or we'd have a hung jury." Another juror, Margaret Lilienfeld, commented on the strategy of the USFL to try to turn the case into a David vs. Goliath situation. She was quoted in the *Los Angeles Times* saying that it was "brilliant on Mr. Myerson's part, but we really must be logical, mustn't we? Some of us were identifying too much with the little guy when there really aren't any little guys. The USFL is a big guy, too." She would also contend that the jury didn't find any overt pressure exerted on the networks and that it "didn't take the Porter testimony too seriously." The jurors would also speak to the discrepancy between the testimonies of Rozelle and Trump. Miriam Sanchez was quoted in the *Los Angeles Times*, saying "Trump had us completely befuddled. Why would he call Rozelle if he wasn't meeting him with some ulterior motive."

Frank Rothman, the NFL's lead attorney, commented, "The dollar verdict is an insult to the USFL. It tells exactly what the jury thought about this lawsuit. It sent a signal that it was preposterous case." Rozelle would ironically thank Donald Trump, Howard Cosell, and Al Davis for their testimony in the case. Jay Moyer adds, "All three had testified against the NFL, each for his own self-serving reasons. Each had accused Pete of trying to hurt the USFL, and he felt they had taken serious liberties with the truth in doing so. But each, in his own inadvertent way, may well have helped the NFL's defense in the long run because none of them had seemed to go over very well with most of the jurors." He summarizes, "That trial was no game. It was an exercise in survival of the NFL as the world knew it." Rozelle would give some last impressions about the trial with the USFL; in an interview in the *New York Times* printed on August 3, 1986, he stated, "I remember after the verdict standing on the courthouse steps, I faced a mob of reporters and cameras. That was probably the most difficult interview I ever had to give. It was extremely emotional because of what the trial meant to the league. It was also so important to me to be absolved from any charges, and I know how much that means to my final years as being commissioner." He added, "We're finally out of a terrible morass of ten or twelve years of litigation. I'm not saying there won't be more litigation. But I don't expect anything as serious as this. Now, we can go forward and create more harmony and togetherness and work to retain our level of popularity."

With the interest added on, the NFL would issue a check to the USFL for $3.76. The check still sits in Steve Ehrhart's desk in Memphis, uncashed. Judge Peter K. Leisure, the United States District Court judge who presided over the case did rule that the NFL had to pay the USFL just over $5.5 million in attorneys' fees and court costs, however. Ehrhart, in retrospect, concedes that moving to the fall might not have been the best idea. He also thinks the USFL might have overreached in the amount of damages it was seeking. Although on the other side of the situation, Ehrhart says he "respected that Rozelle was following the best interests of the NFL and thought he [Rozelle] was masterful in maintaining equity value of his teams." He commends Rozelle for "understanding that the USFL was a greater challenge than the public ever realized." Harvey Myerson, chief counsel for the USFL, would also offer praise of Rozelle, when quoted in *Sport* magazine stating, "He is one of the shrewdest men I have ever met. He has built that league into the most powerful and best-wired organization, politically and economically, that I've ever seen. I give him a lot of credit for having done that." Chet Simmons commented in the *NFL GameDay Program* that commemorated Rozelle's retirement, "With Pete, there was never anything personal in the competition between the leagues. When I took the job as commissioner, he wrote to me, wishing me luck and said that he looked forward to carrying on our friendship. Through all the competition, lawsuits, and court case, I don't think he ever allowed it to get to the personal level."

The verdict would be the final straw for the USFL. On August 4, 1986, the USFL decided to suspend play for that season although it planned to return in the fall of 1987. However, the USFL owners would allow its players to sign with the NFL. Jim Kelly, who had appeared on the cover of *Sports Illustrated* for its July 21, 1986, issue in a Generals jersey holding a Generals helmet, would never wear that uniform in an actual game. Harry Usher negotiated an agreement with the Players Association releasing all USFL players under contract from their obligations to the league and also releasing the USFL teams from their obligations to pay the players. The 530 USFL players with guaranteed contracts would continue to receive their USFL salaries if they chose not to play in the NFL or the Canadian Football League. To be able to sign with the NFL the players simply had to declare that option by August 13 at 10:00 a.m., eastern.

Three weeks after Jim Kelly's appearance on the cover of *Sports Illustrated*, Herschel Walker would appear on the magazine's cover for the August 14, 1986, issue putting on a Cowboys helmet with the headline, "Dallas, Here I Come." Walker, whom the Cowboys had selected in the 1985 NFL Draft with a fifth-round pick that they had acquired in a trade that sent Butch Johnson to the Oilers for Mike Renfro and the pick, would sign a five-year, $5 million contract with the Cowboys. Tex Schramm commented in Bob St. John's book, *Tex*, "I had strong feelings that the USFL would not make it on a long-range basis when we took Herschel. Some of the negative signs that had caused other leagues to fail were there. The league was killing itself by trying to pay the high salaries and not limiting itself on expenses to what it could afford. The signs just indicated the league was going in the wrong direction, and I believed we'd eventually get Walker, although not as soon as we did."

The USFL would never play again. After three seasons it had monetary losses estimated at $200 million. In the end, none of the majority owners of the original USFL teams was still the majority owner in 1986 when the planned fall schedule was cancelled after the verdict. There was, however, a USFL legacy on the NFL. The league had developed some quality players and coaches who would go on to successful NFL careers, people such as Jim Kelly and Hall of Famers, Reggie White and Steve Young. Besides the 250 players from the USFL who would make NFL rosters, rules such as the two-point conversion and challenging officials' calls with instant replay had all been used by the USFL. The USFL also helped increase NFL players' salaries. Prior to the USFL, NFL salaries were increasing at a rate of approximately 7 to 10 percent per year. During the USFL years, player salaries were more than doubling. Even players who were staying with their respective NFL teams were receiving contract extensions and dramatic increases in their pay. In fact, according to Gerald Eskenazi of the *New York Times*, NFL salaries would jump 25 percent in the first two years of the USFL and 19 percent in the third season, but only 5 percent after the USFL.

As for Rozelle, he had once again withstood a challenge, and his vision of the NFL was kept in tact. Although professional football was still the most popular sport in the country, the league had endured some negative publicity. Rozelle would tell the *New York Times*, "I wish we'd be able to stay off the labor pages and the news pages and stay on the sports pages. It's a turnoff to fans to be reading about all this stuff that's not football."

CHAPTER 16

Sad Endings

B Y T H E middle of the 1980s it was abundantly clear that the business climate of the sports world had drastically changed from the environment that Pete Rozelle had become a part of when elected commissioner of the NFL in 1960. Nobody had to explain to Rozelle that lawyers were now a major part of the sports industry, and that fact was unlikely to change. While Rozelle's vision and philosophy had been challenged in court on antitrust grounds by players, team owners, cities, and other professional football leagues throughout his three-decade career as commissioner, he had a simple belief that the issues of the league should be resolved by the parties within the league. As Rozelle told the House of Representatives when testifying in 1982, "The greatest danger lies in the use of the antitrust laws to attack the internal structure of a sports league and to permit even sports league members to second-guess every league operating principle."

Rozelle would later tell Samantha Stevenson of the *New York Times* in September 1994, "The threat of litigation has to be in every decision you make because it will be challenged by someone—a player, an owner, and a city."

In his later years as commissioner Rozelle was spending more time in court than in the office and spending more time working on trial preparations than working on his other areas of interest within the league. The nature of the traditional business relationships had also greatly changed. For example, the informality of dealing with the media had given way to a culture where every word was scrutinized by the press and the public. Because of all of these factors Rozelle was simply no longer relishing the challenges of the job with the vigor that he had demonstrated in leading the NFL to its position as the number one sports league in America.

The trials of the 1980s had clearly affected Rozelle. He didn't like his integrity constantly being attacked or his motivations for decisions being questioned. Jay Moyer explains, "Pete had to shoulder two enormous burdens: the overall responsibility for the result in very expensive and inherently risky antitrust cases, and the lead role in testifying for the NFL in court. In both proceedings, but especially in the USFL case, he had to take the stand and be cross-examined as an adverse witness for days on end about fifty years of NFL history. No one who hasn't experienced that can truly understand the toll it takes. While he came through both cases with flying colors as a witness, given what was at stake I'm convinced that the experiences, collectively, took several years off his life."

There was a visible difference in Rozelle noticed by his family and many of his close friends. His daughter, Anne Marie, recalls at one point during her wedding reception in 1988 seeing her father staring out the window as if he were looking into his future. She remembers thinking then for the first time that her father might be seriously contemplating retirement. Dick Rozelle, who says his brother rarely brought whatever problems he was having in the NFL into the family, also recalls seeing a noticeable difference during the trials. He comments that Pete took the trials very personally because of his great dedication to the NFL. Dick Rozelle explains being commissioner, "wasn't just a job to Pete." Pete Rozelle even admitted that during the trial against Al Davis he would on occasion wake up in the middle of the night and pace. A *New York Times* article on January 22, 1989, featured a headline that read "Owners Contend Rozelle is Slowing." In the article an unnamed owner commented, "There is no question in my mind it has slowed him down. There has been enormous pressure on him, and I've seen the fire leave his belly." The thought was also expressed in the same article that Rozelle's skills of persuasion and public relations were not what the league now needed as much as someone with a more extensive legal background. A small group of powerful NFL executives, Hess, Mara, Modell, Rooney, and Schramm had gathered earlier in 1989 to discuss relieving Rozelle of some of his responsibilities. Rozelle learned of the meeting, but the discussion would not go any further or to the ownership as a whole. At this point even Rozelle, himself, confessed, "It is much harder now to run the league."

More than the job itself, personal troubles began to arise. The Rozelle family would suffer a tragedy in January 1989, when Rozelle's stepson, Jack

Kent Cooke II, died in Los Angeles at the age of twenty-six. The news reached
Pete and Carrie Rozelle on the Friday before Super Bowl XXIII in Miami. In
addition, a long-time habit of Rozelle's also began talking its toll—although
he had quit smoking and gained some weight after years of cigarette smoking,
his health was starting to fail and become more of a concern. Rozelle had
even suffered a mini-stroke, and Anne Marie recalls spending time with him,
quizzing him over and over about league information before a Super Bowl
press conference that he insisted on attending.

In March 1989 the NFL convened in Palm Desert, California, for its annual
league meeting. The meeting would produce a renewal of the NFL's instant
replay system, a strengthened policy regarding anabolic steroids, and one stun-
ning announcement. Encouraged after several conversations with Carrie and
Anne Marie, on March 22, 1989, in a meeting with the NFL owners, the sixty-
three-year-old Pete Rozelle announced his retirement as commissioner of the
National Football League. As Rozelle fought through tears to announce his
retirement to the owners, two emotions would dominate the room: incredible
sadness and complete shock. Rozelle had only told a few people of his decision.
One week prior to his announcement he did have a meeting with Wellington
Mara and Leon Hess to inform them of his decision, but the announcement
would be unexpected to most. His brother and many of his close friends,
even one of his most trusted colleagues within the league, NFL executive Joe
Browne, knew nothing of the announcement until an hour before it was made
to the owners.

For Rozelle it was an incredibly emotional day. It would be one of the most
difficult days of his life; giving up his job, no longer working with people he
cared so deeply about, and to some degree, giving up his identity.

Pat Bowlen, Denver Broncos owner, says the announcement was a
"significant shock to the vast majority of the owners." Carl Peterson recalls
his first thought was, "Oh my gosh, who could possibly replace him, he had
done so much." Upon his announcement Rozelle would receive a standing
ovation from all present in the room. Afterward, several owners approached
him, embracing him with wishes of good luck before leaving the room. Al
Davis, too, shook Rozelle's hand and embraced the departing commissioner.
Davis was quoted the next day in the *Washington Post* about his reaction, saying, "That's normal when you have an emotional feeling about a great job and
a person who has contributed a lot." Art Modell commented, "It's a sad day
for me. We've been colleagues and partners for a long time. He's the finest

commissioner sports has ever seen." Wellington Mara added, "Pete Rozelle will be the standard by which all commissioners will be measured."

Upon Rozelle's retirement, each NFL team was earning $17 million per year in television revenue.

After three decades on the job an explanation for his decision to retire was probably not necessary. However, one reason that Rozelle did not publicly mention or emphasize was his health. Pat Summerall claims that in addition to the trials that had taken so much time away from the office and his family, it was the health problems that ultimately lead to Rozelle's retirement. Summerall declares that although the business was different, "football would not have changed enough for him, football would have never passed him by if it wasn't for his health."

After meeting with the owners, Rozelle would hold a press conference and inform the media of his retirement. Rozelle explained to the press, "I decided in October, but I didn't want to become a lame-duck commissioner. Even my close personal friends did not know. It's going to be a shock to them and that hurts me. I just think you only go through life once. I just think it is the overall period of time that has accumulated." Rozelle would offer one reason for his retirement, stating, "When you talk about three trials in five years, it seemed to never end. And we had to do our job on top of that. These have not been pleasant times for the owners, myself or a lot of people close to football." He continued, "I wanted everything solved on a high note with no outstanding litigation. But in October I just realized it's not going to be like that anymore. There is always going to be something." As he told the press, Rozelle simply wanted "to enjoy more free time, stress-free time." The press conference ended with Rozelle, a person who always wanted to convey a public sense of calm and perfectionism, finally demonstrating a small crack in the facade when, after desperately trying to hold it in, he got choked up and fought back tears before leaving the podium to an ovation by the members of the media.

Rozelle would elaborate on his decision to retire in an article by Paul Zimmerman in *Sports Illustrated*. He stated, "You're playing defense all the time rather than working on anything constructive. My eyes were bloodshot. I wasn't getting enough rest. I looked bad, felt bad. I was smoking two packs of cigarettes a day. I asked myself, is that all there is to life—work, die, and never experience retirement? I wanted at least a few years of leisure without stress." In the same article Carrie Rozelle commented, "What you saw was the combination of fatigue plus cigarettes. He says he smoked two packs a

day, but during that period it was probably three, maybe even more. He'd
devote a whole day to depositions, to attorneys who didn't understand sports
or couldn't care less about football. He'd come home at night and go to bed
around 11:30—he always wanted to watch the eleven o'clock news—and two
hours later he'd be up roaming around, smoking one cigarette after another,
working things out on a legal pad."

In the press conference announcing his retirement Rozelle also reflected
on what he thought were his major accomplishments and what he enjoyed
about the job, particularly citing the growth of the Super Bowl. He stated,
"The most fun I had was watching the development of the Super Bowl because really the game is what it's all about. I felt a high on each Sunday
we played the Super Bowl, with all the glitz, halftime and such." Rozelle
would later tell *Sport* magazine what his proudest accomplishments were:
"One the promotion of the league. Two, the TV aspect, the contracts we were
able to sign. Three, the growth of the Super Bowl." In 1996, he told David
Leon Moore from *USA Today* that his favorite Super Bowl was the Steelers
35-31 victory over the Cowboys in Super Bowl XIII "because of the high
scoring."

With the growth of the Super Bowl as one of Rozelle's major accomplishments, it is only fitting that the Most Valuable Player of that game now receives
a trophy adorned with his name. Paul Tagliabue, upon making the announcement of the Most Valuable Player trophy's new name commented, "No name
is more synonymous with the Super Bowl than Pete Rozelle. It was his imagi-
nation and foresight that made this great event a reality, and his guidance that
elevated the Super Bowl to an unofficial national holiday on Super Sunday."
Jim Murray would write, "Michelangelo has his David, Da Vinci his Mona
Lisa—and Rozelle has the Super Bowl."

Upon his retirement Rozelle would receive many congratulatory letters,
including one from Paul Hornung, the superstar player whom the young
commissioner once suspended. Hornung wrote to Rozelle, as quoted in his
book *Golden Boy*,

Dear Pete,
No one in the history of professional football has ever given more or been more
responsible for the popularity of the game than Pete Rozelle. Long after we're
gone, your name will stand beside the few who really made a difference . . . .
Halas, Rooney, Mara, Lombardi, Lambeau . . . . and not take a back seat. You
can rest knowing that there never was a better commissioner of any sport and

that, during your stay, professional football became the most popular sport in America. I am proud to have known you.

Sincerely,

Paul Hornung

Rozelle's retirement would not be effective until a new commissioner was selected. Lamar Hunt explained the challenge of finding Rozelle's successor as, "I guess what we are looking for is another Pete Rozelle, and we realize that it will be extremely difficult if not impossible to find." It would even be discussed to hire two commissioners who would split the duties and responsibilities. Although the selection process would be nowhere near as tumultuous as in 1960 when Rozelle was tapped to replace Bert Bell, there was still some dissention among the owners. Some of the older owners favored Jim Finks, a veteran NFL executive and then general manager of the New Orleans Saints. Some of the younger owners, who would be referred to as the "Chicago Eleven" after an initial meeting in Chicago, would favor Paul Tagliabue, the younger NFL attorney who had been active in various league functions and was a confidant and advisor to Rozelle.

When the owners met in Cleveland with tension beginning to build and no amicable solution in sight, Rozelle once again intervened, forcing the group to continue to meet until the situation was resolved. Rozelle selected two owners from each camp, Wellington Mara and Art Modell representing the group favoring Finks, and Pat Bowlen and Mike Lynn of the Minnesota Vikings representing the "Chicago Eleven" supporting Tagliabue. Dan Rooney served as the mediator between the two groups. After two hours with little progress, according to Bowlen, Rooney would eventually demonstrate support for selecting Tagliabue. Mara and Modell would concede. On October 26, 1989, Paul Tagliabue was elected commissioner of the NFL.

Bowlen explains that Rozelle liked Tagliabue and tried to stay neutral, not wanting to be outwardly orchestrating the selection of his successor, but once Tagliabue was picked, Rozelle was pleased. Bowlen recalls, "Rozelle felt the league was in a good situation, but he was still concerned with how the league would continue." With Tagliabue as commissioner, Rozelle could easily help with the transition. Tagliabue recalls that Rozelle offered him the simple advice that it is the commissioner's responsibility to do what he thinks best for the game and best for the fans. He says that Rozelle told him that when deliberating about a tough decision to "take a step back and ask, what's best for the game? What's best for the fans?" Tagliabue also recalls Rozelle offering one other piece of advice—that "success is your biggest enemy."

At 12:01 a.m., on Sunday November 5, 1989, Tagliabue would officially take over as commissioner. For the first time since that January day in 1960 when twelve owners hired the relative unknown as the "compromise candidate" to be their commissioner, Pete Rozelle was not the leader of the NFL.

Rozelle retired to Rancho Santa Fe, California, a town just north of San Diego. His first project in retirement was to oversee the building of a new Italian-style house on the land that he had purchased from former San Diego Chargers owner, Gene Klein. The house would have the ocean as a backdrop, and on a clear day one could just about see the city of San Diego. Rozelle spent his summer days at the racetrack, only a few minutes away, or helping Carrie with her film company, Reding-Rozelle Productions. He continued to indulge his love of reading newspapers, subscribing to a half dozen daily papers and having his longtime assistant, Thelma Elkjer, going out every day and picking up others that were not delivered. Rozelle also became involved in a small business, building homes and condominiums in Idaho with the person who built his house in Rancho Santa Fe.

Rozelle did continue to be a consultant to the NFL and kept daily office hours, but that often didn't require much work. Rozelle kept up with the NFL on his three television screens, often inviting friends over on an NFL Sunday. Although he was no longer commissioner, he still possessed one of the essential characteristics he had brought to the job in the first place, the devotion of a fan. Rozelle would keep in constant communication with his friends in the NFL office, bringing things to their attention that he saw watching games on television. But he offered few public statements about the league. He knew that keeping in contact with league personnel wasn't the same as being in the league office on a day-to-day basis in terms of knowing all of the facts about a particular situation.

Paul Tagliabue explains that Rozelle didn't want to even hint at giving the impression of second guessing the decisions that were being made. Out of respect for Rozelle, Tagliabue says that he would alert Rozelle about certain stories that were going to occur in the league, a gesture Rozelle appreciated. Tagliabue comments that in their conversations Rozelle was always supportive and "emphasizing what he thought was positive," for example, applauding Tagliabue when he was able to finally achieve labor peace with the Players Association. Tagliabue does say that he sought Rozelle's counsel on the decision that was made by the NFL to sell the NFC's broadcast package to the Fox network, ending its long affiliation with CBS.

Retirement would not be as fulfilling as Rozelle had hoped. His health problems, which had begun to cause him concern when retiring in 1989, had become much more serious. Rozelle developed a benign brain tumor, which he would undergo surgery to have removed in December 1993. Still recovering from the operation, Rozelle would miss attending the Super Bowl for the first time ever in 1994, when Super Bowl XXVIII was played in Atlanta between Dallas and Buffalo. Carrie Rozelle would undergo a similar surgery. Her tumor would be found to be malignant, but treated through radiation. Rozelle would tell the New York Times, "Every time I look at her, I love her so much I wish mine had been malignant."

Unfortunately, the complications from cancer for Pete Rozelle would continue, and his health quickly deteriorated. Rozelle began to lose his balance and soon needed a wheelchair to get around. He later had trouble speaking. But he remained in possession of his mental faculties, and he courageously fought his illness. Even during the last months of his life he continued going out to restaurants, and he insisted on going to the Republican National Convention in 1996 to support the party's vice presidential nominee, his good friend Jack Kemp.

In his last months, Anne Marie would often sleep on the floor next to his bed. When her father woke they would talk, Anne Marie telling him about his grandchildren or reflecting on a story about her growing up and taking the opportunity to thank him for all his sacrifices, support, and love and telling him how much she appreciated it all. She also recalled her father telling her one day when sitting at the breakfast table and going over things, including funeral arrangements, that he stated, "I'm very lucky. I've had an incredible life. I couldn't have asked for more."

With his health quickly deteriorating, Rozelle's closest friends would receive telephone calls urging them to visit. People such as Joe Browne, Frank Gifford, Jay Moyer, Tex Schramm, and Paul Tagliabue would fly to California to see their dear friend—and, to many, their hero, whom they owed so much—one final time. Jay Moyer recalls that he had been speaking with Rozelle on a fairly regular basis, but with his condition deteriorating rapidly, he received a call from Thelma Elkjer, who told Moyer, "I know you want to see him before he goes, and he wants to see you and Terry [Moyer's wife, whom Rozelle had been quite fond of]." In this conversation Elkjer would tell Moyer, "I think you'd better come now." Moyer and his wife flew to San Diego. Moyer recalls, "It was a very warm, very personal, and very poignant visit. Pete knew exactly where he stood—that he didn't have much longer to go. He knew too, what he had accomplished professionally, and I think he was totally at peace with his life except for his concern for his family he would leave behind." Moyer adds, "When Terry and I got into our car to leave, neither of us was dry eyed. But we agreed that however intensely sad we were, we wouldn't have missed the opportunity to say goodbye for anything."

In his final visit with Rozelle, Paul Tagliabue would ask him who he thought was the greatest player in NFL history. Tagliabue recalls Rozelle's response, "You can't pick one. There have been so many great ones. But the luckiest thing the NFL has had going for it is that the great players on the field have also been great individuals and great contributors to their communities."

Frank Gifford describes his final visit with Rozelle. The two were watching NFL games on Rozelle's bank of television sets and Gifford was thinking how amazing it was what Rozelle had built. Gifford would lean over to Rozelle and tell him, "Pete, you have to be so proud." Gifford, says that Rozelle "had trouble speaking, but he did give a big smile. He knew what I was saying."

On December 6, 1996, Pete Rozelle died.

At his memorial service in Los Angeles, Anne Marie eulogized, "I still have many things my father has given me. His letters, his desk, and the pearl necklace he gave me on my sixteenth birthday. These material things are very special because they remind me of him. But they are not the things I hold most dear. I'm most grateful for the real inheritance my father left me. His sense of humor, his compassion for others, his integrity, his belief that your word is your bond, his conviction that if you're a good person, you'll succeed. And now, I'm trying to live up to his standard. And I'm trying to pass those values onto my own children, Miles and Alexandra, his grandchildren."

Several of the most prominent sports columnists across the country would offer their praise of Rozelle the commissioner and Rozelle the man. Michael Wilbon wrote in the *Washington Post*, "In nearly 30 years as commissioner of the NFL, Rozelle guided, influenced, affected, changed, directed, negotiated and generally led pro football to absolute preeminence in sports, which in turn revolutionized the culture of sports and entertainment as we know it. It's virtually impossible to exaggerate his place in the history of modern sports." Gordon Forbes wrote in *USA Today*, "Rozelle never lost his special touch. Never lost his temper. Never quit being a fan in front of his home TV sets. Never tired of propping a chair backward in some press room and making you feel important with his inflections and that Rozelle smile." For all of his tremendous vision and business savvy, *Sports Illustrated* senior NFL writer Paul Zimmerman said perhaps the most important characteristic that contributed to Rozelle's success was that he was "at heart a fan, the best kind, the kind driven by a love of the game."

On the Sunday after Rozelle's death the Green Bay Packers defeated the Denver Broncos 41-6 in front of over 60,000 fans at Lambeau Field. William Charland wrote in the *Christian Science Monitor* that there were many heroes to celebrate who played in that game for the Packers, "but the real hero of the day for many NFL observers was former league commissioner Pete Rozelle." Charland would contend, "Rozelle was remembered as the foremost champion of revenue sharing in professional sports. Without his pioneering efforts to incorporate this concept during a 29-year career as NFL commissioner, it's doubtful Green Bay, Wis. (population 96,466) would have a pro football team at all." In the article Charland quoted Robert Harlan, president of the Green Bay Packers, who stated, "There are two reasons we can exist in this market. The first is that, back in the 1960s, Pete Rozelle convinced the NFL owners to share their profits. Today 84 percent of the Packers' income comes from revenue sharing." (Harlan cited the salary cap as the second reason.)

Just over one month after Rozelle's death, in Super Bowl XXXI, it would be the Green Bay Packers and New England Patriots who would have the name "Pete" in script on their helmets. Green Bay would win the game, 35-21, and achieve its first Super Bowl championship since Vince Lombardi.

The Vision—The Legacy

N 1985, when marking his twenty-fifth anniversary as commissioner, Pete Rozelle was voted into the Pro Football Hall of Fame. In his acceptance speech Rozelle provided some perspective on his responsibilities, stating, "The commissioner's job, of course, is very unique. You are hired by the owners, but you are called upon to make decisions that can affect them. You can't please everyone, every time." He added, "You simply have to do what you think in your judgment is in the best interest of the game." If Pete Rozelle's judgment over his three-decades as commissioner of the NFL is the final evaluative criterion, it provides substantial evidence of an extraordinary, unprecedented career. Rozelle understood exactly what he wanted to do, where he wanted to take the NFL, and he did it. He was essential in helping build the premier sports league in America, if not the world. Perhaps his greatest achievement can simply be summed up in the fact that people enjoy the game of professional football more because of Pete Rozelle.

The story of Pete Rozelle as commissioner of the NFL is one of a man with a vision, who consistently fought courageously and with conviction to implement and preserve that vision. Rozelle had a philosophy of what a sports league should look like: that the interests of the league always come first. He knew that great things could be accomplished through a collective endeavor. Much of his decision making emanated from his trying to execute and implement this league-first vision. Ideas that are customary now, such as collectively selling broadcast rights to the highest-bidding network as a way to greatly increase revenues, sharing those television revenues equally among all teams, and consistently emphasizing the need for competitive balance, were revolutionary at the time.

Paul Tagliabue explains that Rozelle "had a clarity about what the NFL stood for in terms of sports competition." He adds, "There was clarity about purpose. There was a feeling of team. A feeling of we." David Stern, commissioner of the NBA, says Rozelle was very proud of developing the system of television revenue being shared equally and then extending that economic system to all marketing and licensing agreements. Stern says that through Rozelle's ideas and through his own experience as commissioner of the NBA for more than twenty years, he is "more convinced than ever that we sell competition. Fans have to believe, if well managed, teams can compete and represent them well."

The basic principles of league-first, revenue sharing, competitive balance, and television exposure never changed from the beginning to the end of Rozelle's tenure as commissioner. In fact, Rozelle's business model for a sports league in terms of implementing rules to create competitive balance and the economic system of sharing national television revenue is now the standard practice for all professional sports leagues. Pat Bowlen describes Rozelle's biggest accomplishment as getting the larger markets to equally share television revenue. He calls that accomplishment "the linchpin that made the NFL so successful compared to other sports." Red McCombs, former owner of the Minnesota Vikings, explains that Rozelle "is the reason for so much of the financial success of the league. It is the best financial model for any sports business."

Frank Deford, *Sports Illustrated* writer and reporter for HBO's *Real Sports*, states, "His ability to get the strong big-city owners to give up their preeminent rights for the socialistic good of all was simply brilliant. That could only have been achieved with a combination of persuasion and charm. It may be the single most impressive achievement of any sports commissioner, anytime." In recognizing Rozelle as the most powerful person in sports for the twentieth century, Paul Attner wrote in the *Sporting News*, "Rozelle's obsession about competitive balance, where there would not be obvious haves and have-nots, where every club could envision playoffs and championships, has produced, year after year, a dependable audience delivery system that pleases television and keeps stadiums full in virtually every league city." Rozelle himself told the Hall of Fame audience during his induction ceremony that sharing television money created "the base to compete. The balance has to be scouting, management, coaching, and players. That is the way football should be. It should not be predicated just on money."

In the present day NFL the idea that any team can win in a given year certainly exists. One example that could be used to demonstrate the competitive balance of the NFL is in the league's scheduling. The NFL tries to showcase what it thinks are its best teams in its prime-time games; however, predicting which teams will be good in November can be difficult when the schedule is formulated the previous spring. Because of the competitive balance of the league, for three consecutive years the Super Bowl Champion (the Rams, Ravens, and Patriots—in the first year they won the Super Bowl) did not appear on ABC's *Monday Night Football* during the regular season in the year they won their championships. Carl Peterson, general manager of the Kansas City Chiefs comments that because of Pete Rozelle all teams have the tools to compete. He explains, "What makes our league so extraordinary is that it is legitimate to say at the beginning of the season regardless of the size of your market we have a chance to go to the big show." Peterson says it was Rozelle who convinced owners that "the most important thing is the league, the second most important thing is your franchises."

Visionaries are always looking to the future and the next opportunity; Rozelle was no different. He was always interested in the next frontier for the NFL. Rozelle knew that the frontier often began with television. Knowing that it is the league's greatest source of revenue and exposure, Rozelle was always conscious of how the game was presented through the medium, and his achievements included: ensuring that all teams always had their away games broadcast back to their local market, recognizing the potential of doubleheaders, cocreating *Monday Night Football,* expanding the league's broadcasts into cable, helping to strategically place teams in certain geographic locations to serve a market, and, obviously, overseeing the development and growth of the Super Bowl. Michael Wilbon would write of Rozelle's television prowess in the *Washington Post,* commenting, "Every game on every channel will be a living testament to the greatness of Pete Rozelle."

Rozelle was not correct on every issue that he was confronted with. For example, he fought against home games being televised into the local market, even when they were sold out. On a larger scale, he was also not an active leader on the labor problems with the Players Association and was late in developing a system of free agency for the players. While publicly he often indicated that the decision to go ahead with playing games the weekend of the Kennedy assassination was his deepest regret, it appears that not being a more direct participant in the labor situation was more regretful and frustrating to Rozelle than anything else he was confronted with during his time as commissioner.

Rozelle's intentions, though, cannot be questioned. His motivation was always what he thought was best for the league. Decisions were not made with malice toward any one individual. Even in the situation of Al Davis and the Raiders moving to Los Angeles, Rozelle would comment on many occasions that he was concerned the move would negatively impact the league by threatening its stability and rules procedures. He also firmly thought that the city of Oakland, a community that had enthusiastically supported the Raiders, should receive the support of the NFL in trying to keep its team there. And on the issue of player free agency Rozelle's concern was how the system might impact competitive balance and fan interest in all of the NFL's cities. Art Modell stated in the NFL Films production, *Rozelle: Building America's Game*, "Everything Pete Rozelle did was for the good of the National Football League. At no time did he do anything in a self-serving fashion to benefit himself, benefit his image, create an aura of invincibility, no, the good of the league."

Pete Rozelle also understood the personal relationship aspect of the NFL business better than anyone could have estimated when he was named commissioner. Frank Deford describes Rozelle as extremely charming, and that characteristic was crucial to his success. His ability to cultivate friendships with television network and corporate executives only helped the NFL. Executives from corporations didn't just deal with Rozelle as a means to a relationship with the NFL. Many developed deep friendships with him. To those who knew Rozelle, the characteristics of the man—his loyalty, integrity, humility, and devotion to his daughter—are far more outstanding attributes than his business achievements with the NFL. People such as Pat Summerall, Frank Gifford, Ernie Accorsi, Ed Sabol, and all those who worked with Rozelle at the NFL office speak of not only an extraordinary career, but also an extraordinary man, one whose life inspired and touched so many who knew him.

The characteristic of Rozelle that Ernie Accorsi most admired was his integrity. He says that if he had to sum up Rozelle's legacy in one word it would be integrity, "but right underneath it would be visionary." He was consistent and principled in that if he thought a situation threatened the integrity of the game, he would fight hard for what he thought was best for the league, most notably on the issue of gambling, in his confronting and suspending superstars such as Paul Hornung and Joe Namath. Pat Summerall comments that Rozelle never compromised on his standards, and he stuck to what he thought was right for the NFL. As Paul Tagliabue states, "When he gave you his word or his handshake, that's all you needed." Dave Anderson would write a column in the *New York Times* when Rozelle retired, noting Rozelle's joke to the owners when elected, referring to his repeatedly washing his hands in the restroom, that he came to them "with clean hands." Anderson wrote, "Nearly 30 years later, Pete Rozelle is retiring with the same clean hands. If there's any blood on them, it's his from working to sculpture a sport that transfixes the nation on Sundays and Monday nights during the long campaign to the Super Bowl hoopla that he choreographed so deftly. But more than anything else, Pete Rozelle's clean hands stood for his integrity as commissioner."

Rozelle's legacy reaches far beyond the NFL. Tony Kornheiser wrote in the *Washington Post* when Rozelle retired, "The NFL is sports in America. Pete Rozelle is the NFL. He's the model for the commissioners who came later." Ed Sabol claims the legacy of his friend for over forty years is one of "a new role for a commissioner. He was the first commissioner to value public relations." Peter King says that Rozelle "set a great example for his successor and peers on the importance of the media." Steve Sabol adds that his legacy is that he recognized football as a form of entertainment, but the game has to be competitive, with every team having a chance to win—in essence it is the competition that is entertaining. Finally, the competition and fair play should be marketed, presented, and coached with honesty. Steve Sabol recalls that Rozelle would repeat a mantra to him on many occasions, quoting Shakespeare, "No virtue is so rich as honesty."

Steve Sabol concludes, "He was the right man, right time, right place." As a person skilled in public relations and marketing by trade, he possessed the right set of characteristics for the times, with the NFL needing to receive better exposure on television and better marketing overall. He came along at a time when he could be more informal with the press and build up the important, necessary relationships. Ernie Accorsi, however, somewhat downplays the idea that Rozelle was the right man for only the time in which he served as commissioner, stating, "He would not have adjusted to the times, he would have shaped the times. Because of his many characteristics, notably his intelligence and his being a visionary, he would have been a dominating figure in any era." Accorsi simply calls Rozelle the greatest commissioner in the history of sports. Pat Summerall declares that "he set the standard. Everybody wanted a commissioner like Pete Rozelle."

The story of Pete Rozelle is ultimately a story of how a vision turned into a legacy. Rozelle's legacy is the policies that came out of his vision are still in place. Paul Tagliabue states, "I think he'd be very proud of the league today because I think we've been true to the values that he thought were critical."

On April 15, 2005, the NFL announced that it had signed new television agreements with CBS, Fox, NBC, ESPN, and Direct-TV that starting with the 2006 season and extending for the next six years would pay the NFL $3.75 billion per season. One does not have to speculate about how Pete Rozelle would have reacted to these television contracts. Certainly there would have to be a tremendous sense of achievement and vindication for the system that he was so instrumental in creating, that he endlessly fought to implement and secure. Indeed, Pete Rozelle would be able to take much satisfaction in a vision fulfilled and a legacy unparalleled.

INDEX

INDEX

ABOUT THE AUTHOR

John A. Fortunato, PhD, is an assistant professor at the University of Texas at Austin in the Department of Advertising, College of Communication. Dr. Fortunato has also written *The Ultimate Assist: The Relationship and Broadcast Strategies of the NBA and Television Networks* (2002) and *Making Media Content: The Influence of Constituency Groups on Mass Media* (2005). He has also published articles in the *Journal of Sport Management, International Journal of Sports Marketing & Sponsorship, Rutgers Law Record,* and *Public Relations Review*. Dr. Fortunato earned his PhD from Rutgers University.